Literature and Ideas in America
Essays in Memory of Harry Hayden Clark

HARRY HAYDEN CLARK

1901-1971

LITERATURE
AND IDEAS
IN AMERICA

Essays in Memory of

Harry Hayden Clark

Edited by Robert Falk

OHIO UNIVERSITY PRESS

TABLE OF CONTENTS

v

Contents

PREFACE

THE PRESENT VOLUME WAS ORIGINALLY planned as a tribute to Harry Hayden Clark on the occasion of his retirement from the University of Wisconsin in 1972. His death on June 6, 1971 suddenly changed the book from an honorary to a memorial volume and shifted our emphasis somewhat from a tribute to the man toward a larger, historical purpose not fully seen from the start. His death, of course, saddened his many friends and students who were fortunate enough to share his influence as a scholar and teacher and his warm humanity. As the book progressed toward publication, in a new perspective, Harry Clark's role in American literary scholarship and graduate teaching began to emerge more clearly. At Madison, where he spent his long career, Clark was one of an outstanding tradition of American literary and historical scholars. He added distinction to an already distinguished faculty. He was always an inspiring example to his students, as is testified to by some of the well-known scholars who studied with him and who are represented in this book. These chapters all share Harry Clark's dedication to the thought and expression of American writers and to the American tradition in poetry and prose. They also reflect his interest in the relation of literature to the history of ideas, and they follow his tastes, his favorite authors, and his enthusiasms, even where they differ in style or method from his own work.

Harry Clark received his training at Harvard during the 1920's under the persuasive influence of Irving Babbitt. He completed his M.A. in 1924 when he was awarded the Bowdoin Prize for his essay, "The Romanticism of Edward Young." After three years of teaching at Middlebury College and one year at Yale, Clark was appointed at Wisconsin where he remained for the four decades of his active career. His many distinctions included two honorary doctor's degrees, fellowships from the Guggenheim Foundation and the Library of Congress, and a number of visiting professorships in this country and in Europe. In 1948 he was named chairman of the American Literature Group of the Modern Language Association, a sign that he had won the esteem of his colleagues throughout the nation.

When Clark began his career, American literature as a subject of teaching and research was still in the formative stages. For many critics, both here and abroad, ours was an apprentice literature, derived from the parent England, worthy of study in the case of half a dozen of its acknowledged masters, but hardly to be taken seriously in its total accomplishment. It was often huddled into a single chapter by social historians, or it was something for the journalist-critics and reviewers to haggle over. The subject was in need of literary historians with a sufficiently wide knowledge of men and ideas to assemble large bodies of information and to map out major areas of thought and expression. In the period of Mencken, Beard, Parrington, Van Wyck Brooks, Stuart Sherman, and others the battle lines formed around the then controversial "isms"—nationalism, humanism, Freudianism, Marxism, Darwinism, economic determinism. In his teaching at Madison in the 1930's Clark first took his stand philosophically with the New Humanist group of which Babbitt and Paul Elmer More were the leaders. Their position was conservative, universal in standard, opposed to a narrow nationalism. They looked to the classics. "So you're going to teach American literature?" Babbitt told Clark. "Well, in preparation you'd better study the ancient Greeks."

Critics and historians in and out of the academy were seeking to assess America's unique literary character and to understand the relation of its entire body of thought and writing to world literature and the history of ideas. The direction of this effort was toward broad intellectual synthesis. In 1928 Clark contributed a provocative essay, "American Literary History and American Literature," to a book of joint authorship edited by Norman Foerster which was an early attempt to grasp the backgrounds of the nation's literature in terms of the history of ideas. In this essay in *The Reinterpretation of American Literature* Clark urged a balanced method with close study of the poem or prose work under consideration together with due attention to its background ideas, including "history, religion, economics, and social life." He spoke of the need for the kind of historian-critic who could know and use detailed bibliographical and factual material and at the same time encompass broad areas of intellectual history.

Twenty-five years later Clark himself edited a similar book, *Transitions in American Literary History* (1953), which sought to account for the greater body of research which had been done since the Foerster volume. Recognizing the shift toward analytical criticism of separate works which had grown so rapidly during those years, he stressed the continued importance of intellectual history and backgrounds as a counterpart to the "New Criticism." *Transitions* extended and corrected certain of the assumptions of the earlier book. Clark's purpose was to demonstrate how the accumulated scholarship of a quarter-century had made new terminology and definitions necessary. For the student of literary history, a comparison of these two books can be instructive. And today literary history itself has become a *genre*, subject to analysis, as much written *about* as written.

Meanwhile, Clark had been engaged in the task of enlarging the knowledge of major American writers of the 18th and 19th centuries, especially the bibliographical information upon which evaluation and sound criticism depended.

He steadily encouraged among his students standards of objectivity and accuracy. His approach to an author was always controlled by attention to the genetic growth of his ideas. In a characteristic essay on Lowell, for example, Clark traced three major developments of his thought—his early humanitarianism, his nationalism, and his later humanism as demonstrated in the writings of those three periods in his life. Harry Clark directed more than a hundred Ph.D. dissertations at Wisconsin, yet he himself never completed his own degree. In 1934 he summed up his philosophy of scholarship as follows:

> One must be willing to follow the trail of an author's thought steadfastly, regardless of whether it leads into politics, religion, philosophy, economics, social relations, education, or literary theory. When this has been done, we shall have accomplished, or at least approached, one of the higher tasks of true literary history, which is the re-creation objectively of the contemporary climate of opinion . . . and the discerning of essential intellectual patterns which . . . help motivate writing and which explain why the facts of literary history are as they are.

Clark's own bibliography is impressive indeed (see Appendix) in both the range and variety of the subjects treated. He was a tireless investigator, editor, and interpreter of many different authors, periods, and ideas. He always produced fresh insights into the writers whose work he studied, writers as widely different as Tom Paine, Freneau, Lowell, Whittier, Emerson, Holmes, and Henry James. His most prodigious accomplishment was the general editorship of the American Writers Series, 26 volumes of selections from major and minor American writers. The introductions to these volumes, all carefully directed by Clark and some written by him, were models of precision and completeness. The bibliographies were in most cases the most detailed and annotated that had yet appeared. The series as a whole has not been equalled in comprehensiveness and in high standards of editing. Clark's edition of *Major American Poets* (1936) was also a landmark of its kind. The notes and interpretations of the underlying ideas of the poets represented, from Freneau to E. A. Robinson, were so scholarly and incisive that in using the book one could clearly recognize in it the outlines of an authoritative history of American poetry.

Harry Clark's personal influence in the classroom and his energetic and enthusiastic direction of graduate students were direct results of his published work. He had slight use for doctrinaire methods or subjective criticism, urging upon his students the need for establishing a common ground of factual and established knowledge. He was democratic by temperament, always genial and full of humor. His lectures contained anecdotes, literary jokes, and puns, some of which were not always as funny as his own delight in telling them. He occasionally shocked serious-minded sophomores with this levity. His lectures were so crowded with information as to give a conscientious note-taker the writer's cramp. In his home on Seneca Place there was a long window seat on which was arrayed an "assembly line" of manuscripts, as many as ten or twelve projects in varying states of composition, on which he was always at work. The books in his own library were larded with marginal annotations, underlinings, asterisks, and arrows designating "key" passages and phrases for use in the classroom. His lectures were enriched by his keen memory for significant and apt quotations from the entire range of English and American literature.

Clark was most absorbing and illuminating when he dealt with a given work of literature in terms of intellectual concepts such as puritanism, deism and rationalism, romanticism, and realism. He could bring a seemingly simple poem of Freneau into the mainstream of deistic philosophy by showing its relationship to Newton and Locke. He was particularly at home with such concepts as "physiocratic agrarianism" and "scientific deism" as they impinged on the work of Jefferson, Paine, Franklin, and the 18th century writers and thinkers. Another of his favorite themes was American criticism. Indeed, Harry Clark had many strings to his bow. One feels that his long, impressive bibliography did not satisfy his scholarly ambitions and energies. The reason his work is still influential in the study of American literature and ideas is that he was always working in terms of an even larger and more comprehensive treatment of the subject than he could have, in his busy career, completed. He would have needed four more decades to complete the projects and plans that he conjured up in his vigorous and productive life.

R.F.

I

PHILIP FRENEAU AS ARCHETYPAL
AMERICAN POET

EDWIN H. CADY

TO FORESTALL MISUNDERSTANDING ABOUT "archetypal," I take "archetype" in its common dictionary sense of original pattern or model. Because Freneau was the first true poet American born and educated and the best poet of the Revolution, it was long popular to term him "the father of American poetry." But that left an uncomfortable question on hand: who were Father Freneau's sons? As Hyatt Waggoner says, to find a true father in the main line of American poets one looks to Emerson. It seems better to say "archetypal" because Freneau came first. His life and career set the pattern and shaped the experience of the American poet. Except for a handful of anthology poems, Freneau's example constitutes his chief significance.

To say so is not to deny him merit as an artist. Without that intrinsic worth he could be neither typical nor considerable. The one inalienable claim a poet has upon us is his right to a hospitable hearing. Genuinely heard, Philip Freneau communicates the sense of a mind working with force and resilience. His best poems reveal honest talent—the temperament, the intuitions, the power to register creative impulse in epiphanies, and the technical command of an artist. Lyrics like "To the Memory of the Brave Americans," "The Hurricane," "The Wild Honey Suckle," and "The Indian Burying-Ground" hold place in the permanent American anthology. More of his work will find its way there as perspectives lengthen.

Nevertheless it is true, as the subtitle to Lewis Leary's definitive biography puts it, that the career of Freneau makes "a study in literary failure." His life might have been plotted by Edwin Arlington Robinson. It registers all the twists which that pensive Yankee liked to work into the fates of his frustrated heroes. From wealth, sensibility, brilliant promise, early achievement, and noble sacrifice for the public good in the sustained expenditure of his strength, Freneau fell—repeatedly and a little lower each time—to frustration, disillusion, poverty, defeat, and obsolescence. His life spanned the long gap from the peak of the provincial era of American culture at his birth in 1752 to the onset of the romantic era by his death in 1832. His final quarter century of neglect and obscurity does remind one of Captain Craig and Flammonde. His death by failure to reach home through the snow after a premature Christmas eve at a country tavern recalls Mr. Flood and his party. Freneau's was a career packed with human interest. His literary fate is packed with interest for the American curious about the roots of our culture.

The essential point is subtle enough to require a little care in handling. Freneau's typicality does not consist flatly in having been a failure. In this too his likeness to Robinson's figures is instructive. One of the things Robinson meant is that everyone relatively fails. Nobody wholly satisfies his ambitions or altogether escapes defeat. Therefore, open failure may reveal the human condition more truly than apparent success. And that becomes especially true for a man of the highest talent and aim—such as a poet.

Developments in our understanding of American cultural history have made it possible to understand Freneau more usefully than we might have twenty years ago. For example, R. W. B. Lewis has helped us envision our artists as seekers for American identity; B. T. Spencer has helped with his scrupulous analysis of *The Quest For Nationality*; and Roy Harvey Pearce (though he understands Freneau differently from the way I do) has taken a giant step toward new light in *The Continuity of American Poetry*.

These, and others, have put us in position to see the poet Freneau as archetypal. He is so in his fight to achieve a real career, a place in American life as a poet. He is so more profoundly in his double struggle for identity as an American poet: identity, that is, first to become a poet who was genuinely American; and, second, to achieve authenticity as an artist self in America.

I

Careerwise, as the saying goes, Freneau represented the American poet as forlorn hope. Like shock troops, he dashed with his poetry against the entrenchments of illiteracy and provinciality, of material, military, and religious preoccupation, of political bitterness, and of cultural stagnation in a tangled, revolutionary nation. "An age employed in edging steel/ Can no poetic raptures feel," he lamented, while he clashed political steel with the best. Starting out with the patrimony of a country gentleman and equipped to supplement it from good Huguenot commercial connections and training, Freneau wasted his substance in riotous devotion to democracy and poetry. A poetic career is one of life's greatest ventures, partly because one stakes his most precious inward being on it, and the stakes are generally lost. On the whole, Freneau lost, but with honor.

Perhaps we need to remind ourselves that the poetic career has never been easy. Under feudal or aristocratic patronage the poet seldom rose above the status of public entertainer. Spiritually, if not actually like Papa Haydn, he wore livery. In more self-respecting middle class societies, it has been hard for a poet to make a living. He has had to choose between an uneasy patronage—uneasy for him even when generous—and "making a living" some other way while the life he lived went to poetry. Nowadays we have the irregular patronage of foundations and the government, the quasi-patronage, quasi-something else of the lecture circuits, and what may become other and better than patronage in the universities. In this century great American poets have moonlighted successfully as, in one case, farmer, school teacher, and real estate dealer with lecture circuit and university income on the side; or as Bank of England clerk, publisher's reader, and eventually vice president of a publishing house; as physician; or as successful professional and eventually vice president of a great insurance company.

But in Freneau's America, patronage was as far out of the question as hope of achieving that competency from poetry which would later accrue almost uniquely to Longfellow. With one most honorable exception—it was to be given him to become, if in a minor way, one of the founding fathers of the American republic—Freneau sat originally for the portrait of the young American as poet.

Graduated from Princeton in 1771 the peer of classmates like James Madison, Aaron Burr, and Hugh Henry Brackenridge, Freneau thrashed about in the throes of conflict between the muse and the demands of the world. He twice failed miserably at schoolteaching. He thought about the law, printed poems which he confessed were "damned by all good and judicious critics," and tried to still doubts about his collegiate intention—the Presbyterian ministry—by reading theology. While he was incubating maturer, avant garde poetry, nothing else would quite work. Suddenly (one supposes he had chosen to join the Freneau commercial interests as preferable to farming on the matrilinear New Jersey plantation), he appeared in New York as a conspicuous figure in the prerevolutionary turmoil of 1775.

Here was initiated that cycle—of assault, battle, defeat, withdrawal, and return—which became the fundamental rhythm of Freneau's life. With variations each time around, of course, he passed through his cycle perhaps seven times before he became (after 1809) too defeated to assault again. His objectives were sometimes political—Revolutionary or, later, Jeffersonian—victories, but sometimes personal poetic success. Most often, poetry and politics were passionately mixed. In the phrase a bilingual son of Huguenots would have liked, he was nothing if not *un poète engagé*.

For details one turns to Leary's biography, *That Rascal Freneau*—the title-phrase a quotation from President George Washington. It is the pattern I should like to emphasize. With fine effectiveness, Freneau first jumped into that publicity war which brought about the Revolution, wielding an anti-Tory satire, as he himself described it, "So full of invective and loaded with spleen/ So sneeringly smart and so hellishly keen," that it made an intercolonial sensation. But in the upshot young Freneau made three dismaying discoveries. It was one thing to be sneeringly smart with opponents; it was something else to have them unload spleen on you. As has been said of boxers, Freneau discovered that he could dish it out but he couldn't take it. Tory invective hurt. He felt dirtied and disillusioned.

Even worse, it became evident that political combat signified more than fun and games. People felt serious; there was about to begin a shooting war for which Freneau, as Leary deduces, was not quite prepared. Thirdly, turmoil thwarted his poetic impulse; the angry Muse put confusion in his brain. He withdrew to the Caribbean to think it over. Early in 1776 (when it was still doubtful that a declaration of independence could be secured from the Continental Congress and many American Whigs still hoped for reconciliation), he went to Santa Cruz in the West Indies for two years of sea-faring, commercial activity, and cultivating poetry in an exotic tropical paradise.

That is the period on which I shall focus in this paper. But for the present it ought to be observed that after he grew up, after real if minor combat on land and sea, after a bitter, case-hardening experience aboard an atrocious British prison ship, after years of rugged political warfare editing libertarian newspapers, a mature Freneau would no longer be surprised or disillusioned by warfare actual or verbal. He would know how to fight, lose, and fight again—how even to lose, expended in his cause, with honor in the face of his party's victory. When the libertarian cause, in which Freneau had lost battle after battle, newspaper after newspaper, and sacrificed personal reputation, his fortune, and immense psychological stakes, finally triumphed in Jefferson's election, Freneau would be able to make the gesture which set at nought decades of accusation that he was a venal scribbler. He would accept nothing from the new government: not even, as the story tells, when the President sent James Madison to persuade him.

But what could never be protected, not finally even in periods of withdrawal to the sea or the farm, was Freneau's poetry. Still today the great peril of the moonlighting poet is that he may lose his balance and fall into dilettantism. When Freneau came back from Santa Cruz to plunge into the Revolution, he brought with him the possibilities of a genuine, perhaps a significant contribution to the body of serious poetry in English. That possibility was to be at best fragmentarily fulfilled. Worse, Freneau was to develop little, and then in but a handful of scattered lyrics, beyond his current capabilities. With the first major American poetic talent, Freneau would fail.

The specific circumstances, aside from general career problems, of that defeat are worth summarizing. Freneau's audience was maddeningly inadequate. Potential readers of serious poetry were few, widely dispersed, and preoccupied with practical affairs. Where their cultural interests were not intensely local they were likely to be provincially disdainful of cisatlantic art. Inescapably Freneau became a newspaper poet. That meant an audience largely careless of poetry—Freneau's greatest success was a piece of light verse entitled "The Jug of Rum." And it meant a political audience. As editor-poet, Freneau was tempted to get down in the pit and slug it out with his enemies. His earned reputation as a satiric in-fighter obscured his deserved one as an artist. And even when he designed poetry to be taken seriously, whether as art or as a monument to his services to his country, political considerations damned him.

The most ambitious effort to establish Freneau's fame came with his volume of *Poems Written and Published During the American Revolutionary War* (1809). James Madison and Thomas Jefferson (ten copies each) headed the subscription list. Matthew Carey took two hundred copies, and names from the Middle states and the South mount up to a total of perhaps 750-800 subscriptions. Apparently not a single subscriber came from New England. Yankee sources of reputation were, as William Charvat proved, controlled by Federalists. And they cut Freneau off from the longest, best-knit tradition of American poetry, the one which would dominate the nineteenth century. Concerned with "Early American Poetry" in 1818, William Cullen Bryant's comment, quoted entire, shows how little Freneau was known:

> A writer in verse of inferior [the poets of context are Hopkinson, Church, and the Connecticut Wits] note was Philip Freneau, whose pen seems to have been chiefly employed on political subjects, and whose occasional productions, distinguished by a coarse strength of sarcasm, and abounding with allusions to passing events, which is perhaps their greatest merit, attracted in their time considerable notice, and in the year 1786 were collected into a volume.

Not only was Bryant ignorant of the 1809 edition, he appears to have supposed poet and poetry were dead, though he might in 1818 have learned a good deal from both.

II

It was, of course, not outward circumstance alone which forced Freneau's failure. The poetry suggests a temperament subject to volatile variations, its barometer swinging from sanguine to depressive, pugnacious to hypersensitive. And, yet more fascinating than Freneau's emotional weather, it is plain that both his finest creative impulses and some of his worst difficulties stemmed from a metaphysical crisis long continued and ended only with the decline of his talent.

A colonial poet of parts with an immediate heritage, provincially reverenced, for Dryden and Swift, Pope and Gay, might during the disorders of his country be expected to become a tough and clever satirist. So Freneau did: equally with Wordsworth the heir of Milton and Thomson, sensitive to the breathtaking beauty of an unspoiled American landscape, and patriotically determined to celebrate it, Freneau might be expected to contribute to that Georgic and exact depiction of nature which preceded, perhaps trained, Wordsworth. He did so and moved away from that provincial derivativeness which cursed Mather Byles, Francis Hopkinson, or Timothy Dwight toward imaginative contemporaneity with the freshest stream of English poetry of his time. Insofar as the current of that stream was also to run toward humanity and liberty in the Wordsworth and toward Gothicism in the Coleridge of *Lyrical Ballads*, Freneau leapt ahead of it by a generation in the 1770's.

That is his historical glory—the reality of his and our "might-have-been." Of the three poems which best illustrate this, two had their genesis in the years of struggle toward self-realization just before Freneau's first political venture and were doubtless taken in manuscript to Santa Cruz where the third was begun. It is easy to say that their failure to achieve full artistic resolution was the fault of war-service, the prison ship, the indignant blaze of patriotism which followed, of entrapment in the life cycle, of the impossibilities of career success which killed Brackenridge's fine *United States Magazine* in which two of them first appeared. No doubt there would be truth in such statements.

It is my belief, however, that the secret of Freneau's originality, his promise of poetic greatness, his best poetic achieve-

8

ment, and his ultimate failure was nothing overt, material or common, nothing circumstantial, or demonstrably environmental. It was covert and deeply personal, where the true issues of a poet's life ought to lie. It was a religious tension.

From both his patriarchal Huguenot and his matriarchal Scotch Presbyterian ancestors, Freneau inherited the ideas and sensibility of Calvinism. He went to Princeton to prepare for the ministry at the college which had employed Jonathan Edwards as its early president. But from his cultivated home he must also have taken some awareness of the ideas and sensibility of that great enemy of Calvinism over which Edwards had triumphed—the rather protean, seldom institutionalized, but potent religion of eighteenth century intellectuals, deism. At Princeton he suffered one of the commonest experiences of a bright student. He lost his inherited religion and began an agonizing struggle to find his own.

We know almost nothing about the details of Freneau's religious crises. The best evidences surface in the poetry. His Princeton had become a furnace of political dissent contained by the firebrick of Scottish Common Sense Calvinism. But if Freneau had to lose his parents' religion and find a way to counter Tory with libertarian arguments, he might have seized on one fateful difference between the Calvinists and the "Cosmic Tories" on one side and the liberal Whigs who would one day be democrats on the opposite. The one view of the character and destiny of man and nature despaired in grim foreboding of God's judgment against inescapable sin and folly. The other looked forward, with faith in the mind and heart of man, to obey God in thinking His thoughts after Him and rise to the true happiness He intended throughout creation. For many years Freneau and his poetry were to be caught suspended and oscillating between these two worlds: pessimistic, optimistic.

This division has always been of course fateful to the American mind. Shall we say, and believe in our hearts, that man and nature are essentially, dependably benevolent and, in spite of every error, variation and mischance, designed for goodness? That is the famous American "innocence." Or shall we fix upon a tragic sense of life—the faith that a tiger, always crouched to spring, always ravening forth, possesses the hearts of man and cosmos? That might be the beginning of wisdom—or it might not: is it life-denying? To make room for life we may need to compromise, to trust in the grace of God, in some saving remnant, in checks and balances, in legislation or education, in the gospel of wealth, the gospel of beauty, the moral equivalent of war, or something.

From political arrangements to theology, from primary education to esthetic expression, the cultural life of our nation has been in all generations shot through with this problem. Our archetypal poet led the way. Nowhere was this truer than in those most interesting of his poems, the long, ambitious apprentice works of his period of purest poetic sensibility: "Pictures of Columbus," "The House of Night," and "The Beauties of Santa Cruz." It is to be remembered that these are essentially studio pieces; they bear the same relation to the Freneau who might have been as "Endymion" to the realized Keats. Rich in creative impulse, they sometimes falter in construction. In them derivative lines, even clichés, alternate with fresh, successful expression of direct poetic insight.

III

"Pictures of Columbus, the Genoese," 1774, then as always made a perfect theme for the aspiring American poet. Freneau grasped the romantic significance of a great-souled solitary man forging by the light of genius through the icy fogs of ignorance, superstition, apathy, venality, and cowardice which barred common men from glory. Like figures so disparate as Irving, Lowell, Whitman, Joaquin Miller, and Samuel Eliot Morison to come, Freneau saw that the epic magnitude of the matter transmuted Columbus into a myth heroically flattering to Americans and embarrassing to Europe. In eighteen "pictures" of the hero and his antagonists at crucial moments, Freneau made a fair success of his poem's structure. And the technique permitted him to exploit what would for the better part of a century to come stand among the stock appeals of romanticism: mystic original genius, progress, primitivism, humanitarian sympathy, wild, sublime nature.

Yet of course there is paradox. The fruits of genius and heroism ripen into ambiguity. All unawares Columbus brings a curse upon his wonderful prize. In "Picture XIV" we see two sailors slay an Indian for his crude gold earring: then, enter "Columbus solus," who speaks:

> Sweet sylvan scenes of innocence and ease,
> How calm and joyous pass the seasons here!
> No splendid towns or spiry turrets rise,
> No lordly palaces—no tyrant kings . . . .
> All, all are free!—here God and nature reign;
> Their works unsullied by the hands of men—
> Ha! what is this—a murder'd wretch I see,
> His blood yet warm—Oh hapless islander . . . .
> Is this the fruit of my discovery!
> If the first scene is murder, what shall follow
> But havock, slaughter, chains and devastation
> In every dress and form of cruelty!

Inevitably the hero too is victimized. At last we see him in chains consoled alone by the reward of the future's vision,

> When empires rise where lonely forests grew,
> Where Freedom shall her generous plans pursue.

And so he bids life farewell:

> To shadowy forms, and ghosts and sleepy things,
> Columbus, now with dauntless heart repair;
> You liv'd to find new worlds for thankless kings,
> Write this upon my tomb . . . .

Concerning "The House of Night" I find myself in disagreement with such critics of Freneau as Lewis Leary and Nelson Adkins, and in agreement with Harry Hayden Clark. Recent commentary has held this long, doubly macabre treatment of the Scripturally promised death of Death to be a seriously theological work begun while post-graduate Freneau was reading divinity at Princeton. But careful reading of the poem I think demonstrates that Clark was right in holding this to be a Gothic, or in other words, essentially nonserious poem. In fact, I think it clear that here we see Freneau's metaphysical tug of war pulling against the tragic vision of the Columbus poem. There Calvinist gloom compromised hope and innocence. Here a humanist's reason mocks the dark old solemnities, and the ends are incongruity and fun. "The House of Night" is the kind of poem an ex-Presbyterian might write, exploiting the traditions of grave-yard, epitaph, and evangelical poetry for purposes irreligious.

Gothicism appeals to an evidently ancient and deep-seated emotion—our enjoyment of vicarious terror, safe fear. No one who has experienced it need be told that real fear is no fun. It is psychologically shattering, sometimes more menacing itself than whatever caused it. Perhaps for those very reasons, however, mock fear is great fun. Some of the oldest tales of the race are suitable for scaring their auditors to shivers round the safety of the fire. Even a securely trusting baby will enjoy the safe game of "Let's pretend to drop the baby but don't"—and chortle with glee. Vicarious terror, gothicism, is surefire entertainment.

Mockery was Freneau's game in "The House of Night." He filled it with Gothic devices (not what would become the stock Radcliffian ploys, but fine devices of his own). Representative stanzas show them clearly:

I.

Trembling I write my dream, and recollect
A fearful vision at the midnight hour;

So late, Death o'er me spread his sable wings,
Painted with fancies of a malignant power!

Personified Death struggles erect one last time from his throes:
59.
Then slowly rising from his loathsome bed,
On wasted legs the meagre monster stood,
Gap'd wide, and foam'd and hungry seemed to ask,
Tho' sick, an endless quantity of food.

The narrator flees the awful scene of Death's expiration:
109.
O'er a dark field I held my dubious way
Where Jack-a-lanthorn walk'd his lonely round,
Beneath my feet substantial darkness lay,
And screams were heard from the distemper'd ground.
110.
Nor look'd I back, till to a far off wood
Trembling with fear, my weary feet had sped—
Dark was the night, but at the inchanted dome
I saw the infernal windows flaming red.

One could elaborate upon the tracery of this Halloweenish embroidery, but I think even this little enough to dispel the notion that somehow "The House of Night" represents serious theology. Actually, what the genuinely theological reference of the poem produces is just such an intensification of Gothic effect as Poe recommended. Much of sophisticated Gothicism depends for its power on a technique familiar to the romanticists in several connections—the ability to take an old abstraction and make it "seem real" psychologically. Especially in Gothicism does a paradoxical turn of the abstract and otherwise "unreal" upon a pivot of incongruity, unresisted by the reader, become essential to the best effect. Hence Freneau lets his *persona* reject the confidence of Death that even for him there might be mercy:

" . . . . Much of Theology I once did read,
And there 'tis fixt, sure as my God is so,
That Death shall perish, tho' a God should bleed."

Pauline assurance, however, is precisely not what the actual poem is about. The function in the poem of theological reference is exactly what Poe, discussing his oblique injection of ideas into "The Raven," pointed out: in "subjects so handled [that is, Gothically]," he says, "there is always a certain hardness or nakedness, which repels the artistical eye. Two things are invariably required—first, some amount of complexity, or more properly, adaptation; and, secondly, some amount of suggestiveness—some under-current, however indefinite, of meaning. It is this latter, in especially which imparts to a work of art so much . . . *richness.* . . . " Freneau's pinch of theology dropped into "The House of Night" lends his brew just that "complexity," "suggestiveness" and "richness" which Poe sought. It need hardly be added that, from a nonliterary standpoint, such theology might seem defiant if not blasphemous. And the decidedly deistic-universalist notions of human death with which Freneau ended his poem confirm its note of defiance while suggesting that the inception of the poem was grounded on his own religious conflict.

As effective Gothicism, "The House of Night" was strikingly avant garde. To say nothing of the unborn Poe, whose manner it so strongly anticipated, Coleridge, the author of "The Rime of the Ancient Mariner" and "Christabel" was a tiny boy when Freneau wrote his poem. Walpole's *Castle of Otranto* had been published in 1764. The works of "Monk" Lewis, Ann Radcliffe, and Brockden Brown lay a decade and more in the future. It would be six years after the publication of "The House of Night" before the first Gothic tale would appear in an American magazine.

IV

Structurally, these first two early poems are satisfactory. They have awkwardnesses, but they will do. Their defect is textural unevenness with its danger of falling into bathos. To a degree the opposite is true of Freneau's most interesting, most typical, perhaps most fateful failure. The best lines of "The Beauties of Santa Cruz" reach higher intensities, with smoother consistency and fewer descents to cliché or prosiness. The precision and sensuousness of the nature imagery look forward to William Bartram.

The force of Freneau's romantic appeals to the beauty, glamor, and exoticism of a tropical paradise is registrable still:

> Such were the isles which happy *Flaccus* sung,
> Where one tree blossoms while another bears,
> Where spring forever gay, and ever young,
> Walks her gay round through her unceasing years.

There were incredible tropical fish:

> Some streaked with burnished gold, resplendent, glare,
> Some cleave the limpid deep, all silvered o'er,
> Some clad in living green, delight the eye,
> Some red, some blue; of mingled colors more. . . .
>
> The *Rainbow* cuts the deep, of varied green,
> The well-fed *Grouper* lurks remote below,
> The swift *Bonnetta* coasts the watery scene,
> The diamond-coated *Angels* kindle as they go.

Verdure and fruits seem fabulous, and Freneau succeeds in bodying them forth with notations of taste, scent, and color.

Freneau's trouble was that he did not know what to do with all this poetically, once he had it, because he did not know what to do with it intellectually. His problem with the poem, and the key to its failure, lies in the application of the objective correlative (the sea anemone) with which he concludes his description of the tropic paradise:

> This mystic plant, with its bewitching charms. . . .
> Feast on its beauties with thy ravished eyes,
> But aim to touch it, and—the flower is gone. . . .
>
> Warned by experience, hope not thou to gain
> The magic plant thy curious hand invades;
> Returning to the light, it mocks thy pain,
> Deceives all grasp, and seeks its native shades!

Comparison of the prose setting in which Freneau placed the poem on its first appearance in *The United States Magazine*, February, 1779, with the structure of the poem reinforces one's sense of his difficulties. Introducing his readers to Santa Cruz, Freneau gushed: "Inexpressibly beautiful"; "Inexpressibly charming . . . the vales of Paradise . . . in their primeval beauty . . . an inchanted island, such as we read of in romance." On the other hand, he cautioned, there *was* a solitary "natural failing"—"hurricanes . . . storms of an inconceivable fury." And the sins of man palled paradise over with despair. Slavery on the island was "incredible" in its cruelty. It "blots out the beauties of the eternal spring" and "leaves me melancholy and disconsolate, convinced that there is no pleasure in this world without its share of pain. And thus the earth, which were it not for the lust of pride and dominion, might be an earthly paradise, is, by the ambition and overbearing nature of mankind, rendered an eternal scene of desolation, woe, and horror."

The structure of Freneau's poem shows that he was aware that the lures of sensuous beauty and primitive freedom could be enhanced by contrast with the pains of the world; but he simply could not decide what to think about the snake in Eden. Lines 1-36 form an introduction with an almost Chamber-of-Commerce touting up of the charms of his isle in contrast to the glooms of winter and war at home: "Come, shepherd, haste" he calls. Then follow the 239 lines which form the core of the poem, Freneau's celebration of tropical beauty, with a quick glance at the primitive bliss of Indian lovers wandering in moonlit glades. But then, abruptly after the sea anemone image, fall curses upon "cruel slavery" and its murderous madness, followed, almost as abruptly, by a portentous sketch of the terror and sublimity of a hurricane.

At this point one feels entitled to a resolution of the problems Freneau has set up, though in most unequal balance: natural loveliness, abundance and good—smiling teleology— against natural evil, destruction and death; primitive bliss against cruel tyranny and human evil. But all that eventuates is a welter of rationalizing remarks about the poet's confusing personal situation, and the poem ends in an abject return to the Chamber of Commerce theme. Nothing is resolved.

That the poet himself was aware of his poem's failure is evidenced by the encapsulating lines he later placed between the introduction and the nature celebration and then repeated as a headnote to his poem:

> *Sweet orange grove, the fairest of the isle,*
> *In thy soft shade luxuriously reclined,*
> *Where round my fragrant bed, the flowrets smile,*
> *In sweet delusions I deceive my mind.*
>
> *But Melancholy's glooms assail my breast,*
> *For potent nature reigns despotic there;—*
> *A nation ruined, and a world oppressed,*
> *Might rob the boldest stoic of a tear.*

This is separately a nice little poem which sums up the problem of "The Beauties of Santa Cruz," tightening and clarifying without in the least resolving the difficulty. Neither Freneau's imagination nor his art could, so to speak, make up its mind; and perhaps he did not know how, artistically, to rest with a standing ambiguity.

The real source of the failure of the poem, then, was Freneau's inability to answer his own riddle. He failed to write the metaphysical poem he had posited for himself. That was at once a formal failure and an intellectual one. Success would have been to use the poem as an instrument to explore sentiment and idea, interpenetratedly one, and achieve an answer. Nelson Adkins' *Philip Freneau and the Cosmic Enigma* has refined upon the observation of the poet's ideological inconsistencies earlier pointed out by Clark. But the further point which needs to be seen is that there was also an emotional and imaginative tension troubling the pool of Freneau's creativity and releasing the impulse to poetry. Failure to answer, to resolve, to arrive at a total, personal, and mature response to this challenge eventually thwarted Freneau's career as it did his most promising early poem.

In the long run he did not resolve, he only gave way to tension and moved toward its deistic pole. By the time he was writing perfect redactions of Pope and Paine in his deistic poems of the early nineteenth century ("On the Uniformity and Perfection of Nature," etc.), his successors had moved into the high romanticism, a glorious epoch of the English lyric, of which Freneau had been a prophet and pioneer a generation earlier. He had moved a generation back toward the past from his achievements of the seventies, and he was effectually finished as a poet.

It would make another paper, and a very interesting one, to show how the fine interim lyrics of the 1780's—"The Vanity of Existence," "The Hurricane," "The Wild Honey Suckle," "The Indian Burying Ground"—were products of the decay of Freneau's metaphysical crisis and so of his creativity (though not yet of his maturer technical powers). I should like to close this one by observing that I mean no disrespect in saying that Freneau, a genuine poet, failed. For he failed in an absolutely important attempt—the effort to create himself as an American poet. It is in this that he is most archetypal.

II

DOCTRINE FOR FICTION IN
THE *NORTH AMERICAN REVIEW*:
1815-1826

NEAL FRANK DOUBLEDAY

"IT IS IMPOSSIBLE TO ANTICIPATE," SAID Edward Everett in his 1824 Phi Beta Kappa address, "what garments our native muses will weave for themselves. To foretell our literature would be to create it."[1] It was not altogether impossible; from its beginning in 1815, the *North American Review*, which Everett himself had edited from 1820 through 1823, anticipated something of the nature of our early literature. Our early literary history has as a distinguishing feature the development of a vigorous literary discussion ahead of practice.

Harry Hayden Clark's annotated bibliography of the literary criticism in the *North American Review* during its first twenty-one years is a record of that development.[2] With its aid, I attempt here only to discern the pattern of the *Review's* doctrine for fiction as it was set down in articles and reviews from time to time over its first twelve years.

Now fiction writers cannot boast, as did Swift's spider, that their materials are extracted altogether out of their own persons. What American fiction needed was a way in which American materials might be used in something like a tradition. In helping to work out that way, *North American Review* critics in some sense did foretell our early fiction and help to create it. More than that, they began to develop a concept of realistic fiction that did not come to any full fruition until the 1870s.

Not that these writers were unaware of the difficulties in the way of an American literature, the chief of which seemed to be the short span of American history, the newness of the new country, its lack of legend and tradition. To be sure it had wonderful scenery, but its beauty lacked association with events and persons. And the citizens of the United States, however estimable and hard-working, seemed to offer little of variety and interest for the writer.

Those who despaired of a national literature found these difficulties insuperable. In the *North American Review* Edward Tyrell Channing, for instance, in an 1819 review of William Dunlap's life of Charles Brockden Brown, says that the American scene offers little to the romance writer, for in using it he must deal with "some place or circumstance which is too stubbornly familiar and unpoetical for anything but common incidents and feelings," and to which his readers cannot bring "romantic associations" (IX, 65). Nor is American society developed enough to offer more than "very imperfect materials for a novel" (66-68). And in 1827 William H. Prescott, despite his enthusiasm for Scott, doubts that "our country be yet ripe for the purposes of the novelist." The novel, he thinks, "can only be the product of a highly polished and mature state of society" (XXV, 194-195). Cooper, even after success with American materials, rehearsed in his *Notions of the Americans* (1828) the list of difficulties in the way of an American literature; and the conviction that the United States was too young a country to have a literature persisted long.[3]

The critics of the *North American Review*—and many other writers, too, of course—addressed themselves to the list of often rehearsed difficulties. The literary doctrine that had most to do with the development of fiction affirmed that they could all be surmounted, that there was an American past usable to writers, that there were indeed rich American materials, that American writers, far from being destitute of the elements for literature, were in many ways peculiarly fortunate. And it affirmed that in the quest for American materials and in the manner of their use, the Scottish novels of Sir Walter Scott which deal with a historical period comparable to the span of American experience were the example and guide. Scott's insight into the connections between past and present could show Americans how to realize a continuity in their own historical experience, so difficult of realization in the new republic.

In making that affirmation, the *Review* critics took for granted the preeminence of Scott, not only among readers in general, but in the esteem of the grave and scholarly.[4] In 1827, at the end of the brief period we here examine, William H. Prescott remarked, "We of the present generation can hardly estimate our own good fortune, in having lighted upon this prolific and entertaining epoch" (xxv, 184). Scott had changed, Prescott said, the whole course of literature; he "must of course be considered to have been the most efficient agent in producing this revolution; and from this circumstance he may, like Shakespeare, be taken as the representative of his age" (192). In like fashion, other *Review* writers remarked on Scott's exalted place; they felt no need to contend for it.

Read consecutively today, the pieces that make up the *Review's* discussion of American materials seem repetitious, although doubtless they did not seem so to the readers of the *Review* over a dozen years. But the repetition is indicative, probably of a need on the part of the critics to convince themselves, surely of a strong impulse to convince the public and potential writers that an American literature was not only feasible but emerging. At the time they wrote the pieces we here consider, the critics were for the most part relatively young men, in their twenties or early thirties. The editorial "we," although it is used in expressions of the proclivities of individual critics, often has its reference to the *North American Review* itself; and as the discussion proceeded, the critics were clearly conscious that they were contributing to a body of literary doctrine. The discussion began in 1815 when William Tudor, the first editor, printed his Phi Beta Kappa address on a national literature.[5]

Antiquity for Americans, Tudor wrote, is the period from the close of the sixteenth to the middle of the eighteenth century. Within that period Indians were the most promising literary material—our classic subject—and offered the greatest possibility of a distinctive American literature; most of the address is a disquisition on that possibility. Tudor believed that the Revolution was too close to his present for literary use (II, 14), but that colonial history offered useful and striking scenes and persons. The pervading influence of Scott is apparent not only in two passages that cite his example (29 n.; 32), but in Tudor's very terms: "Perilous and romantick adventures, figurative and eloquent harangues, strong contrasts and important interests, are as frequent in this portion of history, as the theatre on which these events were performed is abundant in grand and beautiful scenery" (28-29). The sentence is at the core of the American materials discussion, and is in substance often repeated. Attached to it is a long footnote specifying persons and incidents American writers might use, and some, as it turned out, they did later use. But Tudor, although he had reviewed *Guy Mannering* (I, 403-436), was writing early enough so that he was thinking of narrative poems like Scott's, or even of poems with epic pretensions; he showed no awareness that his affirmations would have their greatest importance in their application to fiction.

In his 1818 essay, "National Poetry," John Knapp went over much of the same ground that Tudor did, although without always quite agreeing: Knapp, for instance, thought the Revolution might well furnish subjects for literary use (VIII, 171). Yet a central motive in the American materials discussion, a motive connected both with the Associationism of Archibald Alison and the practice of Scott, does emerge clearly in Knapp's essay. That motive is the need to connect story and place.[6] "If we take any glory in our country's being beautiful and sublime and picturesque," Knapp wrote, "we must approve the work which reminds us of its scenery by making it the theatre of splendid feats and heart-moving incidents" (173-174). But in general, Knapp did not greatly advance the discussion. John Gorham Palfrey's ebullient review of *Yamoyden*[7] in 1821 was a much more confident assertion of the resources for an American literature.

Palfrey's review may reveal the same bias that his later *History of New England* has in favor of Massachusetts, but that is a bias other *Review* writers shared. Palfrey contends for "the unequalled fitness of our early history for the purposes of a work of fiction," affirms that in the American Puritans writers have material far surpassing Scott's Covenanters, and offers a long list of Massachusetts Bay personages for the consideration of the fiction writer (XII, 480-483). Palfrey thinks, moreover, that Indians, "a separate and strongly marked race of men—with all the bold rough lines of nature yet uneffaced upon them," offer rich material for the writer in their superstitions, their domestic life, and their heroism. Indians have for Palfrey some qualities of the noble savage; they are "alive to the impressions of natural grandeur and beauty," and they speak "even in their common affairs the rich language of sententious poetry" (483).

With the pieces by Tudor, Knapp, and Palfrey, the American materials discussion takes its initial shape: all three are concerned to point out to writers what is usable in the American past to effect that coming together of story and place, the union of legend and locale for which Americans felt so real a need. But, although we know less about him as a person than we know about most of the *Review* critics,

William Howard Gardiner is the central figure in the American materials discussion.[8] A young man at the time of his *Review* pieces, he was a somewhat arrogant writer, but a highly intelligent one. And he had the advantage of reviewing Cooper's novels, in which the *Review's* doctrine seemed to come to some fruition.

It is in his 1822 review of *The Spy* that Gardiner makes his well-known division of American history for the purposes of fiction. There seem to be, he says, three epochs: "The times just succeeding the first settlement—the era of the Indian wars, which lie scattered along a considerable period—and the revolution" (xv, 255). This division had been at least implicit in the discussion before him; in subsequent discussion it is taken for granted. Like Palfrey, Gardiner thinks the "sterner puritans" of the Bay colony better material for fiction than Scott's Covenanters (255). Like Tudor and Palfrey, he recognizes the high contrasts and important interests in colonial experience: "what would not the author of Waverley," he asks, "make of such materials?" (257)—and he thinks of Indians, "a highly poetical people" (257), as fruitful material for "some future wizard of the West" (258). For the usefulness of material from the Revolution, Gardiner, in a burst of metaphor, points to the achieved success of Cooper, who has "struck into a new path . . . opened a mine of exhaustless wealth . . . laid the foundations of American romance" (281).

In this celebration of Cooper's success, Gardiner makes explicit the *Review's* first assumption in the American materials discussion: fiction of any great appeal must deal with a past, but not necessarily a far past. We need not "revert to any very remote period of antiquity," he says, "to rid us of this familiarity, which forever plays about present things." It is just here that Gardiner finds Scott's example most helpful to the American fiction writer: "Not the least pleasing, perhaps, of the many admirable productions of the great master of romance in modern times, refer to a period hardly so remote" as the days of the fathers of the elder citizens of the United States (255).

But there is another side to the discussion of Scott's example that might surprise some modern readers little acquainted with Scott and misled by depreciations of his work. *North American Review* writers found in Scott models for the treatment of commonplace experience appropriate to the literature of a young republic. From the beginning they recognized in Scott a special skill in dealing with human nature and with common life.[9]

In 1817 Palfrey speaks of Scott's ability to preserve the individuality of his characters and yet to allow his readers to discern in them "the elements of universal human nature": in *Old Mortality*, from Lady Margaret to the little peasant girl, "all is painted to the life" (v, 284-285). In his 1818 review of *Rob Roy*, Edward Tyrell Channing says that Scott "with his love for the picturesque and romantic . . . unites a singular intimacy with men in the practical, common pursuits," that Scott determines accurately "the influence of occupation, accident and every outward circumstance upon character and happiness" (vii, 155). And in this regard Jared Sparks's analysis of the pattern of the "Scottish, or Waverley novels," with which he begins his 1825 review of ten new American novels, is especially instructive.

The Waverley novels, Sparks says, are "for the most part historical," "topographic" in that their scenes are real, and "essentially dramatic" with dialogue in large proportion to incident; "the personages are drawn from models that exist in nature," and they have "not only a human, but a national, and often a provincial character" (xxi, 80-82). Sparks is seeing in Scott a special relationship between story and actuality, a verisimilitude that seems to him a new thing: "the subject of manners and customs," he says, "is one of general interest, and as an adherence to these serves to give individuality to the characters in these narratives, it is so far an improvement on the practice of the older novels, and advantageous to the writer" (82). But Sparks, thinking from the assumption that fiction cannot deal with the familiar, has a reservation: this admirable verisimilitude would be a disadvantage for any reader who happened to have lived "near the place and time of the supposed action," for a man's "own house, his own city, or his own time, can scarcely be made to appear picturesque or romantic to himself"(82).

Now, so long as "picturesque" and "romantic" indicate the desiderata, the prospects for fiction will remain about what we see, for instance, in Gardiner's review of *The Spy*. Yet Sparks does celebrate Scott's verisimilitude in handling common life if that life be enough removed in time and place from the reader. In the same year, William Cullen Bryant takes a step further, and comes close to defining a realistic aim for fiction, long before the term "realism" had a literary application. He sees a possibility for fiction that none of his colleagues on the *Review* save perhaps Willard Phillips[10] quite envisions, but that is recognized in the criticism of Robert Walsh and James Kirke Paulding. Bryant's review of Catherine M. Sedgwick's *Redwood* is a landmark in the history of American criticism, but it needs to be considered in its historical context.

Indeed, Bryant is himself careful to put his review into the context of the discussion of American materials, and to assert the *Review's* part in the discovery of "the fertility of our country, and its history, in the materials of romance." The *Review's* hope, he says, has been amply substantiated by Cooper's success. He finds Miss Sedgwick's novel "in like manner . . . a conclusive argument, that the writers of works of fiction, of which the scene is laid in familiar and domestic life, have a rich and varied field before them in the United States" (xx, 248). The prevailing notion that nineteenth-century American life offers little of interest and variety for the fiction writer is, Bryant thinks, only an unconsidered inference from the fact that no fiction writer had made much of it. "Twenty years ago," he asks, "what possible conception could an English critic have had of the admirable productions of the author of Waverley, and of the wonderful improvement his example has effected in that kind of composition?" (248-249)

Now what Bryant urges is an extension of the wonderful improvement Scott has made—not a revolt against it—and an extension of the search for American materials. It is after all Scott who had taught fiction writers how to deal with characters from all walks of life, to engage our interest in them as "beings of our own species": "It is here that James First, and Charles Second, and Louis Ninth, and Rob Roy, and Jeanie Deans, and Meg Merrilies are, by the great author of the Waverley Novels, made to meet." Fiction writers, Bryant insists, will find ample materials with which to practice what Scott has taught them, to deal with their characters as "objects of sympathy and regard," in the great variety of persons formed "under the influence of our free institutions" (252-253). Americans differ by their religious persuasions, by their geographical locations, and by what they retain of their European inheritances, Bryant says. He suggests an interesting extension of the contrast theme in the fictional study of Europeans recently settled in the United States (253-256). "We shall feel little pride," he declares, "in the sagacity or the skill of that native author, who asks for a richer or a wider field of observation" (256).

But Bryant knows that he is asking for the development of a high skill, and he is quite aware of the assumption that the familiar cannot be made interesting in fiction. He believes that, in dealing with common life, Miss Sedgwick has a difficult but admirable intent: "We have seen the original, and require that there be no false coloring or distortion in the copy" (247). It is, he says as he concludes the review, "a sort of public benefit, to show what copious and valuable materials the private lives and daily habits of our countrymen offer to the writer of genius. It is as if one were to discover to us rich ores and gems lying in the common earth about us" (272). To Gardiner's three epochs, Bryant hopes to add a fourth—his own present, seen in the light of common day.

The American materials discussion in the *North American Review* had an almost immediate effect. The hopes of the critics were not, of course, completely fulfilled. Although they value Irving's achievement and take a considerable pride in it, they seem to see little of importance in Irving's use of American materials.[11] Gardiner, who hopes "to see the day, when . . . the modern historical romance, shall be erected in all of its native elegance and strength . . . and of materials exclusively our own" (xv, 254), is never entirely happy with Cooper's novels, close as they are to critical prescription. Nevertheless, the *Review* writers could be sure of their influence.

Indeed, the *Review* writers were taken aback by the ways and the rapidity in which their affirmation and suggestion came over into practice. Although Gardiner, in a sardonic review of James McHenry's *The Wilderness* and *The Spectre of the Forest* in 1824, complains of characters and scenes not American, and of Americans who speak and act as no American ever did, he complains too of a superabundance of "American materials": "We have wars, Indians, wild beasts, witches, trials, hangings, mobs, pirates, regicides, all conspiring against the reader's peace in every page" (xix, 223).[12] And when in 1825 Jared Sparks reviews that batch of ten new American novels, he writes with a certain resignation. The Waverley novels have brought novel reading into "better favor with the graver part of the community" (xxi, 79), but, unhappily, mediocrity is easy to attain in the Waverley pattern. All that reviewers can do, Sparks thinks, is "to exercise a strict *surveillance* over this department of literature" and to "endeavor to give a beneficial direction to a force, that they cannot resist if they would" (83).

Gardiner, with this overproduction in mind—by one count

twenty-seven novels in 1824 and 1825[13]—and with McHenry's two novels still in his memory, begins his generally favorable 1826 review of Cooper's *The Pioneers* and *The Last of the Mohicans* petulantly: "The experiment of adapting American scenes, events, and characters to historical romance was suggested but a few years ago. It has been since abundantly tried, and is still going on to such an extent, that we should have ample cause to regret the little countenance we may have given it, did we feel ourselves called upon to review, or even to read, half the trash which appears daily under this disguise" (XXIII, 150).

With this review, the discussion of American materials in the *North American Review* comes virtually to an end, and interesting as it is, there is little new in principle. The ideas and contentions of *Review* writers, however, were repeated by others for a decade or more,[14] and their influence went far beyond the rash of romances in 1824 and 1825. There was general acceptance of the *Review*'s three epochs of American romance. The novels of James Kirke Paulding (as a critic he did not share the admiration for Scott) represent all three.[15] Cooper seems to have been impelled to work in all, even where he had no imaginative sympathy, and perhaps *Review* writers should be held partly responsible for his wooden Puritans in *The Wept of Wish-ton-Wish*. Indeed these writers, in their discussion of the resources for fiction in the three epochs, both foresaw and contributed to certain problems in our early fiction.

One of these problems turned out to be what the fiction writer could do with Indians. Tudor's prediction that they would be the classic subject for American writers seems convincing on its face: a distinctive American literature was desired; Indians were peculiarly American. Yet the matter gathered complexities. Palfrey seems confident enough that Indians are good literary material, although he is disturbed that *Yamoyden* makes them the moral heroes of King Philip's War. But his friend and fellow historian, Jared Sparks, in his 1825 review of the long poem *Escalala* by Samuel B. Beach, says that the Indian character is so lacking in interest and variety that he doubts "whether a poem of high order can ever be woven out of the materials it affords" (xx, 211); and Grenville Mellon, in an 1828 review of Cooper's *Red Rover*, makes the same contention in regard to fiction (xxvii, 141).[16] Even Gardiner, with his high hope in Indian material, cannot be satisfied when it is used.

In his review of *The Spy*, Gardiner had said that an account of Indian warfare would be "no mean instrument of the sublime and terrible of human agency. And if we may credit the flattering pictures of [the Indians'] best historian, the indefatigable Heckewelder, not a little of softer interest might be extracted from their domestic life" (xv, 258).[17] But in January, 1826, an article by Lewis Cass, the governor of Michigan Territory, appeared in the *Review* (xxii, 53-119), an article in which Cass is censorious of Heckewelder and, in passing, of Cooper.[18] Thereupon Gardiner, reviewing *The Last of the Mohicans* in the July number, ignores his earlier advice and comments: "The great difficulty is that which we [i.e., Cass] suggested, by the way, in a late article on this interesting subject; namely, that [Cooper] has relied exclusively upon the narrations of the enthusiastic and visionary Heckewelder, whose work is a mere eulogium upon the virtues of his favorite tribe, and contains, mixed with many interesting facts, a world of pure imagination" (xxiii, 166). It will be remembered that Cooper's defense in his preface to *The Leather-Stocking Tales* is to plead that he is writing in the epic tradition. As Tudor had urged, Cooper takes Indians as a classic subject, although Tudor surely did not quite foresee Cooper's Indians.

So, curiously, does Hawthorne accept a theory like Tudor's: he remarks that "no writer can be more secure of a permanent place in our literature than the biographer of the Indian chiefs. His subject, as referring to tribes which have mostly vanished from the earth, gives him a right to be placed upon a classic shelf, apart from the merits which will sustain him there." But with gratuitous emphasis Hawthorne rejects the subject matter for himself: "It has often been a matter of regret to me that I was shut out from the most peculiar field of American fiction by an inability to see any romance, or poetry, or grandeur, or beauty in the Indian character, at least till such traits were pointed out to me by others. I do abhor an Indian story."[19] To understand Hawthorne here and perhaps such attitudes as Sparks's, we need to go behind the text.

Neither Hawthorne nor any other writer could think of Indians apart from their conflict with white men, and their defeat by white men. For any sensitive person the subject was painful, even if it were not consciously so realized. One of Hawthorne's very few mentions of Indians is a bitterly ironic passage in "The Gray Champion"; it comes in the course of a description of a crowd of Puritans: "Here, also, were the veterans of King Philip's war, who had burned villages and slaughtered young and old, with pious fierceness, while the godly souls throughout the land were helping them with prayer." Hawthorne does remark at the beginning of "Roger Malvin's Burial" that "Lovell's Fight" is "one of the few incidents of Indian warfare naturally susceptible of the moonlight of romance," but he uses an incident only peripheral to it. Captain Lovewell was a folk hero in some sort, but only in ballads that kept the focus on his defeat and death. Neither Hawthorne nor any other serious writer subject to the strong influence of literary nationalism could celebrate his career in fiction; the facts hardly allowed celebration.[20]

If the use of Indian material made one kind of problem, a scene in the times of the Revolution made another. Tudor, we remember, ruled out the Revolution as literary material until it should be long in the past. Gardiner, even in his enthusiasm for *The Spy*, still thinks the Revolution "a less prolific source than our earlier history" (xv, 281). If it were to be used, it needed to be made to seem to have an antiquity it did not have in reality. John Knapp foresees the difficulty in 1818 and suggests that "things real may, without offence, be modified and take their form from the hand of an author not strictly historical" (VIII, 175). Hawthorne is an author not strictly historical when he devotes the first paragraph of "My Kinsman, Major Molineux" to obscuring the time—the summer of 1765—in which the action of his tale must go on.

But Hawthorne was uncomfortable with materials as recent as the Revolution. In the frame of "Howe's Masquerade" he complains, "In truth, it is desperately hard work, when we attempt to throw the spell of hoar antiquity over localities with which the living world, and the day that is passing over us, have aught to do." In the "Legends of the Province House" he tried for that spell by Gothic suggestion, an endeavor for which there was some precedent in Cooper's practice and more in Gardiner's comment on it. Cooper, Gardiner says in reference to *Lionel Lincoln*, has the same "sort of magical authority" that Scott, Radcliffe, Walpole and Brockden Brown exhibit; "places . . . familiar to us from our boyhood . . . are boldly seized upon for scenes of the wildest romance. . . . A military conclave at the Province House possesses something of the same interest as if it were holden before the walls of Tillietudlem." This ability to achieve a seeming distance, Gardiner believes, requires the fiction writer's highest skill: "It is the creation and adaptation of a kind of machinery, which may be original in its character, and yet within the narrowed limits of modern probability, that stretch to the utmost the inventive faculties of the novelist" (XXIII, 152-153). Until Bryant, all the *Review* critics assumed that the fiction writer would work in the past; and if 1776 seems antiquity to us, it hardly seemed so in the first decades of the nineteenth century.

The early history of the Massachusetts Bay colony, however, might be made to seem antiquity even in, say, 1825, and thus be the most available period for the fiction writer. Now Hawthorne made Puritan materials so much his own that he has been thought to be their discoverer. But the *Review* critics, from the beginning, held them fruitful, and their prescriptions were accepted. Tudor's suggestion of the use of the legend of the mysterious regicide at Hadley (II, 29 n.), for instance, so appealed to both critics and fiction writers that its extensive history has elements of absurdity.[21] And Puritan materials were used, not only in such forgotten novels as those Sparks reviewed in 1825, but in novels the names of which, at least, we still remember, novels of the 1820's by James McHenry, Catherine M. Sedgwick, John Neal, and Cooper.[22] Hawthorne was not first or alone in seeing the advantages of Puritan material, although he may have been the first to fulfill the predictions of Palfrey and Gardiner that "the sterner puritans" of Massachusetts Bay would be better material than the Scotch Covenanters.

Some of Hawthorne's tales seem to be written to the *Review's* critical prescription—"The Gray Champion," say, or "Endicott and the Red Cross"—except that the ironic reservation in them was not prescribed. Palfrey's long list of personages from Puritan times includes at least four that Hawthorne uses,[23] and much of his reading in the Salem years was devoted to a search for such materials as the *Review* critics recommended. There is a line from the work of Scott through the American materials discussion, and thence through Hawthorne's early work to *The Scarlet Letter*. Indeed Hawthorne, deeply aware of his heritage, early imbued with Scott's novels, found in the American materials discussion something that served him almost as a literary tradition. It may have been in his later career also a limitation. The well-known passages in the prefaces to *The Blithedale Romance* and to *The Marble Faun* come down from the assumption of the *Review* critics that "the familiarity, which forever plays about present things" is inimical to fiction. Hawthorne may have believed, as he says in "The Custom House," that there was a better book in the nineteenth-century actuality of Salem than he would ever write, but his literary habit was formed between his college years and about 1830, and it was hardly to be adapted to a new mode of fiction. Bryant's effort in 1825 to extend and modify the influence of Scott, and to establish a fourth epoch of American materials, was too early to succeed.

But Bryant's review of *Redwood* remains the most surprising document among those we have considered. There is an important difference between the effort of Bryant's predecessors to adapt the example of Scott and Bryant's effort to extend it. His argument for the treatment of common life and central experience is in itself as persuasive (it seems to me) as Howells' argument in *Criticism and Fiction*. But Howells had behind him the example of his own practice— as well as a new movement in Europe. Bryant had only the occasion of the publication of *Redwood*; and Miss Sedgwick, though admirable in many ways, was not that "writer of genius" whose example could establish a new development and show fiction writers that the "familiar and domestic life" of the present might well be the stuff of fiction.

Bryant himself seems conscious of the discrepancy between his discussion of the resources for fiction in the life of his present and his account of Miss Sedgwick's novel. *Redwood*, although it has some interesting figures and uses such contemporary materials as the Shakers, also has a creaking and conventional plot, depending on coincidence and turning on that frayed matter of a mystery in the identity of a central character. Bryant does try to convince his readers, and probably himself, that the plot mechanisms do not spoil the effect of the verisimilitude of persons and scenes in *Redwood*: "As for the Waverley novels," Bryant writes, "they abound in licenses of this sort. After all, the plot of a novel is little more than a convenient contrivance to introduce interesting situations and incidents, well drawn characters and fine sketches from life and nature" (xx, 269). But here the appeal to Scott's example seems ill-judged. Bryant's hope would scarcely be fulfilled, as he must himself have realized, until fiction writers could present convincing contemporary persons with recognizable motives moving in an action equally convincing.

Bryant's eloquent call for the use of American experience in the present is hardly paralleled until that fine passage in Emerson's "The Poet" which begins "We do not, with sufficient plainness, or sufficient profoundness, address ourselves to life, nor dare we chaunt our own times and social circumstance," and which goes on to point out, as Bryant had done, the "incomparable materials" for the writer in the variety of American life. But when Emerson wrote, about twenty years after the publication of *Redwood*, realism seemed as far off as ever.

The *Review* critics were not, of course, everywhere prescient. They did not foresee the development of magazines and short fiction; they did not consider—at least they did not remark—the relationship between a developing literature and publishing in the United States. But they were aware of the needs of the young nation: Willard Phillips speaks for all when he says in his 1824 review of *The Pilot* that just as the pioneer opens the prospect of cultivated fields and habitations, so the writer of a literary work peculiarly American "undertakes a like enterprise; he peoples the regions of fancy and memory" (xviii, 314).

A special interest in the work of this group of *Review* critics, as it seems to me, is that we can see in it an epitome of the American phase of the development of prose fiction into the dominant form. In 1815 Walter Channing writes in a *Review* article that a country with no antiquity is "destitute . . . of the materials for exercising the highest range of dramatick talent, viz. the historical," and for the same reason "we cannot hope much distinction" in the epic (ii, 39-40). He does not speak of fiction; it was not within his purview. In the same year, as Tudor begins the *Review*'s consideration of American materials, he looks forward to a literature in an epic vein; he is denying such contentions as Channing's, but he has not foreseen the development of an American fiction. Yet within ten years, the *North American Review* writers who consider fiction take it for granted that fiction is the dominant form and congratulate the age they live in that it has become so.

[1] Reprinted in *The American Literary Revolution, 1783-1837*, ed. Robert E. Spiller (New York, 1967), p. 296.

[2] "Literary Criticism in the *North American Review, 1815-1835*," *Transactions of the Wisconsin Academy of Science, Arts and Letters*, 32 (1940), 299-350. Professor Clark's bibliography has been so useful to me that I am glad to write in particular reference to it. For studies of early American criticism in larger contexts, see Professor Spiller's anthology cited above; Russell Blaine Nye, *The Cultural Life of the New Nation 1776-1830*, (New York, 1960), pp. 235-267; William Ellery Sedgwick, "The Materials for an American Literature," *Harvard Studies and Notes in Philology and Literature*, 17 (1935), 141-162; G. Harrison Orians, "The Romance Ferment after *Waverley*," *American Literature*, 3 (1932), 408-431.

[3] See Cooper's "Letter #23," reprinted in Spiller, pp. 399-405. For a late survival of this conviction, see James Russell Lowell's essay on James Gates Percival (1867), *Writings*, Riverside Edition (Boston, 1898), II, 148. The most eloquent statements of the negative position, however, are by persons who are restating it in order to oppose it. See William Howard Gardiner, *North American Review*, 15 (1822), 250-253; and William Cullen Bryant's third "Lecture on Poetry" (delivered in 1826), reprinted in *Bryant*, ed. Tremaine McDowell (New York, 1935), pp. 203-205.

[4] See a striking contemporary account of Scott's popularity in the *American Quarterly Review*, 2, 33 (probably by Robert Walsh, the editor), and James D. Hart, *The Popular Book* (Berkeley, 1961), pp. 68-69 and 73-78.

[5] Perhaps one might consider the discussion to begin with Tudor's 1815 review of *Moral Pieces in Prose and Verse* by Lydia Huntley [Mrs. Sigourney] in which he hopefully recommends American materials (I, 111-121).

[6] See a central passage from Alison's *The Nature and Principles of Taste*, as reprinted in Spiller, pp. 493-494; Robert E. Streeter, "Association Psychology and Literary Nationalism in the *North American Review*," *American Literature*, 17 (1945), 243-354. The *Review* critics recognized that Scott showed the way to supply a texture of association for American places. Once, at least, Scott makes his principle explicit: see his introduction to *Sir Tristrem* (Edinburgh, 1804), p. xxvi.

[7] *Yamoyden* (1820) is a long narrative poem concerning King Philip's War by the Rev. James Wallis Eastman and Robert Charles Sands.

[8] William Howard Gardiner (1796-1882) became a prominent lawyer and was the friend and executor of William H. Prescott. He was the Phi Beta Kappa poet at Harvard in 1818 and gave the Phi Beta Kappa address there in 1834 (*On Classical Learning and Eloquence*, Cambridge: James Munroe & Co., 1834).

[9] This recognition was not limited to writers in the *North American Review*; in 1827 Walsh (?) in the *American Quarterly Review* praised Scott for "ennobling persons not only of the ordinary, but of the lowest orders of society, by the magic of his fertile genius" (II, 26).

[10] In 1816, before Scott's example was dominant, Phillips praises a novel called *Rhoda* for its representation of "daily occurrences and observations" (III, 216), and in 1818 he praises Maria Edgeworth for her concern with "men and women, animated by the passions with which real life is glowing, and busy with the pursuits in which we ourselves are interested" (VI, 153).

[11] Richard Henry Dana, Sr. in reviewing the first two numbers of the *Sketch Book*, discusses *Knickerbocker's History* and "Rip Van Winkle" without making any connection with the American materials discussion ("The Legend of Sleepy Hollow" was not, of course, included in the first two numbers of the *Sketch Book*). Dana does remark that Europeans, who have many authors, can hardly understand Irving's importance to Americans: "We, who have only two or three, are as closely attached to them, as if they were our brothers" (IX, 348). Edward Everett, in reviewing *Bracebridge Hall*, complains that Irving might have written the book "without sacrificing . . . all that store of recollections, which he had brought from home" (XV, 214), and that he "might have seen in the preference given 'Rip Van Winkle,' where his forte lies"; Everett therefore prefers "Dolph Heyliger" above the other pieces in the book (215). The *Review* ignores the *Tales of a Traveller*.

[12] In his introduction to *The Spectre of the Forest*, McHenry—with more pertinence than he realized—wrote that "the difficulty arose not from the scarcity but the abundance of materials which every period of the history of this new and interesting country offered."

[13] Orians, "Romance Ferment," p. 423.

[14] See, for example, Rufus Choate's oration "The Importance of Illustrating New-England History by a Series of Romances like the Waverley Novels," delivered at Salem in 1833 (printed in *Addresses and Orations of Rufus Choate*, Boston, 1887). A late survival is W. G. Simms, *Views and Reviews in American Literature, History and Fiction* (New York, 1845).

[15] *The Puritan and His Daughter* (1849); *The Dutchman's Fireside* (1831: concerns the French and Indian War); and *The Old Continental* (1846).

[16] Mellon, however, adheres to the idea that the American past in general furnishes inadequate literary materials.

[17] That Indian material might be "an instrument of the sublime and terrible," a kind of Gothic, occurred to other writers, of course. Charles Brockden Brown in his *Edgar Huntley* had attempted to find an American Gothic in Indians, instead of, as he says in his preface, in "Gothic castles and chimeras." Robert Walsh (?) remarks with some irony that "if . . . a writer of this country wishes to make its history, or its traditions the subject of romantic fiction, high wrought, obscure, and somewhat extravagant, agreeable to the taste of the times, he must go back to the aborigines" (*American Quarterly Review*, 2, 1827, 45).

[18] Cass says that Cooper's "'the last of the Mohegans' [*sic*] is an Indian of the school of Mr. Heckewelder, and not of the school of nature" (XXII, 67). The reference

Neal Frank Doubleday

must be to Indian John in *The Pioneers*: Cass could hardly have read *The Last of the Mohicans* when he wrote his article. Cooper quotes the passage inaccurately in his preface to *The Leather-Stocking Tales*.

[19] "Our Evening Party Among the Mountains," in *Mosses from an Old Manse*, Riverside Edition, p. 483.

[20] See, for example, an account of Lovewell and his men shooting ten sleeping Indians for the bounty on their scalps in Thomas Hutchinson, *The History of . . . Massachusetts-Bay*, ed. Lawrence Shaw Mayo (Cambridge, Mass., 1936), II, 238. What Hawthorne makes his narrator say to his children auditors in *Grandfather's Chair*, Riverside Edition, pp. 467-470 is instructive on Hawthorne's attitude toward the conflict of Indians and white men.

[21] See G. Harrison Orians, "The Angel of Hadley in Fiction," *American Literature*, 4 (1932), 257-269. Gardiner remarks in his review of *The Spectre of the Forest* that "the Spectre . . . appears and disappears in a most astonishing manner on all great occasions, and constantly stands ready to help the author through every difficulty" (XIX, 223), and the remark might apply beyond McHenry's novel. The sanction of Scott's example in *Peveril of the Peak* (1822) may partly account for the popularity of the legend of the mysterious regicide, but it had a remarkable appeal: Palfrey suggests its use; John Neal complains in *Blackwood's* of its pre-emption by Scott (*American Writers*, ed. F. L. Pattee, Durham, N. C., 1937, pp. 191-192); and in a review of James Nelson Barker's *Superstition* in the *American Quarterly Review*, the critic (probably Paulding) says that it "has often occurred to us as singularly striking and dramatic" (I, 354); Washington Irving, we are told, once planned a novel about the regicide judges (Stanley T. Williams, *Life of Washington Irving*, New York, 1935, II, 290). William Leete Stone uses two of the regicide judges in his "Mercy Disborough: A Tale of the Witches" (1834).

[22] McHenry, *The Spectre of the Forest* (1823); Miss Sedgwick, *Hope Leslie* (1827); Neal, *Rachel Dyer* (1828); and Cooper, *The Wept of Wish-ton-Wish* (1829).

[23] Mrs. Hutchinson, Endicott, William Goffe, and Thomas Morton. Palfrey also suggests the Quakers as subject matter for fiction.

III

EMERSON ON THE SCHOLAR, 1838:
A STUDY OF "LITERARY ETHICS"

MERTON M. SEALTS, JR.

WHEN EMERSON DELIVERED HIS PHI BETA Kappa oration on "The American Scholar" in August of 1837 he was partly fulfilling his intention of two years before "to write a chapter on Literary Ethics or the Duty & Discipline of a Scholar."[1] The conception of such a "chapter," which he may at first have thought of in relation to the projected book on "Natural Ethics" that developed into *Nature* (1836),[2] also involved Emerson's image of himself as "the scholar" and his continuing meditations on the scholar's proper relations to nature, the mind of the past, and contemporary society.[3] Another product of his thinking on this subject is the less-familiar "Oration, Delivered before the Literary Societies of Dartmouth College, July 24, 1838," later given the title "Literary Ethics," in which he considers "the resources, the subject, and the discipline of the scholar."[4] Overshadowed by the Phi Beta Kappa oration of 1837 and by the controversial Divinity School Address of 1838, read in Cambridge nine days before the engagement in Hanover, "Literary Ethics" has drawn comparatively little attention from Emerson's commentators. Is it deservedly neglected, or does it contribute to an understanding of his long preoccupation with the scholar's "Duty & Discipline"? These are the questions to be raised in this appraisal.

The letter inviting Emerson to speak at Dartmouth was written on April 20, 1838, three weeks after he had been asked to address the Divinity School seniors in Cambridge.[5] Although he accepted "with great delight" (*JMN*, V, 479), he experienced difficulty in completing his manuscript and had misgivings about its appropriateness for the occasion. During the spring and summer of 1838 he drafted material for both engagements in his journal, but the earlier commitment at Cambridge evidently took priority; the Dartmouth oration was not finished until after he reached Hanover a day before its delivery. In a letter of July 23 he wrote of "the undone address" that it "prospers indifferent well[.] I can't say I admire it much & since I have come hither & seen some of the young men, I think it unfit. But yet is that somewhat about which a wise man will not care when he has done what he could" (*L*, II, 145). Two days later, with the oration duly completed and presented, he asked his wife to tell their friend Elizabeth Hoar that "our speech is better than she thinks, and I have no doubt some of it found ears in the crowd" (*L*, II, 146). After returning home to face new evidence of the stir his earlier address had created in Cambridge, he remarked to his brother William that probably at Dartmouth as well as at the Divinity School "some men hated my speech" while others "said it was true" (*L*, II, 151), but the two works did not have the same incendiary effect on their respective audiences: "If any rumor of the former discourse had reached Dartmouth," as Oliver Wendell Holmes observed, "the audience must have been prepared for a much more startling performance than that to which they listened."[6] Emerson soon published both addresses as pamphlets, but the Dartmouth oration "caused hardly a ripple of excitement" in the midst of the controversy over the Divinity School Address, as Professor Rusk has said, "and was promptly forgotten by all but a few."[7]

Although Rusk classed "Literary Ethics" as "a poor relation" of "The American Scholar," it has affiliations as well
with the Divinity School Address. All three works reflect
the same faith in what Emerson called "the infinitude of
the private man," the "one doctrine" that underlies all his
lectures and addresses of the late 1830's, though to the divinity
students he overtly stressed its religious implications and
at Dartmouth as in "The American Scholar" his primary
emphasis was on secular scholarship. Since "Literary Ethics"
advances many of the same corollary ideas as the Divinity
School Address, the differing receptions of what he had to
say in Cambridge and in Hanover point up the rightness
of his own later remark about his platform appearances in
general: "as long as I call the lecture, Art; or Politics; or
Literature; or the Household," the audience has no difficulty
with its doctrine; "but the moment I call it Religion,—they
are shocked" (*JMN*, VII, 342). The essentially religious character of what he originally planned to say at Dartmouth
is evident from the journal entry of April 30, 1838, that
served as nucleus for its development:

> Could not the natural history of the Reason or Universal Senti-
> ment be written? One trait would be that all that is alive
> and genial in thought must come out of that. Here is friend
> B[arzillai]. F[rost] grinds & grinds in the mill of a truism
> & nothing comes out but what was put in. But the moment
> he or I desert the tradition & speak a spontaneous thought,
> instantly poetry, wit, hope, virtue, learning, anecdote, all flock
> to our aid. This topic were no bad one for the Dartmouth
> College boys whom I am to address in July. (*JMN*, V, 481)

What Emerson calls here "the Reason" he had already
identified in *Nature* with the "universal soul within or behind"
the individual life (*W*, I, 27); his conviction that man has
direct access to immanent Reason was the ground of his
doctrine of infinitude. The term itself is one of several names—
"soul," "spirit," "the moral sentiment," "the Universal," and

so on—that he used interchangeably in the 1830's for the same basic postulate. In "Literary Ethics" he went on to say that the scholar must honor Reason rather than tradition just as at Cambridge he told the divinity students to preach the Soul rather than historical Christianity. The journal passage looks forward to a common theme of both addresses; it even offers the same cautionary example: Barzillai Frost, the uninspired and uninspiring Concord minister, who turns up again in both, though mercifully not by name. In "Literary Ethics" he is present in an adaptation of this same passage, where "B. F." and "he" are generalized into "Men" and "they" (*W*, I, 165-166); in a celebrated passage of the Divinity School Address, as we know from another journal entry, he is the original of the "spectral" minister lifelessly preaching during a snowstorm that seems more real than he (*JMN*, V, 463; *W*, I, 137-138).

The clerical focus of Emerson's thinking is maintained as he continues his preliminary sketch of the Dartmouth oration, reminding himself not to overlook the inhibiting factors against which the scholar must contend even when moved by the Reason.

> Let them know how prompt the *limiting* instinct is in our constitution so that the moment the mind by one bold leap (an impulse from the Universal) has set itself free of the old church and of a thousand years of dogma & seen the light of moral nature, . . . on the instant the defining lockjaw shuts down his fetters & cramps all round us, . . . & the last slavery is even worse than the first. (*JMN*, V, 481)

In just this way all sectarians, including "the new unnamed or misnamed" Transcendentalists, "dogmatise & rail" at others, he observes, "& can not see the worth of the antagonism also. The great common sense (using the word in its higher sense) is the umpire that holds the balance of these kingdoms." Against the "kingdom" of universal Reason, in other words, Emerson sets the contending kingdom that he habitually sought to subordinate or transcend: the world of the immediate, the personal, the finite, illustrated here by religious sectarians with their passion for definition and dogma. In the Coleridgean terms that he often used, the opposition is between Reason and Understanding—and "no doctrine of the Reason," as he was to say prophetically at the Divinity School, "will bear to be taught by the Understanding" (*W*, I, 129). Though acknowledging in the journal that even "antagonism" has a positive value, Emerson is more conciliatory than contentious in the Dartmouth oration itself, where he stands somewhat apart from both opposing "kingdoms," speaking as a kind of surrogate for that "great common sense" that holds them safely in balance. To maintain equilibrium between the two while doing justice to both is an evident objective of "Literary Ethics."

In working out the Dartmouth address, which consists of passages originally drafted in the journal linked together with new matter written specifically for the purpose,[8] Emerson followed the model of the classical oration, as he had done in "The American Scholar" in 1837. The printed version is formally divided into a brief introduction (*exordium*); a long middle section (*exhibition*) consisting of three numbered parts that consider in turn the scholar's resources, his opportunities, and his discipline or ethics; and a short conclusion (*peroration*). The pattern of contrast that runs through the argument is established in the introductory paragraphs (*W*, I, 155-158), where Emerson first shows the scholar as he should appear—"the favorite of Heaven and earth, the excellency of his country, the happiest of men"—and then describes the scholar as he is actually regarded in the America of 1838. American antagonism to "the culture of the intellect," he charges, is responsible for his young country's failure to fulfill in its arts "what seemed the reasonable expectation of mankind." To strike the desired balance in this portion of his account, he carefully distinguishes genuine "service of thought" from mere pedantry, much as he had done in "The American Scholar," affirming now that the scholar's work is not only both sane and reasonable, in contrast to "the despotism of the senses" that leads some men to pursue only "ease or profit," but is also in the best sense realistic. The first and second topical divisions, which grew out of the preliminary journal entry, are also reminiscent of Emerson's earlier writing in their emphasis on the Reason; the third division places the scholar in relation to both the world of Reason and the everyday world of human life and action—the two "kingdoms" he had previously distinguished in the journal.

Emerson's discussion of the scholar's resources (*W*, I, 158-166) develops his seminal idea that what is "alive and genial in thought" must come from the Reason. As in *Nature*, he calls here for an original and primary, not a secondary or derived, relation to the universe; as in "The American Scholar" he addresses not "the inscrutable, obliterated past" of tradition but "the enveloping Now" of the Reason. Growth of the intellect, which is "strictly analogous in all individuals," he identifies with "larger reception" of infinite Reason, noting both the "infinitude and impersonality of the intellectual power." What hinders a man from attaining ideal justice and goodness is "the momentary predominance of the finite and individual over the general truth." When Reason is ascendant, a man exhibits that simplicity which permits free entrance within him of "the spontaneous sentiment"; but when the "too officious activity of the understanding" interferes, the influx of spirit is blocked by "an excess of organization," an inhibiting "disease" that comes between the individual and his potential greatness.

The second numbered subsection, which considers the scholar's "subject," or "the task offered to the intellect of this country" (*W*, I, 166-173), is also written in the spirit of *Nature* and "The American Scholar." It too emphasizes originality and creativity, once again contrasting living Reason and dead tradition. As Emerson had declared in a lecture of 1837, Reason is dynamic and free; it "exists only whilst it creates"; without its continual influx even "the truest state of mind rested in, becomes false."[9] Scholarship must not occupy itself solely with the achievements of past generations, as he had warned there and again in "The American Scholar"; it has the immediate task of looking directly and creatively at nature and history, seeing for itself and not through dead men's eyes. So at Dartmouth, rejecting as "very shallow" any assumption that the only great intellectual work is what was done in former ages, that "all thought is already long ago adequately set down in books,—all imaginations in poems," he reaffirms both the opportunity and the need for further creativity. Each man has yet to "write history for himself" and to sing "his own conversation with nature," he declares exuberantly, and the same unlimited prospect lies open to the creative mind in other fields also. Religion, for example, "is yet to be settled on its fast foundations," which lie "in the breast of man" rather than in received beliefs or established tradition. So too in "politics, and philosophy, and letters, and art"; the work already done is not final: "As yet we have nothing but tendency and indication." For in pursuits such as these, the living Truth is not to be caught or compelled by the systematizers "in any mechanical manner," once and for all time; indeed, no achievement of the finite human intellect, "not mighty Homer and Milton," is great "beside the infinite Reason." Let each generation, each individual, therefore learn not to "hate, or fear, or mimic his ancestors," or to "bewail himself, as if the world was old, and thought was spent," since in every age and in every man, "by virtue of the Deity, thought renews itself inexhaustibly every day, and the thing whereon it shines, though it were dust and sand, is a new subject, with countless relations."

In the remainder of "Literary Ethics," making up a little less than half its length, Emerson is more prescriptive, both in his treatment of the scholar's discipline, "the rule of his ambition and life," and in his brief peroration. Near the conclusion, turning directly to those of his young listeners called "to explore truth and beauty," he admonishes them to honor the "primary duties of the intellect" rather than to follow "the maxims of a low prudence" by seeking "land and money, place and name." The choice of goals is crucial:

> When you shall say, 'As others do, so will I: I renounce, I am sorry for it, my early visions; I must eat the good of the land and let learning and romantic expectations go, until a more convenient season;'—then dies the man in you; then once more perish the buds of art, and poetry, and science, as they have died already in a thousand thousand men. The hour of that choice is the crisis of your history, and see that you hold yourself fast by the intellect. (*W*, I, 185-186; cf. *JMN*, VII, 30)

As these words suggest, the latter pages of the oration, like the introduction, are concerned with the conflict between the intellect and what is called "the domineering temper of the sensual world." In the longest of the three topical sections, that treating the scholar's discipline (*W*, I, 173-185), Emerson explores the issue in terms of alternatives he himself had long been pondering: solitary meditation versus an active life in society.

The implicit premise of the section on discipline is that the great powers and great opportunities open to the scholar make equally great demands upon him. The man dedicated to greatness dares not rest content with the "thin, plausible, superficial existence" of everyday society where others talk at second hand "of muse and prophet, of art and creation," without being themselves creative; out of a "shallow and frivolous way of life," the orator asks, "how can greatness ever grow?" To counteract such mere "seeming that unmakes our being," the Puritan in Emerson prescribes here "a more rigorous scholastic rule," an "asceticism" which "only the hardihood and devotion of the scholar himself can enforce."

He must be "solitary, laborious, modest, and charitable"—solitary first of all, embracing solitude "as a bride," in order to "become acquainted with his thoughts" at their deepest level: "Silence, seclusion, austerity, may pierce deep into the grandeur and secret of our being, and so diving, bring up out of secular darkness the sublimities of the moral constitution." In this introspective and necessarily solitary way the scholar puts himself in touch with the ground of his being and the source of his greatness, the Reason, since a man "is great only by being passive to the superincumbent spirit."[10]

But the case does not rest here, for the withdrawal, meditation, and passivity involved in the Emersonian doctrine of infinitude are by no means the sole requirements of the scholar, nor does the oration advocate "any superstition about solitude" as an end valuable in itself. "Let the youth study the uses of solitude and of society," Emerson declares in a pivotal passage—one not taken from the journal but written directly into the manuscript itself. "Let him use both, not serve either. The reason why an ingenious soul shuns society, is to the end of finding society. It repudiates the false, out of love of the true." The scholar dares not be ignorant of the world about him—particularly if he is a literary man "dealing with the organ of language"; as Emerson had observed in 1837, "life is our inexhaustible treasure of language for thought" (*JMN*, V, 325-326).[11] And though the Reason is still his primary resource, he will find "the richest material for his creations" in the experiences of human life itself. Since the laws of that life are "concealed under the details of daily action," and action is "an experiment upon them," the scholar can pursue them in only one way: not through meditation or reading but by taking some active part in the world of human society and bearing "his share of the common load."

> He must work with men in houses, and not with their names in books. His needs, appetites, talents, affections, accomplish-

48

ments, are keys that open to him the beautiful museum of human life. Why should he read it as an Arabian tale, and not know, in his own beating bosom, its sweet and smart? Out of love and hatred, out of earnings, and borrowings, and lendings, and losses; out of sickness and pain; out of wooing and worshipping; out of travelling; and voting, and watching, and caring; out of disgrace and contempt, comes our tuition in the serene and beautiful laws. (*W*, I, 177-178; cf. *JMN*, VII, 8)

What Emerson is advocating here is not a specific regimen of activity but simply a "mutual reaction of thought and life" that will "make thought solid, and life wise." His withdrawn scholar must return to society and there endeavor, "by punctual action, and not by promises or dreams," to "solve the problem of that life which is set before *him*." Believing in "the presence and favor of the grandest influences," he must now come to "deserve that favor, and learn how to receive and use it, by fidelity also to the lower observances."

On this more mundane level, as Emerson also recognizes pragmatically, the tasks facing a scholar are unavoidably laborious. Having access to the world of Reason by no means warrants his refusal to bear the yoke of study, "to know, if he can, the utmost secret of toil and endurance," since a healthy scholarship must be informed as well as inspired, and therefore requires a certain amount of hard and routine work—Emerson's word for it is "drill." Here too, as in the Divinity School Address, he finds an instructive example in Bonaparte, whatever his "defects or vices": no believer in mere luck but "faithful to facts," Napoleon, "by the calculations of genius," planned how best to apply "means to ends"; at the same time, "whilst he believed in number and weight, and omitted no part of prudence, he believed also in the freedom and quite incalculable force of the soul." So the scholar, recognizing his own "combination of gifts," must not neglect "the work to be done," by way of thorough preparation and steady application, if "the secret of the world is to be learned, and the skill truly to unfold it is acquired."

In the key passage of the section on discipline, growing out of the foregoing discussion, Emerson sums up his conception of the scholar's dual allegiance, to the world of men and the world of Reason, that will make him "not a fragment" but a man both healthy and whole. A "twofold goodness—the drill and the inspiration" will inform his work just as it "characterizes ever the productions of great masters." He must encompass the entire scale of experience, not any one segment of it exclusively.

> The man of genius should occupy the whole space between God or pure mind and the multitude of uneducated men. He must draw from the infinite Reason, on one side; and he must penetrate into the heart and sense of the crowd, on the other. From one, he must draw his strength; to the other, he must owe his aim. The one yokes him to the real; the other, to the apparent. At one pole is Reason; at the other, Common Sense. (*W*, I, 182)

Otherwise, by settling for any one of these paired alternatives without the other as well, "his philosophy will seem low and utilitarian, or it will appear too vague and indefinite for the uses of life."

Emerson's concern with the scholar's greatness is epitomized in this passage on the encompassing wholeness of "the man of genius," which brings together the principal themes of the entire oration in the kind of balance he had envisioned from the beginning, as we know from the first journal entry concerning its central topic. What we also know, now that the journals and lectures of the 1830's have been published in full, is that this is not a passage written especially "for the Dartmouth College boys"; instead, Emerson turned back to a journal entry of 1836 that he had already used in an earlier lecture: that on "Literature" in his course on the philosophy of history, delivered early in 1837.[12] In their original formulation his words had marked a significant development in his thinking about the scholar's role as a functioning member of society; in "Literary Ethics" they constitute a reaffirmation of a position already reached rather than a new development in his thought. Although other parts of the oration were of more recent vintage, the same generalization applies fairly to the work as a whole: like this summary passage, it recapitulates his ideas about the scholar rather than advancing them as "The American Scholar" had so powerfully done.

This is the point made by O. W. Firkins with particular reference to Emerson's discussion of Reason in earlier pages: "though novel doubtless at the time and place," it "contains little that is markedly significant for the habitual traveller on the Emersonian turnpike."[13] Given his original intention of demonstrating that Reason is the source of "all that is alive and genial in thought," he might well have pursued the discussion of the creative process itself, which had been very much in his mind as he set about writing both *Nature* and "The American Scholar." Here, despite the preliminary observation in the journal that "spontaneous thought" immediately releases "poetry, wit, hope, virtue, learning, anecdote," the only illustration of the workings of spontaneity comes not from scholarship or artistry but from extempore debate: "A man of cultivated mind but reserved habits," when once moved to express his feelings, will find it "just as easy and natural to speak" as it had been to remain silent; "for it needs not to do, but to suffer; he only adjusts himself to the free spirit which gladly utters itself through him; and motion is as easy as rest" (*W*, I, 166). Presumably it is the Reason that furnishes him "with thoughts, with pictures, with rhythmical balance of sentences," as Emerson implies, though in a later passage of the address it is not Reason but experience that he identifies as the immediate source of material for literary creation in particular. In treating the scholar's discipline, moreover, despite his reassertion of the importance of "passivity to the superincumbent spirit," his emphasis unmistakeably shifts to the need for various forms of activity: drill as well as inspiration, and beyond that, taking part in the life and work of the everyday world. Thus the original idea of the dependence of thought on Reason might be said to give way to a later insistence on the need for experience and action, and the stress on creative spontaneity in the first half of the oration to be qualified by the ensuing discussion of discipline and drill.[14]

Analyzed in this way, "Literary Ethics" appears open to a charge not infrequently leveled against Emerson's writing, that of inconsistency, though from another point of view the entire oration, building up to the climactic passage on "twofold goodness," exemplifies his characteristic intention to strike a balance between opposites. Whether or not he succeeded, particularly in the extended discussion of the scholar and his discipline, has been the focus of critical disagreement. Firkins, emphasizing "the just weight given to the adverse claims of society and solitude and the almost equal insistence on *drill* and *inspiration*," thought the effort at balance successful, showing "the poise of that equatorial constitution between the attraction of opposite poles";[15] other commentators reaching a less favorable verdict have disagreed among themselves over Emerson's emphasis and meaning. Orestes Brownson, reviewing the first printing of the oration in 1839, found "some difficulty in admitting the notion" he thought Emerson to be advancing: "that the scholar must be a solitary soul, living apart and in himself alone . . . without connexions or sympathies with his race"; being a social activist as Emerson clearly was not, he accordingly professed "no faith in this ascetic discipline."[16] An exactly contradictory reading has been offered more recently by Joel Porte, who concluded in 1966 that Emerson "really leaned" toward the opposite opinion: that "man alone with himself was somehow not to be trusted, and the world's work was preferable to private dreams." Porte dismisses Emerson's argument for a "twofold goodness," calling his injunction to study the uses of both solitude and society "a characteristic equivocation" that had served only to deceive Brownson, who "let Emerson's equivocal advice carry him in the wrong direction. The burden of Emerson's talk had certainly been that scholarship and art are ultimately the means to an end and that solitude is dangerous. Brownson took him to task for saying the opposite."[17]

If either Brownson or Porte, rather than Firkins, has read "Literary Ethics" correctly, then Emerson's scholar faces two mutually exclusive options: a solitary life of thought or an active but unmeditative life in society; certainly there are those in every generation who demand a clear-cut choice between them. But this was not Emerson's way. What to Porte seems characteristically equivocal might with equal justice be called sound psychological realism: recognizing that it is not given a man to dwell wholly in one world, the ideal or the actual, he addressed himself to the never-ending task of coming to terms with both, in practice as well as in theory. Like most of his writing, whether earlier in time or later, "Literary Ethics" reflects his own inner debate over the issues, which he continued to argue throughout his career as speaker and writer. "The worth of the antagonism," to borrow a phrase he had used while planning the oration, was a spur to creative utterance, as he acknowledges in recognizing the existence of such dualities. Though he tried in the oration, as in his own life, to strike a workable balance between them, the equations he set down were at best approximate and relative rather than absolute. In theory, he evidently shared the Platonic conviction that one world, that of the Reason, is primary and "the lower faculties" but tributary and subordinate; in his own experience, as described in the privacy of the journal, he periodically complained of "the feeble influence of thought on life," calling it in one entry, that of May 5, 1838, "a ray as pale & ineffectual as that of the sun in our cold & bleak spring. They seem to lie—the actual life, & the intellectual intervals, in parallel lines & never meet." But following this minimal statement comes a qualifying counter-statement, which in turn is qualified by its successor as though Emerson were indeed balancing the scales:

> Yet we doubt not they act & react ever, that one is even cause of the other; that one is causal, & one servile, a mere vesture. Yet it takes a great deal of elevation of thought to produce a very little elevation of life. How slowly the highest raptures of the intellect break through the trivial forms of habit. Yet imperceptibly they do. Gradually in long years we bend our living towards our idea. But we serve seven years & twice seven for Rachel. (*JMN*, V, 489)

In subject-matter and in method this passage throws light on "Literary Ethics," though the oration begins with a stronger affirmation concerning "the intellectual intervals"; both the method and the movement are representative of Emerson's thinking during the 1830's. Life and thought "act & react ever," as he says in the journal; the scholar's "Duty & Discipline," according to the oration, is to "make thought solid, and life wise," through their "mutual reaction." Here again he is treading familiar ground. As early as *Nature* he had formulated the relation between life and thought in dynamic terms: "The intellectual and the active powers seem to succeed each other, and the exclusive activity of the one generates the exclusive activity of the other" (*W*, I, 22). In "The American Scholar," itself a product of the creative tension between the two, he had seen the mind's polarity in relation to the "principle of Undulation" operating in physical nature: as the sea ebbs and flows or the lungs inhale and exhale, so the mind "now thinks, now acts, and each fit reproduces the other"—and therefore the "great soul" is "strong to live, as well as strong to think" (*W*, I, 98-99). Action is truly a resource, along with Reason. "Literary Ethics" reasserts this fundamental tenet; the difficulty is less in the conception than in the fact of its reassertion. Where "The American Scholar" announces the principle, "under the name of Polarity," with a sense of immediate discovery, placing thought and action in dynamic relation to one another, the Dartmouth oration takes up in turn the claims of passivity and action, solitude and society, but without conveying the same feeling of their reciprocal interplay.[18] There is thus some basis for interpreting "Literary Ethics" in *either/or* language rather than *both/and*, though the critic reading it in relation to what Emerson had been saying elsewhere in the 1830's should hesitate to endorse the findings of Brownson, Porte, or even Firkins without considerable hedging.

If the Dartmouth oration had been Emerson's primary consideration in the spring of 1838, like "The American Scholar" in the summer before, the result would likely have been a more dynamic address, one carrying forward his thinking about the workings of creativity, the reciprocal alternation of thought and action, the transforming power of intellect— all topics opened in the earlier work that would occupy him into the 1840's. But while drafting the oration he was also writing the Divinity School Address, which evidently came first in more than one sense. These same ideas, which might well have received further development in "Literary Ethics" under different circumstances, are explored in the Cambridge address with particular reference to religion and the work of the minister—Emerson's scholar in clerical garb. In Cambridge, moreover, he was to speak at the invitation of young men he knew on subjects he had already discussed with some of them in private conversation; at Hanover, by contrast, he had no close ties, so that his objectives and tactics as an orator must have been harder to formulate. To complicate matters, the most eloquent of his journal passages were finding their way, by accident or design, into the Divinity School manuscript while the Dartmouth oration remained unfinished—and possibly even unfit for its audience, as Emerson feared after reaching Hanover. His uneasiness, though it proved unjustified, is quite understandable. But the finished oration, if not the equal of either of the Cambridge addresses, is a substantial and readable work, representative of his central ideas and in keeping with his developing thought about the scholar and his "twofold goodness." Though it neither raises new issues, as its two predecessors had done, nor says the last word on old ones, it affords a good standing-ground for surveying Emerson's position in 1838—before the storm over the Divinity School Address threatened the equilibrium he had been seeking in his chosen role as the inspired but disciplined scholar.

---

[1] Entry for August 6, 1835, in *The Journals and Miscellaneous Notebooks of Ralph Waldo Emerson*, ed. William H. Gilman et al. (Cambridge: The Belknap Press of Harvard University Press, 1960–), V, 84. Volumes of this edition will be cited hereafter as *JMN*.

[2] Letter to Frederic Henry Hedge, June 25, 1835, in *The Letters of Ralph Waldo Emerson*, ed. Ralph L. Rusk, 6 vols. (New York: Columbia University Press, 1939), I, 447. Volumes of this edition will be cited hereafter as *L*. See also *Emerson's Nature: Origin, Growth, Meaning*, ed. Merton M. Sealts, Jr., and Alfred R. Ferguson (New York: Dodd, Mead, & Co., 1969), pp. 41 ff.

[3] See Merton M. Sealts, Jr., "Emerson on the Scholar, 1833-1837," *PMLA*, 85 (March 1970), 185-195.

[4] *The Complete Works of Ralph Waldo Emerson*, ed. Edward Waldo Emerson, 12 vols. (Boston and New York: Houghton Mifflin Co., 1903-1904), I, 158. Volumes of this edition will be cited hereafter as *W*.

[5] For the invitations, see *L*, II, 144, n. 162, and 146-147, n. 169.

[6] *Ralph Waldo Emerson* (Boston and New York: Houghton, Mifflin and Company, 1884), pp. 131-132. Holmes's comments stress "the extreme difference between the fundamental conceptions of Mr. Emerson and the endemic orthodoxy of that place and time."

[7] Ralph L. Rusk, *The Life of Ralph Waldo Emerson* (New York: Charles Scribner's Sons, 1949), p. 273.

[8] The journal passages drawn upon for "Literary Ethics" comprise a little more than half its total content. All were composed after Emerson's acceptance of the invitation from Dartmouth except for the following entries: (1) *JMN*, v, 249-250 (November 19, 1836), used in W, I, 182; (2) *JMN*, v, 373 (September 18, 1837), used in *W*, I, 168; (3) *JMN*, v, 458-459 (March 5, 1838), used in *W*, I, 171-172; and (4) *JMN*, v, 468-469 (March 27, 1838), used in *W*, I, 167-169.

[9] "The Present Age," in *The Early Lectures of Ralph Waldo Emerson*, ed. Stephen E. Whicher, Robert E. Spiller, and Wallace E. Williams, 3 vols. (Cambridge:

Harvard University Press, 1959; The Belknap Press of Harvard University Press, 1964-1971), II, 158. Volumes of this edition will be cited hereafter as *EL*.

[10] Compare Emerson's poem "The Problem," written in 1839: "The passive Master lent his hand/ To the vast soul that o'er him planned . . . " (ll. 47-48).

[11] This point "ought to have been more distinctly stated" in *Nature*, according to this journal entry of 1837; it is subsequently enlarged upon in "The American Scholar," where Emerson discusses at length the scholar's need for action—in part as providing "a language by which to illustrate and embody our perceptions" (*W*, I, 98).

[12] See *JMN*, V, 249-250; *EL*, II, 61-62; and "Emerson on the Scholar, 1833-1837," p. 191.

[13] *Ralph Waldo Emerson* (Boston, 1915; New York: Russell & Russell, 1965), p. 166.

[14] The scholar's call to create was in his mind late in June of 1838 when he drafted a journal passage used in "Literary Ethics" (*JMN*, VII, 30; *W*, I, 185): "Who forbade you to create?" he asks in one sentence not taken over in the oration.

[15] Firkins, p. 167.

[16] In the *Boston Quarterly Review* for January, 1839; reprinted in Perry Miller, *The Transcendentalists: An Anthology* (Cambridge: Harvard University Press, 1950), p. 432. Among present-day commentators, Sherman Paul also takes exaltation of solitude to be "the message of 'Literary Ethics'": see *Emerson's Angle of Vision: Man and Nature in American Experience* (Cambridge: Harvard University Press, 1952), p. 198.

[17] *Emerson and Thoreau: Transcendentalists in Conflict* (Middletown, Conn.: Wesleyan University Press, 1966), pp. 20-23. To "the would-be man of letters," says Porte flatly, Emerson "offered Napoleon as the man to be emulated."

[18] In using parts of a journal entry of June 12, 1838, Emerson chose to omit the following sentences, among others: "Solitude is naught & society is naught. Alternate them & the good of each is seen. . . . Undulation, Alternation, is the condition of progress, of life" (*JMN*, VII, 14; cf. *W*, I, 175).

IV

A NEW LOOK AT EMERSON
AND SCIENCE

BY GAY WILSON ALLEN

PROFESSOR HARRY HAYDEN CLARK'S IMPOR-
tant study of "Emerson and Science," published in 1931,[1]
has not been adequately assimilated in Emerson scholarship,
though it has been widely cited and praised. In a detailed
survey of the 1909 edition of Emerson's *Journals* and the
"Centenary" Edition of his *Works*, Professor Clark traced
the poet's interest in science through 1838, the "formative
years," during which he read extensively in contemporary
science and was most influenced by scientific theories and
discoveries.

Emerson himself, in summing up the early influences on
him, declared:

> I think the paramount source of the religious revolution was
> Modern Science; beginning with Copernicus, who destroyed
> the pagan fictions of the Church, . . . Astronomy . . . showed
> that our sacred as [well as] our profane history had been written
> in gross ignorance of the laws [of science], which were far grander
> than we knew; and compelled a certain extension and uplifting
> of our views of the Deity and his Providence. . . .[2]

Professor Clark suggested that science, and especially astronomy, emancipated Emerson from anthropomorphic reli-

58

gion, and probably had a great deal to do with his resigning his Unitarian pulpit in 1832. This influence, Professor Clark demonstrated in his essay, also extended beyond Emerson's intellectual crisis in 1832, and may be seen in many of his early writings, including *Nature* (1836).

Late in my own teaching career I discovered that Emerson's first professional lectures (i.e., his first public lectures after he resigned from the Second Church in Boston) can serve as a remarkably helpful approach to *Nature*, which my students had nearly always found difficult. *The Early Lectures of Ralph Waldo Emerson* were not published until 1959-66,[3] and Professor Clark did not have access to the manuscripts at the time of his writing "Emerson and Science." Although his exposition might have been strengthened by inclusion of these lectures, especially the first four, which were specifically on science, his conclusions need not be modified in light of this new evidence.

Emerson had been reading works on science, as Professor Clark showed, before he made his trip to Europe in 1832-33, and it was the scientific lectures which he attended in Italy, France, and England, and the museums of natural history which he examined that made the deepest impression on him[4]—much deeper, apparently, than the art galleries and cathedrals which he dutifully visited. The high point of his experiences in Europe was a visit to the Cabinet [Museum] of Natural History in the Garden of Plants in Paris on July 13, 1833. After describing in his *Journal* the Ornithological Chambers, which he thought finer than anything in the Louvre, and passing through several other collections, he recorded his state of mind:

> The Universe is a more amazing puzzle than ever as you glance along this bewildering series of animated forms,—the hazy butterflies, the carved shells, the birds, beasts, fishes, insects, snakes, —& the upheaving principle of life everywhere incipient in the very rock aping organized forms. Not a form so grotesque, so savage, nor so beautiful but is an expression of some property

inherent in man the observer,—an occult relation between the very scorpions and man. I feel the centipede in me—cayman, carp, eagle, & fox. I am moved by strange sympathies, I say continually "I will be a naturalist."[5]

How seriously Emerson intended to become "a naturalist" one can only guess, but soon after his return to Boston on October 9, 1833, he accepted an invitation from the Natural History Society to give a series of lectures in the Masonic Temple.[6] The first, given on November 5, was on "The Uses of Natural History." Both this lecture and the second "On the Relation of Man to the Globe," were preliminary sketches for *Nature* (1836), which Emerson was planning during his travels in Europe. A third on "Water" was more factual than speculative, but in the fourth lecture, "The Naturalist," he made a strong plea for a recognition of the importance of science in education.[7]

In his first lecture Emerson recounted his experiences in the Cabinet of Natural History in Paris and elaborated the impressions he had recorded in his *Journal* about the "occult relation" he had felt between man and other forms of life. But as in the beginning of his future book called *Nature*[8] he stressed especially the practical *uses* of nature, the first being that "conversation with nature" promotes health, confirming the truth of the Greek fable of the giant Antaeus wrestling with Hercules. "Man is the broken giant, and in all his weakness he is invigorated by touching his mother earth. . . . "[9] Alexander Wilson, the celebrated American ornithologist, had taken up his specialty "for the benefit of his enfeebled health, and in his enthusiastic rambles in the wilderness his constitution was established whilst he enlarged the domain of science." Botany, Emerson said, could be no less beneficial as a health restorer.

In the second place, the uses of nature have made possible what we know as "civilization":

It is the earth itself and its natural bodies that make the raw material out of which we construct our food, clothing, fuel, furniture, and arms. And it is the Naturalist who discovers the virtues of these bodies and the mode of converting them to use. In the most refined state of society, these are most accumulated; but these are now so numerous and the subdivision of labor has removed each process so far out of sight, that a man who by pulling a bell can command any luxury the world contains, is in danger of forgetting that iron came out of a mine, and perfume out of a cat.[10]

Here is Emerson's first warning that technology may interfere with man's healthy adjustment to nature. He did not at that point in his thinking consider the possible relationship between the "broken giant" and his misuses of natural resources, but Emerson saw that labor-saving inventions were undermining men's appreciation of nature. At the moment, however, he was more interested in the contributions of single men, chemists particularly, to the extension of commerce and the increase of mechanical power in modern society, without foreseeable limits. Yet he valued these contributions more for their "general truth" than the "riches which they have acquired."

In fact, Emerson's "third reason for the cultivation of natural history" was the "*delight which springs from the contemplation of . . . truth.*" [Emerson's italics], "for every fact that is disclosed to us in natural history removes one scale more from the eye; makes the face of nature around us so much more significant."[11]

Various scholars have stressed the influence of astronomy on Emerson, but in 1833-34 he seems to have been more influenced by geology.[12] The new knowledge of the vast age of the earth preserved in the rocks had convinced him that the world was more than six thousand years old, and that it had been created not by a sudden Divine command but through countless ages of slow evolution. Coal, for instance, was "the relic of forests which existed at an unknown antiquity before the era of the creation of mankind, and by the overflowing of the sea and other changes of the surface had been buried below the surface at too great a depth to be reached by man."[13] But fortunately earthquakes brought the coal near enough to the surface in some places to be mined and used by mankind. Emerson held in reserve the implication of a Divine purpose in this fact, but he emphasized that "the informed eye" would see in all natural phenomena an ingenious fitness, order, and beauty. Linnaeus, Buffon, Cuvier, Humboldt, and Galileo "used their senses to such good purpose, led on by the mere pleasure of observation," that their "high delight" has become the possession of mankind. This "high delight" also has a "salutary effect upon the mind and character of those who cultivate it. It makes the intellect exact, quick to discriminate between the similar and the same, and greedy of truth."[14]

The fifth use of nature, Emerson said, was to help man understand himself. "The knowledge of all the facts of all the laws of nature will give man his true place in the system of being."[15] Such knowledge will not only enable man to correct his errors and throw off his superstitions, but, most important of all, it will enable him to comprehend the relation of external nature to his "inward world of thoughts and emotions. . . . " This was the beginning of Emerson's theory of nature as a language, which was, first, a means of communicating to the human mind the nature of nature and how it operates; and, second, the power of expression itself, enabling men to share with each other their thoughts and feelings in words. Without words men could not themselves understand their own experiences, and of course not communicate them to other men. Words symbolize aspects of the external world, and metaphors (which embody the very origin of human language) are images of the material world:

> The strongest distinction of which we have an idea is that between thought and matter. The very existence of thought and speech supposes and is a new nature totally distinct from the material world; yet we find it impossible to speak of it and its laws in any other language than that borrowed from

our experience in the material world. . . . And this, because the whole of Nature is a metaphor or image of the human Mind.[16]

This theory of language might have been developed in either of two directions: phenomenologically[17] or mystically (in a Neoplatonic sense).[18] "Where," Emerson asked, "is it these fair creatures (in whom an order and series is so distinctly discernible,) find their link, their cement, their keystone, but in the Mind of Man? It is he who marries the visible to the Invisible by uniting thought to Animal Organization."[19] This statement could mean that all knowledge is empirical, and that nature can only be experienced in the mind as phenomena.[20] The "laws" discovered to govern nature would, therefore, be the laws of appearances. Emerson almost seems to say this in his assertion that "The very existence of thought and speech supposes and *is a new nature* [italics supplied] totally distinct from the material world. . . . "[21] And in a later lecture on "The Humanity of Science" he came even nearer to spelling out phenomenology: "Science is the arrangement of the phenomena of the world after their essential relations. It is the reconstruction of nature in the mind. This is at once its ideal and its historical aspect."[22] But the extent of Emerson's anticipation of twentieth-century phenomenology is his conviction that thought (consciousness) cannot exist without the world's body; thought and nature are co-related.[23]

Emerson did not say that consciousness is "a metaphor or image" of Nature, but exactly the reverse. He quoted a passage from Coleridge's "The Destiny of Nations: A Vision":

For all that meets the bodily sense I deem
Symbolical, one mighty alphabet
For infant minds.[24]

Thus nature is the language that God speaks to men, and

natural scientists learn the syntax of the language. It is not strange, therefore, that Emerson should deduce that "the axioms of geometry and of mechanics only translate the laws of ethics."[25] Such axioms as "A straight line is the shortest distance between two points" and "Reaction is equal to action . . . are true not only in geometry but in life. . . ." Consequently, "A man should feel that the time is not lost and the efforts not misspent that are devoted to the elucidation of these laws [of nature]; for herein is writ by the Creator his own history."[26] Robert Chambers expressed the same thought ten years later in *Vestiges of Creation*,[27] and in general contemporary geologists[28] agreed that in fossils men had a record not only of the evolution of life in the changing ages of the globe, but also a history of Divine creativity. In his closing thought, however, Emerson's imagination soared beyond the teleology of early nineteenth-century science when he speculated that maybe "all this outward universe shall one day disappear, when its whole sense hath been comprehended and engraved forever in the eternal thoughts of the human mind."[29] But however visionary such comprehension may appear to a twentieth-century mind, Emerson did not under-value scientific knowledge.

In his second lecture on science, "The Relation of Man to the Globe," given on January 6, 1834,[30] Emerson drew heavily on his readings in geology, along with some biology and chemistry, and attempted to demonstrate how marvelously the world is adapted for human life. Man, he said, had "been prophesied in nature for a thousand thousand ages before he appeared." This "progressive preparation" was a kind of evolution, more like Lamarck's[31] than Darwin's later theory, for Emerson saw nature adapted to man, not man to nature. Though "the brother of his hand is even now cleaving the Arctic Sea in the fin of the whale, and, innumerable ages since, was pawing the marsh in the flipper of the saurus,"[32] these were merely preparations for "the finish of the rudimental forms" in Man.

According to Laplace, Mitscherlich, and Cuvier, Emerson's chief sources,[33] the whole globe was once in a state of vapor, then a solid mostly covered by water; internal heat threw up mountains and broke the surface of continents, though not necessarily the present ones. Lord Bacon pointed out that the shapes of the coasts of Africa and America so neatly fitted together on a map that they must have once been joined in one huge land-mass.[34] For ages after the globe was habitable to reptiles, palaeotheria, mammoths and mastodons, it was not suitable for man and his domestic animals. But finally, "Man is made; and really when you come to see the minuteness of the adaptation in him to the present earth, it suggests forcibly the familiar fact of a father setting up his children at housekeeping, building them a house, laying out the grounds, curing the chimneys, and stocking the cellar."[35] This domestic parable indicates Emerson's faith in a guiding purpose at work. In every way the globe is exactly fitted to man's structure and needs: the air he breathes, the foods that nourish him, the sounds, sights and forms which delight his senses, and even his difficulties are nicely proportioned to his strength. In all these observations there are echoes of eighteenth-century Deism and Bishop Paley's argument from "design."[36]

There seemed to be a design, too, in the geographical distribution of animals, plants, and minerals, forcing men to travel, explore, and trade to satisfy their wants. Thus nature "acquaints her children with each other, and contrives to impart whatever invention one man makes, to millions."[37] Different parts of the globe also contain a wide variety of beauties, "that the shows of nature might attract so imaginative a creature [as man] from his native spot." Although Emerson thought that natural beauty always surpassed the products of human ingenuity, he did think men had in some ways improved nature, by dredging rivers, draining swamps, planting trees in barren places, thereby sometimes even ameliorating the climate.[38] "Yet," as Shakespeare wrote, "nature is made better by no mean/ But nature makes that mean."[39] Then man's improvements were only repairs.

Emerson believed that the love of nature was innate in all human beings:

> The same organization which creates in the Chayma Indian such thirst and hunger for his boundless woods, which makes a sunny meadow spotted with flowers and visited by birds such a paradise to a child, is the cause in cultivated men of that interest in natural objects and processes which expresses itself in the sciences of botany, of zoology, of chemistry, and astronomy. The pursuit of these sciences has gradually disclosed a new and noble view of man's relation to the globe.[40]

Near the end of his lecture Emerson mentioned two principles which would become primary ideas in his future thinking and writing. The chemist by separating compounds into their separate elements appeared to anticipate "the resolving all created things into a few gases, perhaps two, perhaps one."[41] Emerson's own search for the underlying unity in all natural phenomena would carry him away from physical science into an attempted science of spirit, but he started from theories about the unity of variety in the material world. The second principle was less ambiguous, and would become one of the most basic parallels which he would henceforth find between matter and spirit: "we seem to be approaching the elemental secrets of nature in finding the principle of Polarity in all the laws of matter, in light, heat, magnetism, and electricity."[42]

But Emerson's conclusion in this lecture could have come as much from Paley as from contemporary scientists:

> I conclude . . . that the snail is not more accurately adjusted to his shell than man to the globe he inhabits; that not only a perfect symmetry is discoverable in his limbs and senses between the head and foot, between the hand and the eye, the heart and the lungs,—but an equal symmetry and proportion is discoverable between him and the air, the mountains,

the tides, the moon, and the sun. I am not impressed by solitary marks of designing wisdom; I am thrilled with delight by the choral harmony of the whole. Design! It is all design. It is all beauty. It is all astonishment.[43]

Emerson's third lecture on science was on "Water," given January 17, 1834, before the Mechanic's Institute at the Athenaeum Library in Boston. This was his most technical lecture. He had read up on the geological effects of water, the laws of thermodynamics, the hydrostatic press, and related subjects. In his conclusion he permitted himself to generalize:

> It may serve to enlarge our perception of the boundless resources of the Creator, when we learn that in a bucket of water resides a latent force sufficient to counterbalance mountains, or to rend the planet, and when we trace the manifold offices which one [*sic*] atom of hydrogen and one of oxygen united in a particle of water may perform in the pulse, in the brain, in the eye, in a plant, in mist, in crystal, in a volcano, and it may exalt our highest sentiments to see the same particle in every step of this ceaseless revolution serving the life, the order, the happiness of the Universe.[44]

On May 7, 1834, Emerson addressed the Natural History Society of Boston for the third time.[45] This was the annual meeting and his lecture on "The Naturalist" was more eloquent and imaginative than the one he gave the Mechanic's Institute on "Water." His avowed purpose was to show "the place of Natural History in Education," and he emphasized particularly the study of nature to promote esthetic and moral growth:

> It is fit that man should look upon Nature with the eye of the Artist, to learn from the great Artist whose blood beats in our veins, whose taste is upspringing in our own perception of beauty, the laws by which our hands should work that we may build St. Peter'ses or paint Transfigurations or sing Iliads in worthy continuation of the architecture of the Andes, the colors of the sky and the poem of life.[46]

Nature also taught a lesson in "Composition," constructing innumerable forms of inconceivable varieties out of a few ingredients, illustrating "that rule of arithmetic called Permutation and Combination."[47] But the special beauty derives from the individual form in combination with other forms, which is "composition." The seashell is most beautiful on the seashore, the flower in the meadow, the tree on the hillside.[48] Among the "intellectual influences" of nature study, Emerson mentioned the restraint of "Imitation, the vice of overcivilized communities," and disciplined discrimination, learning "by observing and recording the properties of every individual specie and determining its place in the Universe by its properties."[49]

Emerson thought that the discipline of scientific study might be especially good for the poet, who "loses himself in imaginations and for want of accuracy is a mere fabulist. . . ."[50] On the other hand, the "savant" runs the danger of losing sight of the end of his inquiries in the perfection of his "manipulations" and becoming a pedant. As for himself, "I fully believe in both, in the poetry and in the dissection." And his journals for this period show, as the editors of the *Early Lectures* note, that, "He was checking his own observation of birds, shells, flowers, and other natural objects against their Latin names and classifications in Gray and other technical sources at the same time that he continued to read in such favorite philosophers of science as Coleridge and Goethe."[51]

But what was such activity a *means to*? The great scientists knew their ultimate goal:

> It was the ever present aim of Newton, of Linnaeus, of Davy, of Cuvier, to ascend from nomenclature to classification; from arbitrary to natural classes; from natural classes, to primary laws; from these, in an ever narrowing circle, to approach the elementary law, the *causa causans*, the supernatural force.[52]

To Emerson and many scientists and philosophers of his

period, who hoped to find the *causa causans*, studying nature was also a means of worshipping the Creator. Knowledge of creatures gave "intimations of the inward Law of Nature."[53]

Emerson's lectures on science were not actually trial versions of his book on *Nature*; their value is that they reveal his reading and thinking about science before he had fused his ideas thus derived with the Neoplatonic and "transcendental" ideas of Plotinus, Swedenborg, Wordsworth, Coleridge, Carlyle, and seventeenth-century English Platonists.[54] In his journals he made outlines and wrote down trial passages. These show that his progress was erratic and that he had to struggle for clarity. On May 6, 1834, he was not entirely sure of his reason for studying plants and animals. Perhaps it would console him during times of disappointment, or cheer him in solitude. "Or again say that I am ever haunted by the conviction that I have an interest in all that goes on around me. . . . "[55] He could learn from nature "the laws by which I live." But the strongest motive, to be frank, was "love," meaning personal interest. He was fascinated by the "mysteries" of nature, and believed that "by patient contemplation & docile experiment" he could learn them.

A year later (May 14, 1835) Emerson was thinking of writing a book on "spiritual things," and was contemplating "the parable of geometry & matter."[56] By June 24 his future book was to be "essays chiefly upon Natural Ethics." On January 22-23, 1836, he recorded, "All history is poetry; the globe of facts whereon they [mankind] trample is bullion to the scientific eye."[57] The "scholar" could convey these facts "into a garden of God by suggesting the principle which classifies the fact." This is very ambiguous, but the implications are that he was searching for the *causa causans* of natural phenomena. By March 27 he was outlining Chapters 2-5 of *Nature* and finding that "through Nature is there a striving upward"—a spiral evolution.[58]

On August 8, 1836, Emerson wrote his brother William that his book was nearly finished, but, "There is, as always,

one crack in it not easy to be soldered or welded. . . . "[59]
In a previous letter (June 28, 1836) to William he had expressed the intention of writing a companion essay on "Spirit."[60] This would seem to indicate that he was not yet satisfied with his explanation of the "correspondence" between spirit and matter, the "noble doubt" in Chapter 6 of the "absolute existence of nature."

In his Introduction to *Nature* Emerson says: "The foregoing generations beheld God and nature face to face; we, through their eyes."[61] But a true "theory of nature" may help men once again to see nature "face to face." The evangelical tone of the Introduction also indicates that he is really trying to bring about what William James would call a "religious experience"[62]—to *feel* the presence of the Divine in the observation of its visible creations. In Chapter 1 he follows up this purpose: the stars at night awaken "a certain reverence," and "all natural objects make a kindred impression, when the mind is open to their influence."[63] In the famous "transparent eye-ball" passage Emerson describes the sensations produced by such "open" receptivity of the mind. This passage has often been called a description of a personal mystical experience, but it is more likely an imaginative illustration of the "occult relation" which Emerson had felt to exist between man and the objective world.[64] The emotional delight, so intense as to border on pain (awe, fear), gave him an intuition of the creative spirit sustaining nature.

The "theory of nature" which Emerson attempted to express in *Nature* derived far more from Neoplatonism than modern scientific knowledge, but Emerson was not turning his back on science; he wanted instead to *spiritualize* science, to base science on the theory that the physical world is an emanation of spirit, "the apparition of God" (Chapter 6), or "a projection of God in the unconscious." Here the "unconscious" is the life-force in all existing things except man, who has *consciousness*, which is, as it were, a fragment of the Divine Reason. By cherishing and cultivating his

Reason man can intuit the secrets of nature and the laws of his own existence. Thus Emerson's method of gaining knowledge of nature is now not by patient observation, but by epiphanies—sudden flashes of insight into the Divine mystery. "If the Reason be stimulated to more earnest vision, outlines and surfaces become transparent, and are no longer seen [for themselves]; causes and spirits are seen through them" (Chap. 6). And yet these "higher laws" are curiously paralleled by the laws of physics and physiology: "The axioms of physics translate the laws of ethics." Nature in serving man as "Commodity" (practical use), "Beauty," "Language" (symbol), and "Discipline" teaches him "the will of God."

It is not possible to test these Emersonian hypotheses by the methods of physical science. And yet in defending "Idealism" (Chap. 6) as a pragmatic way of handling the phenomenal appearances of the physical world to the mind, Emerson was attempting to construct a "Natural History of the Intellect," the *magnum opus* he planned for years to write, but got no further than some disconnected lectures which he gave at Harvard in 1870-71, published posthumously (in 1893) as *The Natural History of the Intellect.*[65] What he wanted was "the exhaustive accuracy of distribution which chemists use in their nomenclature and anatomists in their descriptions, applied to a higher class of facts: "laws" for the "intellect" comparable to the laws of science. In this ambition he plainly anticipated Phenomenology:

> In all sciences the student is discovering that nature, as he calls it, is always working, in wholes and in every detail, after the laws of the human mind. Every creation, in parts or in particles, is on the method and by the means which our mind approves as soon as it is thoroughly acquainted with the facts; hence the delight. No matter how far or how high science explores, it adopts the method of the universe as fast as it appears; and this discloses that the mind as it opens, the mind as it shall be, comprehends and works thus; that is to say, the Intellect builds the universe and is the key to all it contains. It is not then cities or mountains, or animals, or globes that

any longer command us, but only man; not the fact, but so much of man as is in the fact.[66]

In *Nature* Emerson defended "Idealism" (Chap. 6) as a phenomenological psychology—and ethics also:

> The advantage of the ideal theory over the popular faith, is this, that it presents the world in precisely that view which is most desirable to the mind. It is, in fact, the view which Reason, both speculative and practical, that is, philosophy and virtue, take. For, seen in the light of thought, the world always is phenomenal; and virtue subordinates it to the mind. . . .[67]

Idealism says that "matter is a phenomenon, not a substance." For this reason Emerson remarks in "Prospects" (Chap. 8) that "Empirical science is apt to cloud the sight, and, by the very knowledge of functions and processes, to bereave the student of the manly contemplation of the whole." This is to say, that the deepest secrets of nature are learned by intuition, not by empirical observation. And unless the scientist himself understands this, his science will not have "sufficient humanity, so long as the naturalist overlooks that wonderful congruity which subsists between man and the world. . . ."[68] When the mind is prepared for this fact, the most common objects will be seen to be "miraculous," for "each phenomenon hath its roots in the faculties and affections of the mind. Whilst the abstract question occupies your intellect, nature brings it in the concrete to be solved by your hands." To illustrate his point Emerson creates a fabulous "Orphic poet" (somewhat resembling Bronson Alcott, partly Emerson himself, but suggested to him by Proclus,[69] the Greek Neoplatonist of the fifth century), who tells him:

> "Nature is not fixed but fluid. Spirit alters, moulds, makes it. The immobility or bruteness of nature, is the absence of spirit; to pure spirit, it is fluid, it is volatile, it is obedient. Every spirit builds itself a house; and beyond its house, a

world; and beyond its world, a heaven. Know then, that the world exists for you. For you is the phenomenon perfect. . . ."[70]

Now of course the basic doctrine here is that, "The foundations of man are not in matter, but in spirit," and that by a *redemption* of his soul (accomplished through *love*, and a new awareness of the nature of the soul) man can transform the "bruteness of nature" into beauty and ideal virtue. Such bold leaping to conclusions based more on faith than objective proof (or at least proof extremely difficult to come by) opens Emerson to the charge of being himself "a mere fabulist," a danger from which he had said in his lecture on "The Naturalist" the poet needed the discipline of science to save him. Such proof is not found in *Nature*.

However, the psychology which Emerson assumed in *Nature* to underlie his theory of the relation of mind to matter, and of matter to the Creative Mind of all nature, including the human mind, he outlined with simple clarity at the end of 1836, three months after the publication of *Nature*, in a lecture on "Humanity of Science."[71] There he said that, "Science is the arrangement of the phenomena of the world after their essential relations. *It is the reconstruction of nature in the mind* [italics supplied]. This is at once its ideal and its historical aspect."[72] The ease with which the human mind can classify the phenomena of nature and by analysis discover the laws of their operation convinced him that "nature proceeds from a mind analogous to our own." Even if one insists on eliminating the transcendental "mind," he would still have to agree on analogies between his own experiences and natural phenomena. For example, man seems to have an instinct for putting things in a row.[73] "This methodizing mind meets no resistance in its attempts." The uniformity of nature makes it possible for the mind to extend one observation to a series in the same class: "as falls the apple, so falls the moon . . . ,"[74] etc. Fossils preserve stages of development of animals which today no longer exist, but those stages of development may still be found in an egg (cf. the "recapitulation theory"[75] in physiology).

Emerson saw "one grand idea" in nature's operation in the formation of the vertebral column in animals, in the shape of leaves, petals, and stems in plants, in the radiation of sound, light and heat, perhaps in the primary cause of electrical and chemical effects.[76] Maybe *one cause* effected all these results. He could not believe that "cause" operated blindly by chance, though it was still a mystery to science. In fact, this seemed to be the place where spiritual assumptions became necessary:

> Behind all the processes which the lens can detect, there is a *Life* in a seed, which predominates over all brute matter, and which irresistibly forces carbon, hydrogen, and water, to take shape in a shaft, in leaves, in colors of a lily, which they could never take themselves. More wonderful is it in animal nature. Above every being, over every organ, floats this predetermining law, whose inscrutable secret defies the microscope and the alembic. The naturalist must presuppose it, or his results are foolish and offensive. As the proverb says, "he counts without his host who leaves God out of his reckoning," so science is bankrupt which attempts to cut the knot which always spirit must untie.[77]

Emerson believed, however, that, "The presence and antecedence of Spirit are impressively taught by modern science." He did not document this assertion, but his personal friend Louis Agassiz[78] would have agreed, and also Sir Charles Bell, whose recently published book on *The Hand, Its Mechanism and Vital Endowments, as Evincing Design* (1835) had been read by Emerson, with other works on comparative anatomy. "Step by step with these facts," Emerson continued, "we are apprised of another, namely, the Humanity of that Spirit; or, that, nature proceeds from a mind analogous to our own." Later, "Indeed, man may well be of the same mind as nature, for he too is a part of nature, and is inundated with the same genius or spirit. He lives by some pulsations of her life."[79]

Darwin would also agree that the human mind is "a part of nature," but there was a vast difference in this agreement. To Darwin the mind had been produced by "natural selection," retaining those aspects of consciousness which had "survival" value, though they had come into being by pure chance. To Emerson no chance was involved, but an undeviating Divine intention and design, inexorably unfolding—a teleological evolution, if that is not a contradiction. Because the unfolding was consistent and predictable, it could be said to have its "laws" and it was these laws that Emerson sought to discover. That was why Emerson called his hoped-for definitive work on consciousness "The Natural History of the Intellect." In spite of the theological bias in this fragmentary work, science caused Emerson to emphasize *Natural* and to search for innate laws. Since he continued to work on this treatise—or at least to think and worry about it—until his mental decay made it impossible to continue, it is incorrect to say that science did not influence him after 1836.[80] Indeed, the two most basic concepts in his philosophy, which he never doubted, were "compensation" and "polarity," both derived from scientific "laws," i.e., for every action there is a reaction, and the phenomena of negative and positive poles in electrodynamics. To these might also be added "circularity," which translated into poetic metaphors the principle of "conservation of energy." In fact, a nearly-complete interpretation of Emerson's thought could be based on these three concepts, but such a study goes beyond the scope of this essay.

---

[1] Harry Hayden Clark, "Emerson and Science," *Philological Quarterly*, 10 (July, 1931), 225-60.

[2] *Complete Works of Ralph Waldo Emerson*, Riverside ("Centenary") Edition (Boston: Houghton Mifflin, 1904), x, 335-36.

[3] *The Early Lectures of Ralph Waldo Emerson* (Cambridge: Harvard University Press, 1964-66), Vol. I: 1833-1836, Ed. by Stephen Whicher and Robert E. Spiller; Vol. II: 1836-1838, ed. by Stephen Whicher, Robert E. Spiller, and Wallace E. Williams.

[4] *Early Lectures*, I, 2.

[5] *The Journals and Miscellaneous Notebooks of Ralph Waldo Emerson*, ed. by Alfred A. Ferguson (Cambridge: Harvard University Press, 1964), IV, 199-200.

[6] *Early Lectures*, I, 5-26.

[7] *Early Lectures*, I, 50-83.

[8] *Nature* (a facsimile of the first edition), ed. by Werner Berthoff (San Francisco: Chandler Publishing Co., 1968); all references are to this edition. Pagination is same as original 1836 edition.

[9] *Early Lectures*, I, 11.

[10] Ibid.

[11] Ibid., 14-15.

[12] Although Emerson frequently mentioned or alluded to astronomy or astronomers, as Clark noted, in his four lectures on science his geological references are usually more concrete. Clark noted also (248) that "In 1835 Emerson read Sir Charles Lyell's *Principles of Geology*." Before this work was published (1830-33), Emerson's sources (see *Early Lectures*, I, 1) were primarily Baron G. Cuvier, *A Discourse on the Revolutions of the Surface of the Globe* (Philadelphia, 1831); R. Lee [Mrs. Sarah], *Memoirs of Baron Cuvier* (London, 1833); and John Playfair, "Illustrations of the Huttonian Theory of the Earth," *Works* (Edinburgh, 1822), Vol. I.

[13] *Early Lectures*, I, 16.

[14] Ibid., 19.

[15] Ibid., 23.

[16] Ibid., 24.

[17] A philosophical movement started by Edmund Husserl in 1905. Bruce Wilshire, in *William James and Phenomenology* . . . (Bloomington: Indiana University Press, 1968) defines the term: "the central thesis of phenomenology is that the world is comprehensible only in terms of its modes of appearance to mind, . . . the relationship of mind to world is necessary and internal."

[18] Neoplatonically, nature symbolizes Divine Reason. See John S. Harrison, *The Teachers of Emerson* (New York: Haskell House, 1966—first edition 1910), and "neoplatonism" in Frederic Ives Carpenter, *Emerson and Asia* (New York: Haskell House, 1968), Chap. 4.

[19] *Early Lectures*, I, 24.

[20] The phenomenologist would say that such a view makes no assumptions about ultimate reality, or what may support "appearances."

[21] *Early Lectures*, I, 24.

[22] Ibid., II, 27.

[23] See note 17, above.

[24] *Early Lectures*, I, 25.

[25] Ibid.

[26] Ibid., 26.

[27] Robert Chambers, *Vestiges of the Natural History of Creation* (Edinburgh, 1844), which Emerson read in 1845. The idea was evidently not original with Chambers.

[28] See note 12, above.

[29] *Early Lectures*, I, 26.

[30] Ibid., 27.

[31] Chevalier de Lamarck (Jean Baptiste Pierre Antoine Monet), *Recherches sur L'Organization des Corps Vivants* (1802), *Philosophie Zoologique* (1809), and other works proposed that changes in environment caused structural, inheritable changes in animals and plants—greater or less use of organs resulting in growth or atrophy.

[32] *Early Lectures*, I, 32. On January 2, 1834, Emerson quoted (*Journals*, IV, 254) Sir Charles Bell, *The Hand, Its Mechanism and Vital Endowments as Evincing Design* (Philadelphia, 1833).

[33] *Early Lectures*, I, 31.

[34] Ibid. Lord Bacon's theory is accepted by modern science; see *Continental Drift: A Study of the Earth's Moving Surface*, by D. H. Tarling and M. P. Tarling (London: G. Bell, 1971).

[35] Ibid., 32.

[36] William Paley, *Natural Theology* (1802).

[37] *Early Lectures*, I, 41.

[38] Ibid., 43-44.

[39] *Winter's Tale*, IV, 4: 89-90; Ferguson, *Early Lectures*, I, 44, note 25.

[40] Ibid., 46.

[41] Ibid., 48.

[42] Ibid.

[43] Ibid., 48-49.

[44] Ibid., 68.

[45] Ibid., 69.

[46] Ibid., 73.

[47] Ibid.

[48] Ibid. See also the poem "Each and All" (1834?) and the entry for May 16, 1834, *Journals*, IV, 291.

[49] *Early Lectures*, I, 79.

[50] Ibid.

[51] Ibid., 69.

[52] Ibid., 80.

[53] Ibid., 81.

[54] See note 18, above.

[55] *Journals*, IV, 291.

[56] Ibid., V, 40.

[57] Ibid., 117.

[58] Ibid., 146.

[59] *The Letters of Ralph Waldo Emerson*, ed. by Ralph L. Rusk (New York: Columbia University Press, 1939), II, 32.

[60] Ibid., 26.

[61] *Nature* (see note 8, above), [5].

[62] William James, *Varieties of Religious Experience* (1902), especially Chap. 3.

[63] *Nature*, 10.

[64] Cf. Berthoff, Introduction to *Nature*, LXI ff. For a different view, see Jonathan Bishop, *Emerson on the Soul* (Cambridge: Harvard University Press, 1964), 10-15.

[65] *Works*, XII, 1-110.

[66] Ibid., 4-5.

[67] *Nature,* 74.

[68] Ibid., 84.

[69] Cf. Harrison, *The Teachers of Emerson*, 246.

[70] *Nature*, 93-94.

[71] *Early Lectures*, II, 22-40.

[72] Ibid., 27.

[73] Ibid., 25

[74] Ibid.

[75] The embryo apparently develops through the evolutionary stages of its species.

[76] *Early Lectures*, I, 29.

[77] Ibid., II, 30.

[78] Louis Agassiz refused to accept the Darwinian theory of the origin of the species, continuing to believe in the special creation of the different species.

[79] *Early Lectures*, II, 35.

[80] Whicher and Spiller, *Early Lectures*, I, 3: "To a considerable extent, as *Nature* (1836) makes evident, his interest in science was absorbed into his interest in moral philosophy and by 1836 no longer served a special function in his thought." While science may not have continued to serve "a special function," it continued to have a pervasive influence.

V

CHURCH, SCRIPTURE, NATURE AND ETHICS IN HENRY THOREAU'S RELIGIOUS THOUGHT

ALEXANDER C. KERN

THE OMISSION OF THOREAU FROM ANY DIS-
cussion of religion in American literature should be corrected. That he seemed pantheistic to Horace Greeley and
James Russell Lowell and irreligious to others is an inadequate justification. Though Transcendentalism seemed radical
even to Unitarians, it was the most religiously oriented of
American literary movements. But Thoreau seemed more
radical than Emerson, and he seemed bad enough. Henry
was never a cleric; he signed off from his church; and he
attacked conventional piety, and even preachers, especially
in *A Week on the Concord and Merrimack Rivers.* Unlike
Emerson, who continued to attend the same First Parish
Church even if with some exasperation, Thoreau would never
have voted in favor of compulsory chapel at Harvard, as
late in life Emerson did. Nevertheless, the exclusion of Thoreau's view from consideration as a part of American religious
thought is based upon the error of orthodoxy in denying
the term religious to any ideas outside its own officially fenced-
in plot.

Now he can be seen as a significant if unorthodox part
and hence product of the American Protestant tradition,

however much he may have struggled against it. While "Thoreau's attitude toward institutional Christianity was one of rank antagonism,"[1] he was a deeply religious man. His spiritually based ethical judgments provide perhaps as cogent a criticism of American materialism as has ever been furnished, and in "Civil Disobedience" he applied the moral criterion to social issues through a method which proved to be the most effective nonviolent technique for producing social change which has ever been devised.

There are of course pitfalls in the path of any attempt to articulate exactly what Thoreau's religious ideas were, because he never felt called upon to state them systematically. Closer to the poet than the philosopher, he said what seemed true and important at each instant, instead of trying to build a system. Consequently he would at one time enunciate a single assumption, at another make an isolated single point, without trying to link the two into a single whole. Like most thinkers, Thoreau was unable to give up some of the older views and terms which he was raised with, though they did not entirely fit the newer viewpoint he had adopted. Nevertheless, the attempt to present his views as they relate to religion will produce, as with Emerson, a more consistent pattern or figure in the carpet than opponents and denigrators seem willing to grant.

Although it produced a superficial impression of being an eclectic gathering of themes from Hindu doctrine to recent German philosophy, this Transcendentalism, which Thoreau was able to take over from Emerson, was based on the American religious experience. The seriousness and moral intensity of the Puritans remained, though the specific doctrines of original sin, predestination to election or damnation, and the revelation of God's truth in the Bible were no longer believed. In their place the Transcendentalists took the certainties of direct divine revelation, which had characterized the earlier Antinomians and Quakers, and held as open to all men what Edwards had held was bestowed only on the elect, a special sense of God's grace, beauty, and benignity. The Transcendentalists were also able to adapt to their use a part of the Enlightenment complex which had held that the universe operated by rational divine plan, that the Creator was best found and understood in nature's laws; parallel to the physical laws there were moral laws and natural rights, the bases for the Declaration of Independence, which all societies must observe. While the austerer and more rational deism of the eighteenth century lost its hold on the populace, who turned to the emotional excess of a revival religion shorn of its predestinarian rigor, the Boston Unitarian clergy held to the gentlemanly rationalities which furnished decorous answers to their problems. Thus the Unitarians were left with the disturbing paradox of accepting both the more mechanical aspects of Lockean psychology and the simultaneous belief in the miracles of the New Testament.

An important piece for the solution of this puzzle was accidentally produced when the Rev. James Marsh published Coleridge's *Aids to Reflection* in the hope of revitalizing Calvinism. Instead the Coleridgean doctrine of Reason offered a parallel to the insights of the prophet or seer for the use of the Transcendentalists, who found that by an intuitive process, they could come into direct contact with the divine through the contemplation of Nature.[2] Thus, in the field of religion, Transcendentalism replaced the traditional belief in the Bible, miracles, election, and the institutional church with direct intuition of an immanent God who wrought within the individual soul. Emerson, having resigned from the ministry in 1832 because he could not conscientiously continue the formalities of religious office, and having achieved a visible position as a result of his little book of philosophy, *Nature* (1836), finally stated his religious beliefs to the Harvard Divinity School in 1838. By disregarding the New Testament, by pushing aside the teachings of the historical church, by insisting that God still speaks to those who are willing to hear, and by saying that Jesus had been taken much too seriously, Emerson shocked conservatives and delighted the young. He was skeptical of most conventional Christian beliefs; yet he conveyed his simultaneous and devout conviction that everything was spiritual.

Thoreau himself, though he had not begun as a Transcendentalist, was able to build upon Emerson's views without having to work them through independently on his own initiative. It became his personal task to put them into effect, to test them by his life, to capture his findings and finally to convey them to others. It will help our understanding of Thoreau's religious responses to order them in terms of his reactions to church, scripture, nature, and value systems.

Recent scholarly attempts to characterize American religion help us to define the nature of Thoreau's rebellion against official and public patterns of conformity. American religious growth was the result of a free tradition which left no established church to rebel against, but which still caused church members to interfere in society by bringing social pressure to bear on their neighbors. What Professor Sidney Mead has called "voluntaryism"[3] assumed that "the personal religious convictions of individuals, freely gathered in churches and acting in voluntary association, will permeate the society by persuasion and example." The image of the "American Protestant Enterprise is that of an intention to embrace the world yet without compromise; to be a sect and yet to mold the whole culture; to reject power and yet be powerful."

Thoreau reacted vigorously against institutional religion, and was anti-church from the time he became a Transcendentalist. Though he had been raised in a pious family and had felt badly about his sins when fourteen, he became a rebel and signed off from the church as soon as it tried to collect a tax from him for its support, and was thereafter a critic of church affairs. So in *A Week* he attacked the church he knew as an institution and the god it created and worshipped as representing only, "the overwhelming authority and respectability of mankind combined."[4] He continued thus: "when one enters the village, the church, not only really but from association, is the ugliest building in it, because it is the one in which human nature stoops the lowest and is the most disgraced. Certainly such temples as these shall ere long cease to deform the landscape. There are few things more disheartening and disgusting than . . . to hear a preacher shouting like a boatswain in a gale of wind, and thus harshly profaning the quiet atmosphere of the 'Sabbath.' "

The narrowness and dogma of New England Protestantism Thoreau felt were not justified by Christian tradition. Christ would be rejected as a "mistaken misguided man, insane and crazed" (*J*, XII, 407). While the church thinks it is free, "all it tolerates is a lifelong hypocrisy. Let us have institutions framed not out of our rottenness, but out of our soundness. This factitious piety is like stale gingerbread" (*J*, XI, 324). Especially when churches advocated restraint so as to stop attacks on slavery, Thoreau expressed extreme disgust, which reached an apex when, in "A Plea for Captain John Brown" he declared, "Away with your broad and flat churches, and your narrow and tall churches! Take a step forward, and invent a new style of outhouses. Invent a salt that will save you and defend your nostrils" (*W*, IV, 420).

Nevertheless Thoreau, though he rejected the religion of his period, was unable altogether to avoid it. He was deeply and permanently influenced by the Puritan conscience, grounded on original sin, the idea that all men are inadequate in the sight of God, and that they are bound to fall short of ideal perfection. The results included soul-searching, sense of guilt, and the view that penitence was needed for individual salvation. This feeling when externalized by the church, set people to looking for evil so as to question and correct the conduct of others. Thus the Christian religion "treated man's spiritual affairs too exclusively," was "too constantly moral," and aimed too much at the next world. (*W*, I, 74). This at worst involved concealment of personal imperfections, public conformity, censoriousness of deviants (the fun is to punish the sinner rather than the sin), and an attempt to impose the kind of tyranny of public opinion which de Tocqueville feared.

Thus, if we look at Thoreau's self-conscious arrogance, his flouting of convention, his attack on the amenities, it becomes clear that these were violent attempts to reject the Puritan attitude towards men. The most obvious example was his response to having set the woods on fire in 1844. At a later time, (*J*, II, 21-25) though he still pretended defiance, he was exorcising guilt. So it is not surprising to find him saying, "It is not worthwhile to let our imperfections disturb us always. The conscience really does not, and ought not to monopolize the whole of our lives, any more than the heart or the head. It is as liable to disease as any other part" (*W*, I, 75).

Undoubtedly, then, one reason why Thoreau found the Hindu scriptures attractive was that they offered a way to his God without penitence for guilt. As for Christianity, "It never reflects, but repents. There is no poetry in it, we may say, nothing regarded in the light of beauty merely, but moral truth is its object. All mortals are convicted by its conscience." But repentance was not sufficiently connected with this world in which Thoreau was trying to live every minute with the utmost vitality: not by being odd or trying to make others good, but by seeking the highest peak in ecstasy. "What," he exclaimed, "after all, does the practicalness of life amount to? . . . I would give all the wealth in the world, and all the deeds of all the heroes, for one true vision. But how can I communicate with the gods, who am a pencilmaker on earth and not be insane?" (*W*, I, 145-46). The means he found was a Brahmin-like purity of continence and restraint. As the chapter "Higher Laws" in *Walden* confirms, the ecstasies of vision came from Hindu asceticism rather than Christian penitence.

While Thoreau did not approve of the Christian church or clergy he showed only a little more respect for the Bible, on which New England religion had been based. His Transcendentalist argument was that all great religions were based on "divine" inspiration and not Christianity only. Thus, as we might expect, he accepted all sacred books as equally valid, and published in *The Dial* a series of excerpts from Ethical Scriptures, which included Saadi, The Laws of Menu, Confucius, Buddha and Hermes Trismegistus.

What Thoreau objected to when he gave the impression of not knowing the Bible as well as these foreign texts was the narrow exclusiveness of Christian dogmatists. He comments as follows:

> I am repeatedly astonished by the coolness and obtuse bigotry with which some will appropriate the New Testament in conversation with you . . . I have seen two persons conversing at a tea-table, both lovers of the New Testament, each in his own way, the one a lover of all kindred expression of truth also; and yet the other appropriated the New Testament wholly to himself, and took it for granted, with singular obtuseness, that the former neither knew nor cared anything about it. (*J*, III, 256-57)

Thus, while Thoreau saw the story of Jesus as a myth like the myths of other great religions, he nevertheless knew the Old and New Testaments especially well, as was proved by his constant references to, rhythmical imitations of, and parodying inversions of Biblical texts. Because knowing the Bible and believing it are two different things, it is clear that Thoreau's religion was not based on a belief in scripture as carrying the true revelation of God.

Though Thoreau never tried to work out a systematic and coherent theological scheme, but depended upon successive flashes of insight, his religion can, not unfairly, be called a religion of nature. When he applied what we may loosely call the Romantic Imagination considered as a spiritual faculty to Nature, Nature became a symbol as fact flowered into truth. But because he was rather mystical, his views are difficult to define. Was he a pantheist? Was he a theist? Was he a humanist? Though he might at times show some of each, we can find a major consistency in him despite the difficulties.

He only occasionally mentions God. In the poem "Inspiration" God has changeless power, offers insight, life, eternal truth and untold love. It is interesting that this one of Thoreau's better poems should sound so conventional with a God of love. This is confirmed by a *Journal* statement of 1856 "God could not be unkind to me if he should try," (*J*, IX, 160) and by the God of love implied in "Paradise (to be) Regained." But some ambiguity is introduced in the wry twist of a beatitude expressed in one of his final letters to Parker Pillsbury, "Blessed are they who never read a newspaper, for they shall see nature, and through her God" (*Corr.*, 611).[5]

On the whole the thing he sought was a feeling of union with Nature, a correspondence which made him feel that she was congenial with man because the same force or spirit was behind both. But he was not perfectly protected against a threat of man's personal insignificance in an alien universe. Thus when he first encountered the vast, awesome, unfinished summit of Mt. Ktaadn he was profoundly shocked, because it was of a different order, not one bound to be kind to man. In this early reaction he anticipated the later American literary naturalists who likewise responded with pessimism to the discovery that man no longer appeared to be the aim and center of creation.

Though this disillusion has been emphasized, the fact is that it proved temporary. It was perhaps only one element which led to a crisis when his hopes of successful authorship were temporarily shattered by the crushing failure of *A Week*. It was the recovery from this gloom which Sherman Paul celebrates in his eloquent introduction to *Walden*;[6] John F. Jaques in addressing himself particularly to the Ktaadn crisis convincingly claims that it was resolved when Thoreau was made to search his own life "and the results were soon recorded in the much revised masterpiece *Walden*."[7] This recovery is attested by a letter to Harrison Blake in 1857 when the incapacitation of Thoreau's climbing companion prevented an ascent of Ktaadn:[8]

> The aspect of the world varies from year to year, as the landscape is differently clothed, but I find that the *truth* is still *true*, and I never regret any emphasis which it may have inspired. Ktaadn is there still, but much more surely my old conviction is there, resting with more than mountain breadth and weight on the world, the source still of fertilizing streams, and affording glorious views from its summit, if I can get up to it again.

Despite some ambiguity here as to whether it is the mountain or his conviction which offers the chance of brilliant prospects, and even ambiguity whether he would ever get up again, this passage has an affirmative and positive rhythm and tone. Thoreau then seems to have ended with a relatively optimistic interpretation of Nature.

Death is a natural fact which so ineluctably confronts every man that some deep anxieties are sure to result. While Thoreau on the surface seems to have been relatively cheerful about the threat of destruction, recent scholars have emphasized the subconscious forces at work. By considering first Thoreau's responses to the death of close relatives and then to his consciousness of his own mortality, we can come to see the issues and answers. While editing the unpublished Journal covering the death of Henry's brother John, Perry Miller naturally raised the problem of Thoreau's difficulty in coming to terms with the shattering experience of John's fatal attack of lockjaw. And while recognizing that Henry achieved a solution in the writing of *Walden*, Miller magnified the importance of the crisis.[9] Henry did not refuse to face the issue and in a letter of May 23, 1843, he sent to his sister Helen a poem which suggests the assuagement of a belief in immortality.

> Brother, where dost thou dwell?
> What sun shines for thee now?
> Dost thou indeed fare well
> As we wished here below?
>
> What season didst thou find?
> 'Twas winter here
> Are not the Fates more kind
> Than they appear?
>
> Is thy brow clear again,
> As in the youthful years?
> And was that ugly pain
> The summit of thy fears?

Joel Porte points out along with Miller that Thoreau not only learned that each death of a relative was an assault on his vital force, (*J*, XVII, 438-9) but found the thought of death intolerable and wished to dispose of it in haste.[10]

Of course Thoreau was perfectly aware of the religious answer to the problem and wrote that death and funerals keep the churches going (*J*, III, 120). That he did not accept the simplest view of resurrection and personal immortality, is indicated by suggestions about 1851, of earlier incarnations and of the transmigration of souls (*J*, II, 27, 303). But this seems to have been only a temporary belief, and most of the time he adhered to the view that only human beings have souls. Consequently, Thoreau was able to accept the disgusting process of the decay of animal bodies though it was allied to the unpleasantness of cleaning animals or fish and became one of the reasons he advocated vegetarianism. But this was multiplied in the case of large bodies like those of men or of the horse he mentioned in *Walden*. At one extreme he advocated returning corpses to the soil in such a way as to help the fertility of agricultural land; at the other he approved of cremation as a quick process which was clean. But death he saw as physical only and of no lasting importance. "There is no continuance of death. It is a transient phenomenon" (*W*, IV, 327-28). Porte is on stronger ground in suggesting that Thoreau's advance from home life to country life at Walden, his retreat to the life in nature, and his emphasis on the cycle of the year all represent his consciousness of death's chariot coming near.[11] Nevertheless we should be skeptical that Thoreau believed that the soul as an epiphenomenon of the body disappears on death. All evidence indicates that Thoreau showed a remarkable serenity as his own death approached. This was attested by his friends as well as Sam Staples, who had jailed him for not paying his poll tax. So he was able to joke about immortality with Parker Pillsbury, and indicated to his farmer friend Edmund Hosmer, "This is a beautiful world; but I shall see a fairer."[12] Because he accepted some sort of supremacy of the spirit, Henry had no difficulty in accepting physical death and the dissolution of the body because this was in the process of Nature and followed her laws.

For present purposes of analyzing Thoreau's complex responses to the natural world it is valuable to introduce the scheme worked out by Jonathan Bishop in his original study *Emerson on the Soul* (Cambridge, 1964): within the soul there "seems to be three main realms: intellectual perception, moral individuality and organic instinct,"[13] all of them loose and flexible in meaning. The physical response to nature varying from bare consciousness to ecstatic enjoyment, the area emphasized by Porte as the purely sensuous life, is that based on organic instinct. Conversely, the realm of science would be based upon intellectual perception. Finally, the moral sense would find particular expression in the area of social and ethical relations.

For Thoreau, aspects of the first and third of these categories produced particular problems. If we begin with the instinctual we discover not only that a normal decline of sensitivity resulted in fewer ecstatic moments for Thoreau, though they did not totally cease, but also that some problems ensued. Less certain than Emerson that intuition would give the answers, Thoreau sought a program of action to reconcile man to god[14] by leading a saintly life. In his early career Henry believed in both intuitive and scientific and moral avenues to Nature, and was convinced that fact would flower into truth. In "Natural History of Massachusetts" he said that the true man of science would "know nature better by his finer organization, by a more perfect Indian wisdom" (*W*, I, 131), which is really instinct. Moreover he thought that man could learn enough to "anticipate" the rhythms of nature and so keep time with them. Nature's cyclical organization made this anticipation seem possible. So while Thoreau used the cycle of the year successfully for *Walden*, the attempt at a day-by-day calendar did not get him any closer to the spiritual meaning of nature, any closer to God, and so offered no new, successful, structural principle.

At the same time, Thoreau was discovering that science was developing in a direction which was equally frustrating. While Emerson bridged the Cartesian gap by making the perceiver central to the understanding of Nature, science grew more interested in the external fact, and increasingly uninterested in its impact on the mind of the perceiver. Thoreau, perfectly aware of this, wrote that the scientific ideal was to "cooly give your chief attention to the phenomenon which excites you as something independent of you and not as related to you" (*J*, x, 164-65). So he often attacked science, in the romantic idiom of Keats or Poe. But through some change which he could not control, Thoreau became increasingly interested in the recording of facts, with the result that his later *Journals* become relatively less engaging. But when Thoreau was personally concerned, he was able to perceive relations and so to become a pioneer ecologist, and in "The Succession of Forest Trees" was able to suggest ways of managing woodlots. So he opposed science at the very time he was resorting to it. Thus, while Thoreau undoubtedly had an empirical side and showed a real interest in nature for its own sake, science did not give him ultimate answers.

And while neither the instinctual nor the sensual proved permanently satisfying, Thoreau nevertheless felt an important connection between the heightened responses to nature and intimations of the higher moral law. Though he could not articulate any logical relation between the two, he nevertheless asserted it. When he heard the superlatively lovely song of the thrush, he wrote, "This is the gospel according to the wood thrush. He makes a sabbath of a weekday. I could go to hear him, could buy a pew in his church. Did he ever practice pulpit eloquence? He is right on the slavery question." (*J*, VI, 225.) Three years later in 1857, in reminiscence of his night in jail he wrote, "I ordinarily plod along a sort of whitewashed prison entry, subject to some indifferent or grovelling mood (*J*, IX, 364) . . . But suddenly, in some fortunate moment, the voice of eternal wisdom reaches me even in the strain of the sparrow and liberates me" (*J*, IX, 365). "Methinks," he records earlier in the same sequence, "I hear these sounds, have these reminiscences only when well employed" (*J*, IX, 364).

Another particularly long and exciting passage makes a similar connection in more general terms: "It was a serene, elysian light in which the deeds we have dreamed of but not realized might have been performed . . . It was such a light as we behold but dwell not in! . . . And then it was remarkable that the light-giver should have revealed to me, for all life, the heaving white breasts of two ducks within this glade of light" (*J*, x, 133-34; 10/28/57). Nothing could appear more useless, more irrelevant to slavery and abolition than this vision of light. Nothing could seem more useless or more irrelevant, as Emerson said, than being the captain of a huckleberry party. Yet Thoreau out of such visions linking nature and an ethical call was able to work out a position of belief.

We are told that he did not vote, and we know that he refused to pay his poll tax, and so spent a night in prison. We know that he helped fugitive slaves on the underground railroad; we know that he gave vigorous speeches on slavery, we know that he helped one of Brown's band of raiders to escape to Canada, though this was an act compounding treason. But it was the writing and publication of "resistance to Civil Government" or "Civil Disobedience," as it came to be called, which was an act of worldwide significance.

As a Transcendentalist, Thoreau believed in living by the higher laws and in judging institutions and people by ideal rather than historical or relative standards. Consequently he turned to a self-conscious and resentful rejection of what most of his neighbors approved. The virtues of thrift, industry, and prudence which were acclaimed by conservative public opinion he found wanting. The long "Economy" chapter of *Walden* showed that he was more interested in life than in money. Indeed though he might have gained wealth through marketing his superior quality plumbago, he was unwilling to give up his calling to do it.

Passing over his well-known attack on industrialism and his Walden attempt to simplify his life, let us concentrate for a few moments on "Civil Disobedience," in which we see the operation of Thoreau's transcendentalist ethic, one based on the highest point of view, rather than on expediency; "They who know no purer sources of truth . . . stand by the Bible and the Constitution," which were both used to justify slavery. But for Thoreau, "it is not desirable to cultivate a respect for law, so much as for the right. The only obligation which I have a right to assume, is to do at any time what I think right." There are times "in which a people, as well as an individual must do justice, cost what it may. If I have unjustly wrested a plank from a drowning man, I must restore it though I drown myself (a sentiment later denied by the post-Darwinian Justice Holmes). This, according to Paley would be inconvenient. But he that would save his life in such a case, shall lose it. This people must cease to hold slaves, and to make war on Mexico, though it cost them their existence as a people."

He then continued: "Action from principle—the perception and performance of right,—changes things and relations; it is essentially revolutionary. . . . " Abolitionists should not wait for a numerical majority; "it is enough if they have God on their side . . . Moreover, any man more right than his neighbors constitutes a majority of one already." "A minority is powerless while it conforms to the majority; it is not even a minority then; but it is irresistible if it clogs by its whole weight. If the alternative is to keep all just men in prison, or to give up war and slavery, the State will not hesitate which to choose . . . This is in fact the definition of a peaceable revolution, if any such is possible." Such optimism is based upon the assumption that governments are composed not only of "brute force" but of people, so that "appeal is possible, first and instantaneously, from them to the maker of them, and secondly from them to themselves."

This ethical appeal, religiously based upon the highest intuitions of man or of his Maker, we know has had the most widespread effects. The language was obviously more important than the quixotic incarceration, but even that had its value. The tradition in the Emerson family, characteristic of the men, has it that Emerson exclaimed "Henry, what are you doing in there?" to which Thoreau replied, "Waldo, what are you doing out there?" Thoreau earned the right to speak by his ethical action. Not willing to confine the right of revolution to the time of Washington and Franklin, he took it on himself to disobey the law and to suffer the consequences. When Gandhi decided that this technique would work on a public scale he was embracing the ethics of Thoreau, who was himself an admirer of the high, table-land grandeur and sublimity of the Hindu scriptures, the Laws of Menu and the Bhagvat Geeta. And when the ideas of Thoreau and Gandhi were taken up again in America to combat the evils which slavery introduced and abolition did not remove, the wheel had come full circle. The prophet was not without honor even in his own country.

Since the religious attitudes of American intellectuals have been much less conventionally orthodox than is generally thought, Thoreau's position has been attacked with shock and outrage. Perhaps not too strangely, skepticism of religious dogma is no more acceptable, is really rather less acceptable, to the American middlebrow than it was in Thoreau's day. And this seems true because the twentieth century is not a religious age. Consequently, when middle-brow groups are faced with serious thought, with honest doubt, with sup-posedly irreverent criticism of their passively accepted dogma, they react with shock and pain.

Moreover, political and social conservatives are as irritated today by Thoreau's "rage to reform" as they ever were. He is still seen by some as a mere rebel, impractical, wrong-headed, and bent on minority tyranny, but as a man too fragmented to have even been able to write with real effect.[15]

Conversely, Thoreau has more serious readers today than ever before. Most critics see that his asceticism was not a withdrawal from life but a means of living it to the full. His ethical challenge to simplify, to wedge deeply, to front life and drive it into a corner has been taken up, in a time of the organization man and the lonely crowd, by people who insist on individuality, not convention. It is the spirit of Thoreau which animated some passive resistance and civil rights causes like that of Martin Luther King, in our time.

Now he is seen as a religious figure, ethical in his rejection of material gains and his ecological faith and spiritual in his emphasis upon a direct access to the divine through contemplation of nature.

[1] Roy Meyer, "Thoreau and Christianity", (unpublished master's thesis, University of Iowa, 1949), p. 57.

[2] Alexander Kern, "The Rise of Transcendentalism," in H. H. Clark ed., *Transitions in American Literary History* (Durham, 1954), pp. 275-84.

[3] William L. Miller, "American Religion and American Political Attitudes," in James Ward Smith and A. Leland Jamison, eds., *Religious Perspectives in American Culture* (Princeton, 1961), pp. 81-91. Sidney Mead is quoted on p. 89.

[4] Henry David Thoreau, *The Writings of Henry David Thoreau* (Boston, 1906). 20 volumes. In this article reference to the writings will be inserted into the text in parentheses as (W, I, p.—). Since they are separately published, the *Journals* will start with volume I, as (J, I, p.—).

[5] Walter Harding and Carl Bode, eds., *The Correspondence of Henry David Thoreau* (New York, 1958), p. 611.

[6] Sherman Paul, editor, *Walden and Civil Disobedience* (Boston, 1960), p. xxxv.

[7] John F. Jaques, "'Ktaadn'—A Record of Thoreau's Youthful Crisis," *Thoreau Journal Quarterly*, 1 (1969), 6.

[8] *Correspondence*, p. 491-92.

[9] Perry Miller, editor, *Consciousness in Concord* (Cambridge, Mass., 1957), pp. 55-76.

[10] Joel Porte, *Emerson and Thoreau* (Middletown, Conn., 1966), p. 185.

[11] Ibid., p. 200

[12] Walter Harding, *The Days of Henry Thoreau* (New York, 1965), p. 462.

[13] Jonathan Bishop, *Emerson on the Soul* (Cambridge, Mass., 1964), p. 21.

[14] Nina Baym, "Thoreau's View of Science," *Journal of the History of Ideas*, 26 (1965), 221-234.

[15] Leon Edel in Sherman Paul, editor, *Six Classic American Writers* (Minneapolis, 1970), pp. 188-94.

VI

COVERDALE'S CONFESSION, A KEY TO
MEANING IN *THE BLITHEDALE ROMANCE*

RICHARD DILWORTH RUST

THE BLITHEDALE ROMANCE IS AN ANOMALY
in Hawthorne's fiction. It was written in the most intense
artistic period of his life when he was in full control of
his powers. Furthermore, Hawthorne was working with rich
materials with which he was intimately familiar. Yet of the
three novels written from 1849 to 1852, *Blithedale* has received the least praise.[1] In fact it has been faulted for alleged
flaws in its basic components: questions have been raised
about the function, value, and reliability of the narrator;[2]
early reviewers objected that it lacked a fusion of romantic
and realistic parts and that it failed to give an accurate
and detailed account of Brook Farm;[3] some critics have been
distressed by apparent weaknesses in the plot such as the
multitude of mysteries and confusing character relationships;[4]
and others have objected to various structural elements, particularly the conclusion.

The weight of critical dissatisfaction with the totality of
the novel (although not necessarily with elements such as
imagery) compels one to admit it is not a successful work
in the category of *The Scarlet Letter*. Nonetheless its weaknesses lie not in lack of talent, ability, or conception on
the part of Hawthorne. Rather, it falls short because Haw-

thorne was experimenting with new methods and techniques, such as the first-person point of view and the fictionalizing of current events, and because he was overly subtle in major areas of the novel.

Of all elements in *Blithedale*, the conclusion has come under the most severe attack. W. C. Brownell calls it "an idle boast."[5] William Van O'Connor says that "most readers presumably are offended or shocked" by it.[6] Terence Martin thinks it is "the saddest (and most maddening) confession in Hawthorne's fiction, a last second attempt to make whole in retrospect a figure who has sacrificed himself to the story as pleasantly as he could."[7] Nina Baym bluntly asserts, "Coverdale, when he claims to be in love with Priscilla, is lying."[8] Other critics are content to discount or ignore the confession. Yet Coverdale says that the knowledge he reveals of his love for Priscilla "will throw a gleam of light over my behavior throughout the foregoing incidents, and is, indeed, essential to the full understanding of my story."[9] This puzzling statement does indeed provide a key to understanding the novel, precisely as Coverdale says it will, although it is not readily comprehensible because of Coverdale's narrative methods and Hawthorne's concealment of his own emotional involvement in the story.

Early readers of *The Blithedale Romance* were inclined to see Coverdale simply as a fictional portrait of Hawthorne, and some modern critics have persisted in reading the novel as a *roman à clef*.[10] There are of course numerous elements of self-portraiture in Coverdale just as there are scenes taken straight from Hawthorne's experiences at Brook Farm. Yet the characteristics of Coverdale at the end of the novel are very different from Hawthorne's during the period in which he wrote *Blithedale*. In "Miles Coverdale's Confession" the elements emphasized are Coverdale's lonely bachelorhood, inactivity, lack of purpose, disuse of artistic gifts, and loss of human ties. In 1851-52 when he wrote *Blithedale*, Hawthorne was a devoted family man; he had recently achieved wide acclaim with *The Scarlet Letter* and had followed that success with intense literary activity; and he had become, in the Boston area to which he had moved, a more social person than he had ever been before.

The nature of these differences between Hawthorne and Coverdale underlines the single most important aspect of Hawthorne's life during and following the Brook Farm period —the love he and Sophia Peabody had for each other and the fulfillment of that love in marriage. This love in fact serves as a controlling theme for much of Julian Hawthorne's biography of his father and is a dominant theme in Randall Stewart's biography. On one level, then, Coverdale's confession is the answer to a number of "What if" questions Hawthorne posed for himself as he imaginatively explored roads not taken. What if, as a man in his late 30's, he had not found Sophia? What if he had remained a bachelor? What if negative tendencies in his personality, such as "Paul Pryism," skepticism, and detachedness had been allowed to develop unchecked? What if he had not committed himself fully to his artistic vocation?

As he says in "The Old Manse," Hawthorne could not be "one of those supremely hospitable people who serve up their own hearts, delicately fried, with brain sauce, as a tidbit for their beloved public."[11] Rather, in examining sensitive and important factors in his life as he does in *The Blithedale Romance*, his method was to choose as a narrator a caricature of himself who would mask the author's true intentions while allowing him to explore personal tendencies. When Hawthorne has his serio-comic narrator say, "I exaggerate my own defects" (p. 247), he is also describing his own autobiographical methods.

At many points "Miles Coverdale's Confession" is relevant to Hawthorne's life. Coverdale says: "I am now at middle-age— . . . a bachelor, with no very decided purpose of ever being otherwise; . . . [I am an] old bachelor, . . . a man in his afternoon . . . with these three white hairs in his brown mustache" (pp. 246-47). We learn that he is about 37—the same age as Hawthorne when he joined the Brook Farm community.[12] In other words, at the age at which Coverdale's bachelor life had "come to rather an idle pass," Hawthorne had just begun to live. Again, Coverdale laments his "colorless life" and his lack of purpose which has rendered his life "all an emptiness" (pp. 245-46). His lament is reminiscent of many of Hawthorne's: In an 1837 letter to Longfellow he speaks of having "no share in either [the world's] joys or sorrows. For the last ten years, I have not lived, but only dreamed about living."[13] And in a letter written to Sophia in September, 1841, Hawthorne believes, "If, in the interval since I quitted this lonely old chamber in Salem, I had found no woman (and thou wast the only possible one) to impart reality and significance to life, I should have come back hither ere now, with the feeling that all was a dream and a mockery."[14] Coverdale's confession that he flings an "unsatisfied retrospect" back on life and a "listless glance towards the future" might have been Hawthorne's own fate had he not married Sophia. In a journal entry of March 31, 1843, Hawthorne tells of a visit to Salem "where I resumed all my bachelor habits for nearly a fortnight, leading the same life in which ten years of my youth flitted away like a dream. But how much changed was I!—at last, I had caught hold of a reality, which never could be taken from me. It was good thus to get apart from my happiness, for the sake of contemplating it."[15] In like manner, *The Blithedale Romance* is in part Hawthorne's contemplation of the period surrounding his Brook Farm experience and his marriage to see how different circumstances might have denied him his "reality" and happiness.

A vital distinction between Hawthorne's life and Coverdale's experiences may be seen in Hawthorne's symbolism of the dove—which most likely was intended for his wife's private appreciation. From a window of his Boston boarding house, Coverdale becomes fascinated with a dove perched on a dormer window of the house in which Priscilla is staying. While Coverdale watches, the dove flies straight toward his own window sill, but then suddenly swerves aside, flies upward, and vanishes. (In the experience from which this scene was taken, the dove did not vanish but instead remained visible on the roof of the house in which Hawthorne was staying.)[16] The dove is linked with Priscilla: Coverdale dreams that Priscilla had peeped in at the chamber window but then "had melted gradually away" (p. 153); upon arising he notices that the dove had remained at its perch. Then at the end of the same chapter Coverdale tells us that although Priscilla "disappeared from the boudoir," the dove "still kept her desolate perch" (p. 159). Realizing that "Dove" was one of Hawthorne's pet names for Sophia during their courtship, one can see a private source of the symbolism. Coverdale's great sorrow is that his dove, Priscilla, swerved aside and left him desolate. Hawthorne's joy was that his dove, Sophia, came to him.

Because it comes as such a surprise, Coverdale's admission at the end of his narrative of love for Priscilla at first seems incredible. Earlier in the novel, however, he had hinted of it: while convalescing, Coverdale regrets that Priscilla did not make him out "for the third place in her regards" (p. 50). In his tree-hermitage Coverdale flings to a passing bird a message for Priscilla, warning her against Zenobia and Hollingsworth, and admitting, " 'If any mortal really cares for her, it is myself' " (p. 100). At the first Eliot's pulpit scene he dislikes Hollingsworth's "necromancy" which wins the affections of the two women and leaves Coverdale "to shiver in outer seclusion, without even the alternative of solacing himself with what the more fortunate individual has rejected" (p. 126). And when Coverdale leaves Blithedale he asks only Priscilla for a "parting keepsake" (p. 142). Ten years after the event when Coverdale finally does confess, he does so reticently: "As I write it, the reader will charitably suppose me to blush, and turn away my face:—I—I myself—was in love—with—PRISCILLA!" (p. 247). Coverdale's secretiveness and his belated confession of love are in character as final manifestations of his Prufrockian detachment and unwillingness to commit himself until the time for doing so has passed.

These veiled feelings of Coverdale are only a part of a series of secrets and mysteries which pervade the novel. On one level these mysteries are merely irritating, and they have caused William Hedges to complain: "Throughout most of *Blithedale* mystery functions as a distraction sidetracking the adventure from its avowed purpose."[17] Rather than being gratuitous, though, the mystifying functions help characterize Coverdale. The narrator's preoccupation with mystery begins with his saying that interest in the Veiled Lady was "wrought up by the enigma of her identity" (p. 6). He has this same type of interest in Priscilla who is for him "an object of peculiar interest, a riddle" (p. 35). On his sick bed he perplexes himself "with a great many conjectures" to discover "whether Zenobia had ever been married" (p. 46); and when he overhears the Westervelt-Zenobia conversation he thinks it "the design of fate" to let him "into all Zenobia's secrets" (p. 103). Coverdale begins Chapter IX, "Hollingsworth, Zenobia, Priscilla," by saying that his three friends "were separated from the rest of the Community, to my imagination, and stood forth as the indices of a problem which it was my business to solve" (p. 69). In his hermitage, Coverdale believes that "the many tongues of Nature whispered mysteries, and seemed to ask only a little stronger puff of wind, to speak out the solution of its riddle" (p. 99). He tells us that his reason for seeking an interview with Old Moodie was to ascertain "whether the knot of affairs was as inextricable, on that side, as I found it on all others" (p. 174). And the reason Coverdale gives us in Chapter XXIV for returning to Blithedale is that he had "a yearning interest to learn the upshot of all my story" (p. 205). Coverdale's concern for solving mysteries thus displays his skeptical and prying nature, and justifies Zenobia's stricture that he has an "insolent curiosity" and a "meddlesome temper" (p. 170).

In spite of Coverdale's overwhelming attention to mysteries, they often remain unsolved or only partially solved. This has brought Mark Van Doren's complaint that Coverdale is a "distressingly pale character" who tells his story "so badly that when he is not forcing scenes he is suppressing them altogether, with the result that we do not know what the story is."[18] Actually, this suppression of facts enriches Hawthorne's characterization of Coverdale as a person reticent in drawing conclusions. An example of this is found in Old Moodie's first visit to Blithedale. The only questions Coverdale asks are about the identity of the person who made Moodie's silk purses. This brings Hollingsworth's comment, " 'Why do you trouble him with needless questions, Coverdale? . . . You must have known, long ago, that it was Priscilla' " (p. 85). Another manifestation of this trait in Coverdale occurs in the scene in which Coverdale awakens Hollingsworth and Silas Foster to help him look for Zenobia:

> I showed Hollingsworth a delicate handkerchief, marked with a well-known cypher, and told where I had found it, and other circumstances which had filled me with a suspicion so terrible, that *I left him, if he dared, to shape it out for himself.* By the time my brief explanation was finished, we were joined by Silas Foster, in his blue woollen frock.
> "Well, boys," cried he, peevishly, "what is to pay now?"
> "Tell him, Hollingsworth!" said I.
> Hollingsworth shivered, perceptibly, and drew in a hard breath betwixt his teeth. He steadied himself, however, and *looking the matter more firmly in the face than I had done,* explained to Foster my suspicions and the grounds of them, with a distinctness from which, in spite of my utmost efforts, *my words had swerved aside.* The tough-nerved yeoman, in his comment, put a finish on the business. . . .
> "And so you think she's drowned herself!" he cried.
> *I turned away my face.* (p. 230 [italics added])

Coverdale's reticence and weakness in this scene is best imaged forth in his turning away his face, an action that is repeated in his confession at the end of the novel.

The same process Coverdale uses in telling Hollingsworth and Silas Foster about Zenobia's death applies to the relationship between Coverdale and the reader. Coverdale gives all the clues needed to establish identities and then leaves it up to the reader to formulate the conclusion. Thus a perceptive reader who is aware of Coverdale's methods can have a feeling of success in linking the parts of the mystery into an understandable whole. In fact, the reader often is able to discover truths which Coverdale perceives only much later or not at all, such as Priscilla's identity as the Veiled Lady. Although Priscilla is shrouded in mystery when she comes to Blithedale, she is soon linked with the Veiled Lady by clues such as her being called "spiritual" and a prophetess and her going into a mesmeric trance when she hears a voice calling. Eventually Priscilla's identity as the Veiled Lady is revealed to the reader in Zenobia's legend which, like Hamlet's "Mousetrap" play, allows Zenobia to confirm the truth of what Westervelt had told her in their forest interview. Coverdale nevertheless appears unaware of the Priscilla-Veiled Lady identity, and shows no signs of having recognized it in the Fauntleroy story. It is not until the village hall scene that Coverdale makes "a quick association of ideas" (p. 200) which confirms the identity for him.

Coverdale's reflections in the chapter "Miles Coverdale's Confession" not only help characterize him and clarify his narrative methods, but also cause us to reexamine his motives and the whole process of his change and development. As he tells us in the chapter "Blithedale," the major reasons Coverdale first went to Blithedale were to find a place where he could "be true" and to join a group of people who believed that love and not economic competition should be the basis of human relationships. When he started out for Blithedale,

Coverdale rejoiced in leaving behind the "dusky city" with its "falsehood, formality, and error" (p. 11); and upon arriving declared his hope to produce poetry that was as "true, strong, natural, and sweet" as the life the Blithedalers were going to lead (p. 14). Another appeal of the Blithedale society for Coverdale was that its members had divorced themselves "from Pride, and were striving to supply its place with familiar love" (p. 19). One test of this love is found in Hollingsworth's challenge concerning Priscilla: " 'As we do by this friendless girl, so shall we prosper!' " (p. 30)

Coverdale's moral change and regeneration into a new life do not come easily, however. The "hot-house warmth" of his former "luxurious life" had taken "much of the pith" out of his physical system, resulting in his getting a bad cold which reduces him to "a skeleton above ground" (pp. 40-41). He is brought back to life, though, mainly through Hollingsworth's ministrations which at first seemed to Coverdale "the reflection of God's own love" (p. 43). Because of this love, which is a particularization of the brotherly love he sought at Blithedale, Coverdale emerges into a new existence in which he is, "in literal and physical truth, . . . quite another man" (p. 61).

A letdown in Coverdale's hopes begins with his suspicion that perhaps Hollingsworth had demonstrated friendship toward him in order to make him a proselyte to Hollingsworth's views. Coverdale's disenchantment is continued when he realizes he has grown physically, but that the mental change accompanying this growth has been debilitating. Also he is distressed that Hollingsworth's earlier challenge is slighted; instead, "Priscilla found but scanty requital for her love" (p. 50). Hollingsworth comes dangerously close to crushing "the tender rosebud" of Priscilla's heart, and Zenobia demonstrates her lack of love in the "malignant weed" scene, during Old Moodie's visit, and at the end of the legend of the Veiled Lady.

Of the four major characters, Coverdale is the person most

changed by the events of the three central chapters. Although he may have given the reader the impression he was merely a skeptical and detached observer, in truth he is strongly affected emotionally. As he says in a veiled statement at the beginning of Chapter xv, the summer "went deep into my heart" (p. 128). And looking back on the conflict with Hollingsworth, Coverdale says, "There is still a sensation as if Hollingsworth had caught hold of my heart, and were pulling it towards him with an almost irresistible force" (pp. 133-134).

The "crisis" between the two men which produces Coverdale's most drastic change is Hollingsworth's being false to the Blithedale experiment and his betrayal of Coverdale's love. Following this "tragic passage-at-arms," Coverdale finds that "Blithedale was no longer what it had been. Everything was suddenly faded. . . . The change will be recognized by many, who, after a period of happiness, have endeavored to go on with the same kind of life, in the same scene, in spite of the alteration or withdrawal of some principal circumstances" (p. 138). Some readers may be led into accepting as the sole reason for Coverdale's leaving Blithedale his later statement that he planned to get a "new observation" from an "old stand-point." Others may point to his disaffection with Blithedale as the cause of his leaving.[19] Instead of being causes, though, Coverdale's lessened idealism and desire to reexamine his position are results of the deep hurt inflicted by Hollingsworth. In fact, this in part is what happens throughout the novel—Coverdale reexamines from a distance the interplay of human emotions, including his own. Up to this point in the novel Coverdale's relationship with the other major characters has been relatively cordial and tight-knit. Following the conflict with Hollingsworth, though, Coverdale realizes he will never again be able to show and give his affection as freely, nor will he ever again be able to trust fully the affection of others.

The chapters set in the city show Coverdale now detached

from the other three major characters and presumably removed from the sphere of their influence. Before this he was emotionally involved with others, but now he goes to a hotel "situated somewhat aloof" from his former track in life where instead of being involved in the "muddy tide of human activity" he can "linger on the brink, or hover in the air above it" (pp. 145, 147). Now the most Coverdale feels he can do is observe sympathetically what happens to his friends. Counteracting Coverdale's sympathy for his friends, though, is his reluctance to enter within their sphere. This forms part of Coverdale's dilemma. He has strong affections; yet his weaknesses are a selfishness in resenting his own pain, a desire to know merely for the sake of knowing, and a reluctance to participate fully.

Coverdale's stay in the city gradually changes him back into the worldly person he was before he went to Blithedale. It is not surprising, then, that in the last section when Coverdale returns to Blithedale he at first finds the place to be "nothing but dream-work and enchantment" (p. 206). Whereas Coverdale before saw Blithedale as a place for regeneration and life, now he is overwhelmed by the number of images he sees or premonitions he has which remind him of death.[20] Then, when he stumbles upon Hollingsworth, Zenobia, and Priscilla at Eliot's pulpit, he at first feels that he has "no right to be or breathe there" (p. 214).

Soon after meeting his three friends, however, something happens which makes Coverdale feel it *is* his "right to be there" to witness Zenobia's solitary suffering (p. 222). As a veiled hint at what had caused the change, Coverdale says, "It suits me not to explain what was the analogy that I saw, or imagined, between Zenobia's situation and mine; nor, I believe, will the reader detect this one secret, hidden beneath many a revelation which perhaps concerned me less" (p. 222). But just as Coverdale has given clues to the solution of mysteries which concerned him less, so he has given clues to solving this secret. The secret, of course, is Coverdale's love for Priscilla which Coverdale refers to in his confession as having "something to do with these inactive years of meridian manhood, with my bachelorship, with the unsatisfied retrospect that I fling back on life, and my listless glance towards the future" (p. 247). With this knowledge of Coverdale's love, the "analogy" he speaks of becomes clear. Coverdale's witnessing the emotional conflict between his friends has reactivated his own emotions which he had smothered while in the city. Now Coverdale sees in Zenobia's being rejected by Hollingsworth a parallel with his own situation in being rejected by Priscilla. Furthermore, just as Priscilla's "blind, instinctive love" for Hollingsworth removes the possibility of conflict between that love and love for Zenobia, likewise there is no room in Priscilla's heart for love of Coverdale.

Coverdale had earlier imagined that an appropriate remedy for Zenobia's sorrow would have been for her to die. His thoughts on the subject, however, could well be prompted by his own feelings as well as by sympathy for Zenobia. After her departure he flings himself down at the base of Eliot's pulpit and remains there while the sun goes down and night comes on. This figurative death comes, as Coverdale tells us, because "I was listless, worn-out with emotion on my own behalf, and sympathy for others" (p. 228). Nevertheless, there is an important distinction between Zenobia's motivation and Coverdale's. Zenobia had earlier told Coverdale, "'You have really a heart and sympathies, as far as they go'" (p. 226). This is exactly Coverdale's problem—his emotions do not go far enough. Because Coverdale is not fully committed, he does not actually die, but rather is awakened by his intuition of "some tragical catastrophe" which involves real death. Coverdale had been denied a keepsake of love from Priscilla when he departed from Blithedale, but at the edge of the "Black River of Death" he receives Zenobia's shoe as a keepsake of death. Soon afterward the parallel between Zenobia's death and Coverdale's figurative death is most forcefully made when Hollingsworth wounds Zenobia's heart with his pole and at the same time Coverdale feels a sharp pain in his heart "as if the iron hook had smote my breast" (p. 234).

The ending of *The Blithedale Romance* is the disclosure of Coverdale's tragedy just as it is that of Zenobia's. Zenobia's tragedy is to love and lose; and because she has staked all on her love, the only alternative upon losing is death. Coverdale's tragedy is that he had not loved enough, nor had he loved fully and openly; consequently he is doomed to waste away his remaining years in a kind of death-in-life. Hawthorne summarizes this fate in his reference in the Preface to Coverdale as "the Minor Poet, beginning life with strenuous aspirations, which die out with his youthful fervor" (pp. 2-3).

In his final confession, Coverdale exposes his overarching purposes in writing his narrative. In many ways *The Blithedale Romance* is a love story;[21] and Coverdale desires to see from the perspective of years what had happened to his friends in this regard and, most of all, to learn why he did not find love for himself—especially in a community which encouraged falling in love. Inherent in Coverdale's narrative is the recognition that he is addressing his account to a reader who knows the external facts of the Blithedale experiment. (This is suggested by Coverdale's comment, "Dr. Griswold—as the reader, of course, knows—has placed me at a fair elevation among our minor minstrelsy" [p. 246].) Since even the other major characters often impute wrong motives to Coverdale (both Zenobia and Hollingsworth call him a skeptical balladeer), it is likely that the reader he is addressing has misjudged Coverdale's role in the Blithedale affairs and misunderstood the other major characters as well. Thus one of Coverdale's purposes is to tell the world the true nature and motives of Hollingsworth, Zenobia, Priscilla, and himself, with the hope that the reader will give him the same degree of sympathy he has given his friends. Most of all, Coverdale

is trying to solve the mystery of his own personality and
present lifeless existence. Earlier in the novel Coverdale had
said he felt impelled "to live in other lives, and to endeavor
. . . to learn the secret which was hidden even from themselves" (p. 160). Although Coverdale is sometimes successful
in discovering the secrets of his friends, like them he has
a secret hidden from himself. Through emphasizing the themes
of love and sincerity and through showing us Coverdale's
narrative motives and interests, Hawthorne discloses that the
secret hidden from Coverdale is that like Blithedale he failed
because of "infidelity" to his own "higher spirit" (p. 246).

---

[1] For a survey of the reception and later critical evaluation of *Blithedale*, see
Hans-Joachim Lang, *"The Blithedale Romance:* A History of Ideas Approach"
in *Literatur und Sprache der Vereinigten Staaten*, ed. Hans Helmcke, et al. (Heidel-
berg, 1969), pp. 88-106.

[2] See especially Frederick Crews, "A New Reading of *The Blithedale Romance*,"
AL, 29 (May 1957), 147-70.

[3] See particularly reviews numbers 81 and 85 in J. Donald Crowley, ed., *Hawthorne: The Critical Heritage* (New York, 1970). Also see Donald A. Campbell,
"A Critical Analysis of Nathaniel Hawthorne's *The Blithedale Romance*" (unpubl.
diss., Yale, 1960), pp. 30 ff.

[4] As an example of this see William L. Hedges, "Hawthorne's *Blithedale*: The
Function of the Narrator," *NCF*, 14 (March 1960), 316.

[5] *American Prose Masters* (New York, 1909), p. 93.

[6] "Conscious Naiveté in *The Blithedale Romance*," *Revue des langues vivantes*,
20 (Feb. 1954), 37.

[7] *Nathaniel Hawthorne* (New York, 1965), p. 159.

[8] *"The Blithedale Romance:* A Radical Reading," *JEGP*, 67 (Oct. 1968), 553.

[9] *The Centenary Edition of the Works of Nathaniel Hawthorne*, ed. William
Charvat et al. (Columbus, Ohio: Ohio State University Press, 1964), III, 247. All
subsequent page references to *Blithedale* are to this edition, and will be cited in
parentheses in the text.

[10] See Robert C. Elliot, "*The Blithedale Romance*," *Hawthorne Centenary Essays*,
ed. Roy Harvey Pearce (Columbus, Ohio: Ohio State University Press, 1964), pp.
103-17; Rudolph von Abele, *The Death of the Artist: A Study of Hawthorne's
Disintegration* (The Hague, 1955), p. 76.

[11] *Mosses from an Old Manse* (New York, 1846), I, 29.

[12] John Shroeder in "Miles Coverdale's Calendar; or, A Major Literary Source
for *The Blithedale Romance*," *EIHC*, 103 (1967), 363, points out that at the beginning
of the novel Coverdale is said to be three or four years younger than Hollingsworth,

and Hollingsworth is later said to be about 30. The reference to Coverdale's volume of poetry being published 10 years previously thus dates Coverdale at about 37.

[13] Quoted by Annie Fields in *Nathaniel Hawthorne* (Boston, 1899), p. 41.

[14] *Love Letters of Nathaniel Hawthorne*, ed. Roswell Field (Chicago, 1907), II, 35.

[15] *The American Notebooks*, ed. Claude M. Simpson (Ohio State University Press, 1972), p. 368.

[16] *American Notebooks*, p. 508.

[17] Hedges, p. 316.

[18] *Nathaniel Hawthorne* (New York, 1957), p. 189.

[19] Two critics who maintain this are Crews, p. 162, and Daniel G. Hoffman, *Form and Fable in American Fiction* (New York, 1961), p. 206.

[20] For a discussion of the death imagery in the last section see Hedges, pp. 310-14.

[21] William B. Pike, who Julian Hawthorne says "probably knew Hawthorne more intimately than any other man did," identified love as the major theme of *The Blithedale Romance*: "In this book, as in *The Scarlet Letter*, you probe deeply,— you go down among the moody silences of the heart, and open those depths whence come motives that give complexion to actions, and make in men what are called states of mind. . . . Love is undoubtedly the deepest, profoundest, of the deep things of man, having its origin in the depths of depths,—the inmost of all the emotions that ever manifest themselves on the surface. . . . In 'Blithedale' . . . you show how such things take place, and open the silent, unseen, internal elements which first set the machinery in motion, which works out results so strange to those who penetrate only to a certain depth in the soul." (Quoted in Julian Hawthorne, *Hawthorne and His Wife* [London, 1885, I, 444-5]).

VII

THE NOVELS OF OLIVER WENDELL HOLMES:
A RE-INTERPRETATION

JOHN STEPHEN MARTIN

THE LITERARY IMAGE OF OLIVER WENDELL
Holmes, Sr., has changed very little since his own day.
Along with Lowell and Longfellow, Holmes seems simply
part of the New England triumvirate that protected the genteel
virtues of the so-called Brahmin class. His wit of the Breakfast-
Table series, his *vers de societé*, and his poems of occasions
all tend to support the innocuous conclusion that Holmes
possessed a serene and patrician mind, but a mind—dare
one say it—that was not very profound nor based upon
vigorous emotions. Furthermore, when Holmes ventured
from poetry and the essay to write three fictional romances,
the assertion appears to be even more plausible. These three
romances—*Elsie Venner* of 1859-1860, *The Guardian Angel*
of 1867, and *The Mortal Antipathy* of 1885—are virtually
unknown entities today, but the judgments made of these
romances have generally, in an unexpected fashion, contributed to the overall impression of Holmes' superficiality.
It is not my intention to make a case for Holmes' intellect
that might be unappreciated, but to point out in the three
novels how Holmes addressed his talents to a complex problem of his generation not properly noticed in existing commentaries.

111

There are two basic views of the romances. On the one hand, they have been called "medicated" romances because they ostensibly are concerned with medical data and diagnoses. In Holmes' own day, readers called them "medicated" because at least two of the romances evidenced contemporary interest in physiological speculations and experiments.[1] Some two decades ago a professor of psychiatry revived this idea of "medicated" art when he cited from the remaining romance, *The Guardian Angel*, statements to show that Holmes was a "precursor of Freud" in the exploration of the subconscious.[2] More recently R. W. B. Lewis summed up this view when he wrote that "while Emerson and Whitman were trying their best to convert medical facts into inspirational poetry, Holmes was converting a literary form into a vehicle for a medical case history."[3]

But the trouble with this view, as I will show in some detail, is that there is no sustained desire by Holmes to treat his characters as a "medical case history." He is liable to introduce melodramatic twists at crucial moments, and the reader finds that Holmes has a peculiarly unmedical, highly moralized view of man. Finally, the very details referred to as "medicated," often are highly ludicrous and completely implausible.

A summary of the plot and characters of the novel *Elsie Venner* is sufficient to show how negligible are the novel's "medicated" intentions. Elsie Venner's mother, we are told, received a bite from a rattlesnake when Elsie was *in utero*. But instead of being poisoned, as one might fear, Elsie survives though deformed mentally and morally, because of an apparent genetic change. Instead of walking, Elsie has a "peculiar undulation;" when she sleeps, she "coils up;" she lisps despite no organic cause (v, 77-8, 145, 147). When aroused, her diamond-shaped eyes narrow, and her head "flattens" and draws back to strike; she has been known to bite persons although no one has died (v, 77-8, 99, 160). She is very much subject to the seasons; in winter she is dull and only after "basking for whole hours in the sunshine" of spring is she able to exert herself (v, 184, 261). Despite these characteristics, the cause—the prenatal rattlesnake bite—is known only to three persons of Elsie's rural Massachusetts village: Elsie's father, the faithful Negro servant Old Sophy, and the family doctor, Dr. Kittridge. These three persons, however, think that Elsie must be kept apart from people because she has dangerous nonhuman impulses. Thus it is that when the young medical student Bernard Langdon attempts to diagnose the medical case of Elsie, Holmes already has prejudiced the case against a "medicated" conclusion, for the secret is merely used to set up the climax. When Elsie misinterprets Bernard's interest in her as a medical subject, she believes that she is loved and violently courts Bernard; but he cannot reciprocate and in a moment of conscience, refuses her. Elsie, unable to understand the meaning of reciprocal love, or Bernard's conscience, becomes ill with a mysterious fever and dies. In her last moment, however, she is said to resemble her mother and seems human, as if Elsie was cured only by a resignation to death (v, 152, 151, 194, 453-54, 457).

This account of the melodramatic elements of plot and characterization should sufficiently contradict the view that *Elsie Venner* is a worthy "medicated" novel. Moreover, Holmes' preface to the 1861 edition was clearly emphatic in denying that this "scientific doctrine" of the transference of material characteristics from one organism to another has "his absolute belief." The doctrine of transference was adopted, Holmes continued, only as a "convenient medium of truth" (v, vii). What that "truth" might be, was left unanswered by Holmes until the 1883 preface, but what Holmes wrote then is not immediately clear and has unexpectedly given grounds to the second major interpretation of the three romances.

In the preface of 1883, Holmes said that his intention was to pose a question for the reader that concerned the nature of man's morals.

> Was Elsie Venner, poisoned by the venom of crotalus [rattlesnake] before she was born, morally responsible for the "volitional" aberrations, which translated into acts become what is known as sin, and, it may be, what is punished as crime? (v, ix-x)

One might reduce Holmes' words to a series of statements: If the reader were to condemn Elsie for her nature, he condemns her despite her inability to determine her choices of action. And, if the reader does pity her, he might also pity any person who commits a sin or a crime because those actions are not self-determined.

Central to this interpretation is the assumption that Holmes as a medical doctor accepted science as a form of deterministic thought, and such determinism in nature is considered a telling argument against the possibility of man's free will. Holmes did say apparently as much in regard to Elsie, but as I will point out, it is very questionable whether this interpretation expresses Holmes' intention about free will or the purpose of the novel as a whole.

However this second assessment is harder to refute because it is interwoven with another matter—the question of a proper theology for modern Americans. Professor Harry Hayden Clark and several of his students—Samuel Hayakawa, Arnold Goldsmith, and Charles Boewe, have argued persuasively that Holmes believed scientific determinism was experiential proof in any attack on the Calvinist doctrines of original sin, the will, and pre-destined election.[4] The argument is said to be, that by showing man's will as predetermined through nonmoral forces, Holmes wished to expose the shoddy logic of Calvinist orthodoxy by which man was held responsible for his sins and his crimes without first having that moral freedom necessary for a personal decision deserving of "election" or "damnation." This argument seems to fit the case of Elsie exactly.

But there are two flaws. First, the argument ignores the fact that Puritanism had radically changed since 1750. In particular, this argument neglects the development of New England Unitarianism which viewed man's will as being free and commensurate with man's rationality. Holmes subscribed to this view, as did many others; and even Congregationalism of the day allowed for a similar view of the will. The point is, the old Calvinism was virtually a negligible opponent for Holmes.

Secondly, the argument is based on an incorrect reading of three important essays that Holmes wrote on the subject of moral freedom. Those are: the 1870 Phi Beta Kappa address entitled "Mechanism in Thought and Morals," the 1875 essay "Crime and Automatism," and the 1880 essay entitled "Jonathan Edwards." It is true that each essay makes a case that if the mind is bound with the body, the causality of nature and man's internal impulses could control the will so that moral freedom is a mere illusion. But on closer analysis, Holmes can be seen to begin with this point, rather than to end with it. Holmes goes on in each essay to speak of what he called "character"; "character" creates that freedom necessary for moral decisions. For men with "character," the moment of moral decision is "attended by a sense of effort, and followed by a feeling of fatigue."[5] In short, for Holmes, the "character" of moral persons can be proved experientially, even if the moral causality of the majority of men is predetermined and untraceable. Moreover, because of its reality, "character" can be attained by the practice of self-discipline so that physical energies are exchanged for psychic energies.[6] This is actually good Calvinist doctrine, to the extent that it asserts that the Elect alone are free to choose to the degree that they are obedient to spirit. Thus, in the 1880 essay "Jonathan Edwards" Holmes nowhere attacks the arch-spokesman of the Puritan doctrine of the predetermined will, but is surprisingly conciliatory to Edwards —a fact which is largely ignored in existing commentaries, and in one of the key passages at the close of the essay, Holmes introduces the medical concept of "interstitial action" as a metaphor to convey his belief of Puritan doctrines of moral freedom. That is, just as decaying tissue of the body is replaced by new tissue and the organism lives on though with different cells, so too man's moral nature is ever the same although changed in details to suit the new environment. "Interstitial action" is an important metaphor because by it Holmes says that religion has been updated to reflect the potentialities of the American individual living after the Civil War, and this modernization has been implied from the first in Puritanism. So it is that most men are in fact determined, predetermined, and unable to make moral distinctions; and at the same time there exist select individuals—the Elect— with "character" able to exercise freedom despite the non-moral pressures of the modern world.[7] This is Holmes' view of religion but it is also a social view of the new American of the day. By the same view, Holmes can show that the mores and beliefs of the Brahmins were evidence of the moral freedom of this class of leaders, and there was a clear line of succession from the colonial theology to the modern social hierarchy. In this scheme the unfortunate Elsie is merely a token of general humanity who lived outside the Brahmin code. She is an object of pity but she also induces terror in a Brahmin reader.

Consequently, it would seem, the assertion of Holmes' anti-orthodoxy tends to read passages of the novel *Elsie Venner* out of their true context. In the novel, this case has rested upon a misreading of the words of Dr. Kittridge, the Reverend Honeywood, and the medical professor at Harvard who narrates the frame story of Bernard Langdon's attempt to diagnose Elsie's calamity. In particular, commentators make a great deal of a letter from the professor to

Bernard to have us think that Holmes intended to let humanity slip through the noose of its Calvinistic responsibility, but it should be analyzed more closely. The professor writes:

> I do not know in what shape the practical question may present itself to you; but I will tell you my rule in life, and I think you will find it a good one. *Treat bad men exactly as if they were insane.* They are *in-sane*, out of health, morally. Reason, which is food to sound minds, is not tolerated, still less assimilated, unless administered with the greatest caution; perhaps, not at all. Avoid collision with them, so far as you honorably can; keep your temper, if you can,—for one angry man is as good as another; restrain them from violence, promptly, completely, and with the least possible injury, just as in the case of maniacs,—and when you have got rid of them, or got them tied hand and foot so that they can do no mischief, sit down and contemplate them charitably, remembering that nine tenths of their perversity comes from outside influences, drunken ancestors, abuse in childhood, bad company, from which you have happily been preserved, and for some of which you, as a member of society, may be fractionally responsible. I think also that there are *special influences* which *work in the blood like ferments.* . . . (v, 228)

The professor's words mention charity towards the less fortunate, which is what Holmes suggested in the 1883 preface, cited earlier. But what is here unusual, is that the unfortunate are really outside the pale of humanity; they are to be subjugated by those who "have happily been preserved" from detrimental influences which they themselves may have unwittingly created. In this case, that superior individual is Bernard, who is the son of a Brahmin. My point is, that one does not find in the novel any attack on the Puritan doctrine of moral determinism, for the reason that the doctrine has been modified so as not to apply to Bernard and to the professor.

This interpretation is supported by an analysis of a conversation between Dr. Kittridge and the orthodox minister, the Reverend Honeywood. It is true, as has been contended, that the minister attacks the new doctrine of natural causality as the determinate of man's moral nature because it is "degrading and dangerous" to excuse men from their moral responsibility. But it has not been noted that it is the minister who insists that people, in fact, are free to choose only what they are able to choose. The minister, in short, believes in limited freedom of the will despite Elsie's apparent condition. The problem of interpretation is further complicated when Dr. Kittridge, in the same conversation, makes a subtle distinction. He does not agree with the minister's theology based on limited freedom of the will, because he himself accepts the doctrine of natural causality, but the medical man is "charitable" because not all persons share the same ability to be free. Dr. Kittridge insists that such persons who might be governed by necessity do not

> degrade or endanger us, for this reason, that while it makes us charitable to the rest of mankind, our own sense of freedom, whatever it is, is never affected by argument. Conscience won't be reasoned with. We feel that *we* [the more enlightened persons] can practically do this or that, and if we choose the wrong, we know we are responsible; but observation teaches us that this or that other race or individual has not the same practical freedom of choice (v, 317).

Nevertheless, the words of the minister and the doctor are not two separated positions, of religion against science, as sometimes has been argued by those who see Holmes as an iconoclast.[8] Actually, both speakers share the same view of Elsie's moral fatality but assume that *they* personally have moral freedom despite the nonmoral pressures present in the modern world. This agreement is the key to Holmes' larger intention for the novel. The dialogue and plot of the novel confirm the professor's belief that the Brahmin class has grown "by the repetition of the same influences, generation after generation," so that heredity achieves maximum moral freedom. The professor admits that a "large uncombed youth" may arise from a family having little more free will than a Hottentot might have, and he may even startle "the hereditary class-leaders by striding past them all"; this is "nature's republicanism," the professor continues, but it should not make one "illogical" to proclaim the end of those cultivated features that have gifted the Brahmins alone with the possibility of free will (v, 5).

Consequently, Elsie does not carry the burden of Holmes' intentions. The real focus is on the "character" of Bernard Langdon. Holmes' first title for the novel was "The Professor's Story" in order to draw attention to the ambiguity of moral responsibility faced by Bernard. The professor makes clear at the start that Bernard is putting aside his medical studies for a time in order to support his family that is having temporary financial difficulties, but he believes that Bernard will return to school as long as he does not in the meantime meet a girl who will want him to marry before he has a career. Thus Bernard must fulfill his "duty" by helping his family as well as by securing his own status, and Bernard must show "character" to refuse the love of Elsie, blinded as she is by the deformity of her will. Bernard's refusal of Elsie is a sign of his superior sensibilities that ought to bring him far through life.

Holmes' second novel, *The Guardian Angel*, comes to a similar conclusion. But it begins with a "medicated" interest in the possibility of the inheritance of psychological characteristics. At the opening, fifteen-year old Myrtle Hazard is being treated by Dr. Fordyce and the kindly middle-aged Brahmin Byles Gridley for what appears to be a form of schizophrenia. On closer examination, Myrtle seems to be acting out a personality that is uncommon to her as the snake-like characteristics were said to be uncommon to Elsie.

In a long flashback, we learn that Myrtle, as an orphan of parents who died in a pestilence in India, was living with her Aunt Silence Withers and her cousin Cynthia Badlam. Both women had forced Myrtle to repress her own natural impulses and conform to a cheerless Calvinist view of the universe. Aunt Silence is misled, but cousin Cynthia is malicious because she detests Myrtle's good looks, joy and courage. The completeness of their control over Myrtle is evidenced when Myrtle sings hymns celebrating man's damnation as a sign of the glory of God. But as a result of this repression, Myrtle one day enters her "misty dream" to have a "Vision" of persons which she believes are her ancestors.

This "Vision" is a crucial point in the novel, because up until now it may seem that Holmes is writing a "medicated" novel in a way that *Elsie Venner* was not. Holmes initially seems to be hinting of psychosis, especially so because those ancestors will struggle among themselves to gain mastery over the psyche of Myrtle. But Holmes did not note these demonic aspects of his plot, and in fact he led the reader away from such a conclusion. Indeed, Holmes told his reader to view such ancestors, generally, as the potential guardians of the present personality of Myrtle in her moment of repression by her relatives. Holmes writes: "It is by no means certain that our individual personality is the single inhabitant of these our corporeal frames" and "some, at least who have long been dead, may enjoy a kind of secondary and imperfect, yet self-conscious life, in these bodily tenements which we are in the habit of considering exclusively our own." These ancestors—which are personal, not racial—"often account for looks and actions which may, at times, surprise both ourselves and others" (VI, 22-3). Consequently, for Holmes, the case of Myrtle has become simply a matter of which voice she will heed, as if she might freely choose what her personality will be; further, in making this choice there is a moral implication, (the Freudian aspect of sublimation resulting from repression is partially negated) which nullifies the medicated interpretation of the novel.

The rest of the flashback concerns which ancestors Myrtle did in fact choose to emulate up through the time that she becomes a subject for Dr. Fordyce and Byles Gridley. There

is her great grandmother Judith Pride, the vain beauty of
the county; her grandmother Virginia Wild, an impulsive
girl because of her part-Indian heritage; an unnamed witch
who was brought to trial and burned; and, most important,
Ann Holyoake, a sixteenth-century religious martyr under
Queen Mary. At first, Myrtle was guided by the beauty Judith
Pride, and she became a coquette; for a time Myrtle felt
that her destiny was "to please, and so to command" (vi,
277). But when Myrtle almost stabs a girl with a knife for
challenging her gaining the role as Pocahontas in the school
play, it is evident that Virginia Wild, for the moment, was
in control. Only at the last moment was Judith Pride able
to restrain Myrtle to prevent her own ruin (vi, 281). Yet
Judith Pride is no longer in control after Myrtle falls in
love with the young Brahmin sculptor Clement Lindsay. It
is then that Holmes presents another crucial twist to his
story that nullifies any serious "medicated" intentions for
the novel.

When Myrtle falls in love, she is said to be free of her
bondage to the vain Judith Pride and at the end of her
long transformation into her mature personality. In full possession of "character" facing "duty," Myrtle's "visions of worldly
enjoyment had faded before the thought of sharing and ennobling the like of one who was worthy of her best affections,—of living for another and of finding her own noblest
self in that divine office of woman." But the literary problem
of this climax is, that while Myrtle's action seems satisfactory
to the reader, Myrtle in fact has chosen a new guardian
from the past. She has permitted, Holmes says, "a transfusion
of the martyr's life [Ann Holyoake's] and spiritual being . . .
to manifest itself" in her, and it is this "transfusion" of a
high moral nature which permits Myrtle to follow her husband
into the battlefields of the Civil War to aid the sick and
wounded (vi, 409-10). If Dr. Fordyce, Byles Gridley, and
Clement Lindsay see Myrtle as "cured" of the obsessions
of her mind, yet it is evident that Myrtle has been adopted

by the martyr, and the question is: is Myrtle finally in possession of her real personality? This question of the conclusion to the novel is excused by Holmes perhaps because he approves of certain moral values characterized by Ann Holyoake. But it is a moral rather than a "medicated" conclusion.

It is also a conclusion that does not agree with those commentators who would want to find a special case for psychological determinism by which Holmes argued against Calvinist doctrines of original sin, moral responsibility, and the Elect. Some sort of determinism is present, but in terms of the entire romance—which presents Brahmin ideals—just the opposite intention must be concluded. Myrtle is of the Brahmin class, and while her will is controlled at first by Aunt Silence and cousin Cynthia and later by undisciplined ancestors, that time is said to be her sole period of illness. But when Myrtle chooses Ann Holyoake, she chooses a "guardian angel" by which she is able to exercise moral freedom as Holmes defined it in the essays. As Ann Holyoake, Myrtle has the "character" able to suffer physical fatigue and pain to fulfill her sense of "duty." In fact, the hereditary relation existing between the martyr and Myrtle is a good illustration of the words of the professor in *Elsie Venner* which suggested that moral freedom could pass to succeeding generations of the Brahmin class.

Holmes' last romance, *The Mortal Antipathy*, follows the same pattern of the first two novels. It begins as a "medicated" novel; at the crucial moment, it negates this concern as well as determinism; and it concludes with evidence that Holmes believed moral freedom exists for Brahmins alone.

Ostensibly the plot considers how environmental events can set up conditioned reflexes which control man's perceptions and decisions of the mind and will. Maurice Kirkwood, a young Brahmin, had been dropped as a baby by his pretty cousin Laura. Since that time Maurice has had an uncontrollable antipathy towards attractive young women, and is a victim to fainting spells in their presence. As the novel opens, no one understands the cause of such fainting, but the Brahmin Dr. Butts is attempting to find the cause in order to determine a cure.

The novel promises a "medicated" view of behavior, but from the very start there is much playfulness in the plot as if Holmes was conscious of quite a different goal. Miss Lurida Vincent—nicknamed "The Terror" because of her unfeminine interest in intellectual reasoning—speculates that Maurice might have been bitten by a lower organism, such as that of a tarantula, much in the manner that Elsie Venner's mother was bitten by a rattlesnake. Even Dr. Butts explores the possibility that Maurice may have been frightened by a cat or dog, or even be a victim of the superstition of the evil eye (VII, 63-65, 176). It would seem, in these examples, that Holmes is spoofing the "medicated" detective work for which some persons would commend him.

However, Dr. Butts is serious about the moral implications of Maurice's illness. When he discovers the cause of this sickness, he attempts to define the nature of conditioned reflexes in the commonplace image of how a path is made. He writes:

> How does a footpath across a field establish itself? Its curves are arbitrary, and what we call accidental, but one after another follows it as if he were guided by a chart on which it was laid down. So it is with this dangerous transit between the centre of inhibition and the great organ of life [between the reflex center of the brain and the heart]. If once the path is opened by the track of some profound impression, that same impression, if repeated, or a similar one, is likely to find the old footmarks and follow them. Habit only makes the path easier itself in a timidity which shames the manhood of its subject (VII, 236).

Dr. Butts's words are value-laden. "Conditioned reflexes" as "dangerous" and as a "habit" can negate man's moral freedom in action. These considerations lead him to believe that Maurice is living within "a second nature" that robs him of his powers of free choice. In this situation, Maurice is an example of what the Calvinists had called "inable" man: a man who knows intellectually the truth but is unable to have it transform his will. Perhaps with this situation in mind, Dr. Butts speaks of trying "to change" the "nervous current" in Maurice as one might effect a "reversal of the poles in a magnet" (VII, 237). However it is only by a fortuitous accident—that reveals Holmes' real intentions for the "medicated" plot— that the required antidote is given Maurice. Miss Euthymia Tower—nicknamed "The Wonder" because of her graceful gymnastic skills,—rescues Maurice sick with fever from Dr. Butts's burning home, and Maurice falls in love with his savior. A beautiful woman has plausibly reversed the reflex that another had set for Maurice. But when Dr. Butts writes of the cure, he drops the earlier metaphor of the path for a metaphor with new implications. Dr. Butts writes:

> The river which has found a new channel widens and deepens it; it lets the old watercourse fill up, and never returns to its forsaken bed. The tyrannous habit was broken (VII, 279).

Maurice is pronounced free of the shameful tyranny. And yet, because Dr. Butts, perhaps unwittingly, speaks of how one "watercourse" is dried up as another one begins, it is also true that there is no possibility of returning to any sort of "true" self that existed prior to experiences that might warp men's wills. No man is ever free of such reflexes, but this is not Holmes' concern. Similar to the ambiguous "cure" of Myrtle Hazard, Maurice's "new existence" is simply one which Holmes would commend (VII, 277). That is, when Maurice falls in love with Euthymia, he shows that he properly values her daring risk of safety, and he passes the test of "character" facing persons of the Brahmin class. Seemingly Maurice is free of the natural reflexes that deprive the ordinary individual of his freedom of choice, and Maurice's history of the conditioned reflex is actually a third parable of the threat of secular experience to Brahmins of even the best hereditary qualities. Once again Holmes fails to satisfy the requirements of a "medicated novel," and those commentators who would persist in saying that Holmes is building a case for deterministic influences shaping man's moral decisions have only failed to read the novel as literature.

Holmes' concerns about free will, "character," and "duty" dominate the three novels, and for good reason. In his 1870 Phi Beta Kappa address, Holmes clearly was warning the children of the Brahmins not to falter in seeking for themselves the moral sanction of "conscience" that he thought necessary for their continued leadership in the postwar society. Without such a moral mandate, the Brahmins were undistinguishable from any other persons who were scrambling to amass wealth in the new industrial America. Holmes had a clear understanding of how much the Brahmin oligarchy depended for its status on inherited wealth, but when he saw the "new wealth" as threatening the status of this oligarchy, he concluded that the New England "conscience" was fatiguing, and it was fatiguing because of the weight of abstract doctrines that defied experiential verification. The metaphor of "interstitial action" served to describe a concept by which truth endured unnoticed because of a naturalistic flux of events and details that seemingly prohibited persons from seeing that truth; in the conversation between the Reverend Honeywood and Dr. Kittridge, the point is clear that science is perhaps able to render experientially convincing the truths of theology which, if understood properly, will permit that awareness of moral freedom necessary for a person to become a Brahmin in a secular world. It is, indeed, the peculiar dilemma of Americans to live in a secular environment and amidst the artifacts of culture while insisting on a transcending moral order that might structure society and its leadership. Thus, if Holmes found fault with Calvinist orthodoxy in the romances, it was not because Calvinism was illogical in itself, but it was illogical for a Brahmin to accept its doctrines if they were not valid in experience: Calvinism simply had not evidenced in the everyday world that condition of moral freedom necessary for choosing in the face of naturalistic forces, and so the Brahmin would unwittingly default in his "conscience" and the development of "character." Calvinism was content with the abstruse doctrine of Election before creation, but for Holmes Calvinism was primarily a presentation of how a truth had lost its visibility in the modern world. Holmes' romances were to be new testaments in the new era, and if this is Holmes' intention, then the artistry of the romances is apparent and crucial. The use of the frame-story and the shifting points-of-view, melodrama, and allegorical details—such as Elsie's rattlesnake features, Myrtle's ancestors, and Maurice's conditioned reflex—served the genteel reader as rhetorical confirmation of his moral righteousness in an amoral world, and it assented to his holding an inherited position in society in which all men were compelled to seek power.

---

[1] *The Works of Oliver Wendell Holmes* (Boston and New York, 1892. Standard Library Edition, 15 vols.), v, p. ix, discusses how the term "medicated" arose in response to his novels. Hereafter this edition is cited by volume and page within parentheses in the text.

[2] Clarence P. Obendorf, *The Psychiatric Novels of Oliver Wendell Holmes* (New York, 1943), pp. v, 6-13.

[3] R. W. B. Lewis, *The American Adam: Innocence, Tragedy, and Transition in the Nineteenth Century* (Chicago, 1959), p. 35.

[4] Many of these arguments are first suggested in Harry Hayden Clark, "Dr. Holmes: A Re-Interpretation," *NEQ*, 12 (March, 1939), 19-35, esp. 28, and in the same author's *Major American Poets* (New York, 1936), p. 886. But see Samuel I. Hayakawa, *Oliver Wendell Holmes: Physician, Poet, Essayist* (unpub. Ph.D. dissertation, Wisconsin, 1934), esp. pp. 54-121; a concise summary of Hayakawa's views is to be found in S. I. Hayakawa and Howard Mumford Jones, ed., *Oliver Wendell Holmes: Representative Selections* (New York, 1939), Part III of "Introduction." See also Arnold Louis Goldsmith, *Free Will, Determinism, and Social Responsibility in the Writings of Oliver Wendell Holmes, Sr., Frank Norris, and Henry James* (unpub. Ph.D. dissertation, Univ. of Wisconsin, 1953), esp. pp. 1-23, and Charles Ernest Boewe, *Heredity in the Writings of Hawthorne, Holmes,*

and Howells (unpub. Ph.D. dissertation, Univ. of Wisconsin, 1955), esp. pp. 167-170, which assert that Holmes did not believe that free will was incompatible with determinism, but which conclude that Holmes sought merely to show that Calvinism made for moral non-responsibility rather than allowed the Brahmin to have responsibility in a non-responsible world, as I argue.

[5] *Works*, VIII ("Mechanism in Thought and Morals"), 294; see also VIII, 301-2: "The moral universe includes nothing but choice: all else is machinery." *Works*, VIII ("Crime and Automatism"), 333, describes Prosper Despine's analysis of the will: "His test of free-will, or self-determination, is the sense of effort by which a desire is overcome, and the self-approval or self-approach which follows a right or wrong action. But desire is only overcome by a sense of duty. . . . There is no struggle between desire and the sense of duty before the commission of a crime, and no remorse after it, in persons destitute of the moral instinct." *Works*, VIII ("Jonathan Edwards"), 380, speaks of limited free will for those who are aware of an act of duty requiring effort.

[6] *Works*, VIII, 382. On p. 381, Holmes wrote: "In spite of the strongest necessitarian doctrine, we do certainly have a feeling, amounting to a working belief, that we are free to choose before we have made our choice. We have a sense of difficulty overcome by effort in many acts of choice."

[7] *Works*, VIII, 401. On v, 253, Holmes said that "a soul . . . was born to a full sense of individual liberty, an unchallenged right of self-determination on every new alleged truth offered to its intelligence"; unfortunately, "Asiatic" or "Oriental" aspects had usurped man's freedom of choice in previous eras.

[8] *Works*, v, 327, 323; Holmes chastizes both ministers and doctors for inferring that the culturally deprived (e.g. Digger Indians) have liberty of the will.

VIII

MARK TWAIN ON SCIENTIFIC INVESTIGATION: CONTEMPORARY ALLUSIONS IN "SOME LEARNED FABLES FOR GOOD OLD BOYS AND GIRLS"

HOWARD G. BAETZHOLD

MOST STUDENTS OF AMERICAN LITERATURE know that Samuel L. Clemens was fascinated most of his life by science and technology. But relatively little has been written about his satires on scientific investigation. This study, then, hopes to add to the information on that genre in the Mark Twain canon.

At various times, especially early in his career, Clemens was inspired to poke fun at the pretensions of learned investigators, as well as at the admiring populace who received their pronouncements with applause and wonder. Some of these burlesques and satires owe a good deal to other humorists like John Phoenix and Dan DeQuille for their form and for some elements of their content.[1] But almost always their initial inspiration came from contemporary events or news items. "A Washoe Joke," for instance, was born in 1862 when the author observed that Nevada and California seemed to be "running wild about extraordinary petrifactions and other natural marvels." To burlesque this "petrifaction mania," and incidentally to needle the new justice of the

peace and coroner of Humboldt, with whom he had had
a "temporary falling out," Mark Twain concocted an elaborate story of the discovery of a petrified man. Justice Sewall
entered the picture in the ridiculous role of an official who
traveled some 150 miles over dreadfully rugged terrain in
order to conduct an inquest on a man who supposedly had
been dead and turned to stone more than 300 years before.[2]
It is a tribute to Mark Twain's skill, but even more to the
gullibility of the public, that many readers took this hoax
seriously, even though a careful reading would have shown
that the "petrified man" was thumbing his nose at the on-
lookers.

Two years later, a news item in the San Francisco *Alta
California* prompted Mark Twain to write "A Full and Reliable Account of the Extraordinary Meteoric Shower Last
Saturday Night." On November 11, 1872, the *Alta* published
a telegram from Professor Benjamin Silliman, Jr., Yale professor and editor of the *American Journal of Science*, who
was then in California after conducting mineralogical experiments in the gold and silver mines of Nevada. Interested
in the mineralogy of meteorites, Silliman noted that "meteoric
showers" would be especially spectacular on the nights of
November 12 and 13 (as indeed they were), and urged observers in Nevada and California to report their observations
for his journal, "where they will be published for the good
of science."[3] Mark Twain's sketch, submitted as a letter to
"Professor Silliman, Jr." appeared in the San Francisco *Cali-
fornian* on November 19. With an observer whose sobriety
was open to considerable question, it burlesqued scientific
jargon, and played with a wild chain of associations based
on the words "science" and "star". Needless to say, this report
was not among the several that Silliman later published.

The most notable of Twain's early burlesques of scientific
investigation, however, was "Some Learned Fables for Good
Old Boys and Girls," which he wrote sometime between
his return from England late in January, 1874, and the follow-

ing September 2, when he sent the story to William Dean Howells, editor of the *Atlantic Monthly*. Although this tale has received little notice, save for Gladys Bellamy's examination of Twain's debt to John Phoenix, it is worth further attention both for its subject matter and for what it reveals about Mark Twain's literary methods. Because "Some Learned Fables" is not widely known, I shall summarize the principal events so that the relationship of the various episodes may be clear.

Typical of the fable in its assembling of a non-human cast of characters, and employing a Swiftian *reductio ad absurdum* by making the "scientists" insects, the story begins,

> Once the creatures of the forest held a great convention and appointed a commission consisting of the most illustrious scientists among them to go forth, clear beyond the forest and out into the unknown and unexplored world, to verify the truth of the matters already taught in their schools and colleges and also to make discoveries.

After mentioning certain earlier expeditions the author describes the noble procession of:

> Tortoises heavily laden with savans, scientific instruments, Glow-Worms and Fire-Flies for signal-service, provisions, Ants and Tumble-Bugs to fetch and carry and delve, Spiders to carry the surveying chain and do other engineering duty . . . ; and after the Tortoises came another long train of iron-clads—stately and spacious Mud Turtles for marine transportation service; and from every Tortoise and every Turtle flaunted a flaming gladiolus or other splendid banner; at the head of the column a great band of Bumble-Bees, Mosquitoes, Katy-Dids and Crickets discoursed martial music; and the entire train was under the escort and protection of twelve picked regiments of the Army Worm.[4]

After three weeks, the expedition emerges from the forest and looks upon "the great Unknown World." The next day they reach "a great avenue," containing "two endless parallel

bars of some hard black substance," a phenomenon that
Professor Mud Turtle finally announces to be a palpable
manifestation of the parallels of latitude. When "a vast terrific
eye . . . with a long tail attached" shoots by with demoniacal
shriek, the old geographer calms the terrified laborers by
explaining that they had been permitted to witness nothing
other than the Vernal Equinox. A similar apparition from
the other direction brings about a quandary, but after much
discussion, including a sneering dismissal of Professor Woodlouse's surmise that this was the *Autumnal* Equinox, Lord
Longlegs proposes that the phenomenon must have been
the transit of Venus. When Chief Inspector Lizard objects
that Venus was supposed to transit the sun, not the earth,
Lord Longlegs grandly proclaims that though former scientists had honestly believed that the transit of Venus consisted
in a flight across the sun's face, the present party had been
"granted the inestimable boon of proving that the transit
occurs across the earth's face, *for we have* SEEN *it*."

The party then finds that the "transit" had dropped a
"hollow cylinder" containing "a pungent liquid of a brownish
hue, like rainwater that has stood for some time." Tasting
the contents, the whole company soon become "exalted with
great and pleasurable emotions," and go staggering about
"singing ribald songs, embracing, fighting, dancing, discharg-
ing irruptions of profanity, and defying all authority." The
next day it is determined that this liquid was "without question
that fierce and most destructive fluid, lightning."

The explorers set out again—after another day of rest
and recuperation—and soon encounter a series of strange
trees, extending in a single rank and "bound together, near
their tops, by fourteen great ropes, one above the other,"
which stretched from tree to tree, "as far as . . . vision could
reach." Chief Engineer Spider reports that these are merely
a web hung there by some immense member of his own
species. With this information the expedition's naturalist is
able to identify a fragment of a vertebra from one of the

131

huge insects and from this relic builds a beautiful model of the colossal spider, for "he knew exactly what the creature looked like, and what its habits and its preferences were, by this simple evidence alone." The grateful conference names the monster after the naturalist, "since he, after God, had created it."

A week later the expedition discovers a number of "vast caverns of stone" rising "singly and in bunches out of the plain by the side of the river." It is soon decided that these formations belong to the Old Red Sandstone Period, for they are composed of layered strata, each two layers of Old Red Sandstone separated by "a thin layer of decomposed limestone," and even more strangely, every sandstone stratum "pierced and divided at mathematically regular intervals" by *vertical* strata of limestone.

In and around the "caverns" were countless inscriptions in a mysterious tongue, of which Professor Woodlouse, the philologist, has facsimiles made and subjects them to linguistic tests, in the hope of deciphering this strange language. In comparing numbers of them, he notices that some occurred especially often: "For Sale Cheap," "Billiards," "Try Brandreth's Pills," "S.T.—1860—X," "Keno," "Ale on Draught," etc.

The most interesting and rewarding of the "caverns" bore the inscription "Waterside Museum. *Open at All Hours. Admission 50 cents.* WONDERFUL COLLECTION OF WAX-WORKS, ANCIENT FOSSILS, ETC." This was a truly great discovery, for inside there were rows of figures, soon identified as "the long extinct species of reptile called MAN, described in our ancient records. . . . perfectly preserved in a fossil state." (Professor Woodlouse had earlier explained that "Museum" meant "Burial Place.") Labels on the figures read "Captain Kidd," "Queen Victoria," "Abe Lincoln," "George Washington." The scientists proceed to dissect these specimens and make thorough notes on the nature of this remarkable animal.

All about the Burial Place, too, is evidence that Man had lived "in the earliest ages of creation with the mastodon, the icthyosaurus, the cave bear, the prodigious elk." The investigators also examine some charred bones and ashes behind the Museum, observing that Man had obviously been in the habit of splitting the bones of his own species in order to extract the marrow. There is evidence, too, of Man's artistic endeavors—items marked with the untranslatable words "Flint Hatchets, Knives, Arrow-Heads, and Bone-Ornaments of Primeval Man," some of which "seemed to be rude weapons chipped out of flint." And behind the Burial Place is a mass of ashes, "showing that Man always had a feast at a funeral—else why the ashes in such a place? and showing also, that he believed in God and the immortality of the soul—else why these solemn ceremonies?" All of these findings were summarized in the official notes of the expedition, with the conclusion: "Let us not laugh; there may be creatures in existence to whom we and our vanities and profundities may seem as ludicrous."

The next discovery, near the river, was a large stone with a carved inscription commemorating a great flood in the year 1847. Citing the fact that the waters had inundated the entire township, destroyed many homes, and killed more than 900 cattle, the inscription concluded: "The Mayor ordered this memorial to be erected to perpetuate the event. God spare us the repetition of it." This "Mayoritish Stone" was a particularly valuable find because it enabled Professor Woodlouse to provide the first successful translation of the mysterious language. Though "slightly marred by one or two untranslatable words," the message was generally clear: "One thousand eight hundred and forty-seven years ago, the (fires?) descended and consumed the whole city. Only some nine hundred souls were saved, all others destroyed. The (king?) commanded this stone to be set up to . . . (untranslatable) . . . prevent repetition of it."

The professor's success at deciphering this document not only brought him great personal fame, but marked "the origin of the school of scientists called Manologists, whose specialty is the deciphering of the ancient records of the extinct bird termed man." [They had now decided that Man was a bird rather than a reptile.]

The party then finds a "vast round flattish mass, ten frog-spans in diameter and five or six in height." Professor Snail discourses learnedly upon this "isoperimetrical protuberance" and decides that it is "one of those rare and wonderful creations left by the Mound Builders." When excavation unearths no relics, it is declared to be a "Monument" rather than a mausoleum. Whereupon the Tumble-Bug laughs and declares that "to the shrewd keen eye of science" it may be a Monument set up by the Mound-Builders, but "to an ignorant poor devil who has never seen a college it is not a Monument, strictly speaking." Yet it is still "a most rich and noble property; and with your worships' good permission I will proceed to manufacture it into spheres of exceeding grace and—."

Driving the Tumble-Bug away with blows and derision, the scientists proceed with their measurements and finally load the Monument onto the backs of four of the largest Tortoises, to send it home to the king's museum.

The weather now growing harsh, the expedition prepares to travel home, but on their last day they discover one additional treasure in "an out-of-the-way corner of the Museum" —"nothing less than a double Man-Bird lashed together breast to breast by a natural ligament and labeled with the untranslatable words, 'Siamese Twins.'" This discovery they declare to be a new and distinct species, particularly adapted to regions of danger, since one of the pair could watch while the other slept. Near the Double Man-Bird they also find "an ancient record of his, marked upon numberless sheets of a thin white substance and bound together," in which Professor Woodlouse immediately notices the sentence

"In truth it is believed by many that the lower animals reason and talk together."

Astonished that there could be lower animals than men, the expedition then journeys homeward, to receive a "mighty ovation" by the whole country. And the story ends:

> There were vulgar, ignorant carpers, of course, as there always are and always will be; and naturally one of these was the obscene Tumble-Bug. He said that all he had learned by his travels was that science only needed a spoonful of supposition to build a mountain of demonstrated fact out of; and that for the future he meant to be content with the knowledge that nature had made free to all creatures and not go prying into the august secrets of the Deity.

When Mark Twain submitted "Some Learned Fables" to the *Atlantic Monthly* in September, 1874, Howells turned it down. Explaining his refusal, he said that in regard to religious matters, the *Atlantic* was "just in that Good Lord, Good Devil condition when a little fable like yours wouldn't leave it a single Presbyterian, Baptist, Unitarian, Episcopalian, Methodist, or Millerite *paying* subscriber" and that "all the deadheads would . . . abuse it in the denominational newspapers."[5] Publication of the tale thus had to wait until the appearance of Mark Twain's own collection, *Sketches New and Old* (1875).

Though Howells' reservations may seem over-cautious, he knew his magazine's clientele. Some comments in the story would surely have offended the "unco 'guid" in 1874. When the insect "scientists" find the whiskey jug, for instance, and the Tumble-Bug and Lord Longlegs lie soddenly drunk, the official notes of the expedition comment, "Thus inscrutable be the ways of God, whose will be done!" When the explorers attempt communication with the "timid, gentle race" of "heathenish" spiders in the multi-storied "caverns," they detail "A great detachment of missionaries to teach them the true religion." Within a week, the "precious work" of these missionaries creates a situation in which fewer than three families are at peace with one another or have a firm belief in *any* system of religion. Shortly thereafter, Professor Woodlouse, analyzing some of the inscriptions on or near the "caverns" concludes that messages like "For Sale Cheap," "Billiards," "Ale on Draught," "Boats for Hire Cheap" must be religious maxims. Finally, an analysis of the "Burial Place" and the mass of ashes, bones, and other relics behind it results in the opinion that the now-extinct creature, Man, once cooked and ate the young of his own kind, that "he bore rude weapons and knew something about art," and that he "imagined he had a soul, and pleased himself with the fancy that it was immortal." In addition, some readers who would not have been offended at the religious quips might have considered a serious breach of good taste the expedition's activities with the cow-manure "Monument."

Though these touches were probably enough to warrant Howells' rejection, they are interesting now as early expressions of opinions and themes that Mark Twain would develop at some length in later years. Furthermore, his use of the Tumble-Bug as a "realistic" commentator upon the "savants' " high-flown speculations represents a stage in the humorist's development from the "Mr. Brown–Mr. Twain" relationship (in both the Sandwich Island letters and *Mark Twain's Travels with Mr. Brown*) to Huckleberry Finn's common-sense deflations of Tom Sawyer's romantic flights of fancy. But much more fascinating are the hidden allusions to people and events actually featured in the news shortly before and during the time that Mark Twain was writing his story.

The sketch's first paragraph is so allusive as to be worth quoting almost in its entirety. After the announcement of the expedition's purpose, the narrative continues:

It was the most imposing enterprise of the kind the nation had ever embarked in. True, the government had once sent

Dr. Bull Frog, with a picked crew, to hunt for a north-westerly passage through the swamp to the right-hand corner of the wood, and had since sent out many expeditions to hunt for Dr. Bull Frog; but they never could find him, and so government finally gave him up and ennobled his mother to show its gratitude for the services her son had rendered to science. And once government sent Sir Grass Hopper to hunt for the sources of the rill that emptied into the swamp; and afterwards sent out many expeditions to hunt for Sir Grass, and at last they were successful—they found his body, but if he had discovered the sources meantime, he did not let on. So government acted handsomely by the deceased, and many envied his funeral.

The matter of scientific exploration was very much in the news during the early 1870s. In the United States, a number of government-sponsored expeditions, such as those led by geologist Francis V. Hayden, Lt. George M. Wheeler, and Major J. W. Powell, were exploring the western territories. Professor Othniel C. Marsh of Yale was conducting yearly palaeontological research parties to investigate the fossil deposits of Wyoming and Colorado. Reports of all these ventures appeared periodically in the press. The "Editor's Scientific Record" in *Harper's* magazine for January, 1874 (an issue which Mark Twain may well have seen since its "Editor's Drawer" contained a brief but complimentary account of his Sandwich Island lectures in London) mentioned no fewer than twenty-four different expeditions recently completed or currently under way in many parts of the world. One of them in particular may have caught the humorist's fancy—a military contingent "sent out toward the Yellowstone . . . for the protection of the working parties along the line of the Northern Pacific Railway." Noting that "a corps of scientific men" accompanied the military party, the report concludes:

> Owing to the impediments caused by the heavy rains, the Indiana difficulties, and the necessarily rapid movements of the party, less was accomplished in the line of natural history than was

hoped; but the specimens collected were important, and will serve as the basis of a report which will materially extend our knowledge of the resources of that country.[6]

Two other projected expeditions, however, probably supplied the major impetus. Either of them could have evoked Mark Twain's comment that "earlier expeditions were mere trifles compared with the present one." The first was the voyage of H. M. S. *Challenger,* which sailed from England in December, 1872, with biologists, chemists and geologists, on a four-year journey that would ultimately cover most of the Atlantic and Pacific Oceans and collect enough data to fill some fifty volumes in the *"Challenger" Report* (London, 1880-95). Preparations for this project, which the *Encyclopaedia Britannica* has called "a voyage without parallel in the history of scientific research,"[7] were frequently in the news during the months preceding the *Challenger*'s sailing.

During 1873 and 1874, also, there was an even greater stir over international plans to observe the rare astronomical phenomenon, the transit of Venus across the face of the sun, which was to occur on December 8, 1874. The transit had last occurred in 1761 and 1769, and would again be observable in December, 1882. But after that it would not recur until the year 2004. What scientists hoped to secure from their observations was data that would permit a really accurate measurement of the earth's distance from the sun. Preparations for the 1874 observations were especially elaborate since the sun was to be in a much better position for the sightings than it would be in 1882. And by that December no fewer than fifty expeditions, from all of the major countries, had set up observation posts in remote corners of the globe.[8] Given the many notices concerning these preparations in newspapers and magazines, and since Mark Twain memorialized the event by having Lord Longlegs identify the passage of the second railroad train as the transit, this project may well have provided the author's primary inspiration.

The two earlier expeditions specifically mentioned in Twain's first paragraph allude to explorations that had occurred in years past. But here, too, current news items almost certainly provided a reminder of those ventures. The search for the "northwesterly passage through the swamp" and the many expeditions sent to hunt for Dr. Bull Frog obviously suggest the ill-fated Arctic voyage of Sir John Franklin and its aftermath. Sir John's ship, which sailed in May, 1845, had last been sighted, by a whaler, in July of that year. Between 1848 and 1859 some twenty-seven expeditions, both public and private, had embarked from England and America, five of them supported primarily or entirely by Lady Jane Franklin, the explorer's wife. Search parties in 1851 and 1855 found some of the group's articles, and finally, in the spring of 1859, the crew of the *Fox* (one of the ships financed by Lady Jane) recovered the skeletons of most of the crew and a journal which showed that the expedition had reached a point from which, had they been able to proceed, they would have accomplished the Northwest Passage. That journal also recorded the death of Sir John on June 11, 1847, but if his skeleton was among those recovered, it was never specifically identified. Following this news, the British government erected a monument to Franklin in London's Waterloo Place, and though it did not "ennoble his mother," as Mark Twain indicates, it did award the explorer's widow a gold medal in 1860, confirming Sir John as discoverer of the long-sought Northwest Passage.[9]

In the intervening years, Arctic exploration was seldom mentioned without some reference to Sir John Franklin, but Twain's inspiration probably came from news items that appeared during the autumn of 1873, while he was still in England. That October the British papers carried notices of the death of Sir Robert McClure, another Arctic explorer, who in 1850-51 had verified the existence of a Northwest Passage. The London *Times* account, which credited McClure with *discovering* the passage, stimulated a letter from Lady

Jane Franklin, reminding the editor of her husband's "incontrovertibly proven claim" to the discovery some two and one-half years earlier than Sir Robert's. Mark Twain would certainly have noticed that item, and he may also have seen an article in the London *Contemporary Review* that same month, which urged the British government to underwrite a new Arctic expedition. Besides deploring the efforts of "the croakers" to "raise the cry of danger" by citing the fate of Sir John Franklin, the writer further argued that the search for the Northwest Passage had been "thoroughly practical and useful" not for trade but "for the sake of all the numerous, valuable observations in every branch of science."[10]

The second Twain expedition—Sir Grass Hopper's "hunt for the sources of the rill that emptied into the swamp," the search for Sir Grass, and the finding of his body—alludes to the African explorations of Dr. David Livingstone's continued explorations in 1872-73, and his death in May, 1873 (which was not confirmed until January, 1874).[11]

The prototype for the "rill" was the Nile River, whose ultimate sources were still a mystery when Twain wrote his story. Though Europeans had early traced the Blue Nile, and J. H. Speke in 1862 had established the Kagera River as the source of the White Nile's main stream, the sources of the Kagera and of other feeder streams remained to be found: Livingstone, during his explorations in the early 1870s, mistakenly thought that those sources lay far to the south. After the death of Livingstone, it remained for Henry M. Stanley to explore the Kagera and other tributaries. In 1875 he camped at the foot of the Ruwenzori range, unaware that he had actually reached the "Mountains of the Moon," cited by Ptolemy centuries earlier, as the probable home of the glaciers whose melting fed the Nile headwaters. (Actually, at the time of his visit clouds masked the snowy peaks). Hence not until 1888 would he actually see the mountains whose glaciers feed the streams that ultimately feed the Nile.

Stanley's search for Livingstone, had, of course, evoked world-wide interest. Sponsored by the New York *Herald*, the reporter-turned-explorer landed in Zanzibar on January 6, 1871, and began the hazardous trip inland on March 21. Eight difficult months later, at Ujiji in western Tanganyika, he finally greeted the "missing" Scotsman with the now-famous "Dr. Livingstone, I presume?" He then accompanied Livingstone on further explorations of the Nile basin for some two months before beginning the long trek back to Zanzibar. Arriving there on May 7, 1872, he sailed for England, carrying messages and mementos to Livingstone's family and others.

Twain obviously had followed the accounts of Stanley's trip, for in July, 1872, he submitted "The Secret of Dr. Livingstone's Continued Voluntary Exile" to the Hartford *Courant*. Signed "Ujijije Unyembembe, Interpreter to the Expedition," the burlesque report of the news that Stanley had brought to Livingstone listed numerous unpleasant events that had occurred during Livingstone's absence and ended with the explorer's decision to remain in Africa where life was immeasurably simpler. Early that September, too, the humorist entertained the Whitefriars Club in London with a short speech "On Stanley and Livingstone," in which he asserted that it was really he who had found Livingstone first, but that he was graciously allowing Stanley to receive the credit.[12]

Stanley was in London at the time, and a great celebrity. Interestingly enough, however, when he first arrived, his story had been received with a good deal of skepticism, a reception that had infuriated him. But once Livingstone's family had verified the journals that he brought back, he was applauded and honored. Queen Victoria thanked him personally, presenting him with a jewel-encrusted gold snuffbox, and Mark Twain noted the occasion in one of his journals. In late October, the Royal Geographical Society held a dinner in Stanley's honor. Writing to his wife the following day, Twain, who was present at the dinner, remarked particularly on how impressed he had been by the ceremony and by the presence of so many of "the renowned men of Great Britain's army, navy, and schools of science."[13]

Besides the indirect reference to Stanley's "search expeditions" in "Some Learned Fables," another allusion occurs in Twain's description of the "bald and venerable geographer, Professor Mud Turtle," who, though "born poor, and of a drudging low family, had, by his own native force raised himself to the headship of the geographers of his generation." Though not "bald and venerable" at the time of the story— he was 34 in 1874—Stanley was the illegitimate child of the son of a well-to-do Welsh farmer and a maidservant. Baptized John Rowlands, he was brought up first by his maternal grandfather, and then boarded around at his mother's brothers' homes until the age of seven, when he was taken to the St. Asaph Union workhouse. In 1859, after working for a haberdasher and then a butcher, he signed on as cabin boy on a ship bound for New Orleans, where he was befriended and later adopted by Henry Morton Stanley, a wealthy merchant whose name he took. But his patron died shortly thereafter without making any provision for his adopted son. Following a brief military service in the Civil War, a return to England (where he was turned away from his mother's door), and a tour at sea, Stanley returned to America and began his career as newspaper reporter. Here he found his niche. His vivid stories soon brought him to the attention of James Gordon Bennett, of the New York *Herald*, who gave him a roving commission and, in 1871, sent him on the search for Livingstone that made him world-famous, both as a writer and as an explorer.

As for the object of that famous search, Dr. Livingstone had again been in the news in January of 1874. In that month the reports of his death in May, 1873, were finally confirmed. And Mark Twain's comment (re: Sir Grass Hopper) that "government acted handsomely by deceased, and many envied his funeral" doubtless reflects the ceremonies attending the explorer's interment in Westminster Abbey, April 18, 1874.

Most of the other contemporary allusions in the story are related in one way or another to the discovery of the "caverns" of Old Red Sandstone. The analysis of these ruins and their contents reflects Mark Twain's longtime interest in palaeontology that had begun at least as early as his piloting days on the Mississippi. More recently, in the summer of 1871 shortly after he finished "A Brace of Brief Lectures," Mark Twain and his old California friend Joseph T. Goodman had spent many interesting hours during Goodman's visit to Elmira collecting fossils from a nearby quarry and following "random speculations to far-lying conclusions, developing vague humors of phrase and fancy, and having altogether a joyful good time."[14]

The materials and attitudes Twain had expressed in "A Brace of Brief Lectures on Science" find special reflection in "Some Learned Fables" when the "scientists" discover "The Waterside Museum." Besides some of the items regarding the bones, artifacts, and burial customs already cited, Twain drew directly on his earlier article for his investigators' assertion that some of the charred bones, split lengthwise, showed Man's liking for the marrow of those bones, "since no tooth-mark of any beast was upon them." And then he had the practical Tumble-Bug suggest that probably "no beast could mark a bone with his teeth anyway."

The details of the "Flint Hatchets, Knives, Arrowheads and Bone Ornaments of Primeval Man" also lead directly to another contemporary reference, made explicit in Mark Twain's description of the "untranslatable legend on a thin, flimsy material" that the explorers find "in a secret place." Addressed to "Jones," the message read: "If you don't want to be discharged from the Musseum, make the next primeval weppons more careful—you couldn't even fool one of these sleapy old syentiffic grannys from the Coledge with the last ones. And mind you the animles you carved on some of the Bone Ornaments is a blame sight too good for any prim-eveal man that was ever foaled—Varnum, Manager."

If the contemporary reader had not already related the "Waterside Museum" with its wax-works and collections of ancient fossils to P. T. Barnum's famous establishment in New York City, that note would have directed him. Even the point about the charred bones behind the Burial Place is pertinent here, for fires at the Barnum museums must have been all but legendary at the time.

Barnum's Museum had been an institution in New York ever since the entrepreneur purchased Scudder's American Museum in 1842 and moved it from Chambers Street to Broadway and Anne. After that building burned in July, 1865, Barnum's New American Museum opened the following September at 539 and 541 Broadway, continuing to attract large crowds until it, too, burned down on March 3, 1868. Moving again, Barnum reopened on the south side of Fourteenth Street in a building previously known as the Hippotheatron and Lent's Circus. And again the building burned, this time on December 24, 1872. Finally, on April 28, 1874, after a good deal of advance publicity (and probably before Mark Twain had finished his story), New York witnessed the gala opening of Barnum's Great Roman Hippodrome which occupied an entire square block between Fourth and Madison Avenues.[15]

Mark Twain was well acquainted with Barnum's Museum, for he had visited it in 1867, and had provided the readers of the *Alta California* with a burlesque description of its exhibits in much the same vein as in "Some Learned Fables." He also knew P. T. Barnum personally and had probably been pleased to learn that the showman was among those present at his opening lecture in England in October, 1873. The pair corresponded periodically, particularly during the remainder of the 1870's, and Barnum's letters in the Mark Twain Papers show that he did not take offense after "Some Learned Fables" appeared in *Sketches New and Old* (1875).[16]

The final discovery of the waxwork "Siamese Twins" indirectly suggests another connection with Barnum. Born in Bangkok of Chinese parents in 1811, the famous original Siamese Twins, Chang and Eng, had toured England and the continent for a number of years, and then had been a feature attraction of Barnum's Museum from 1850 to 1855. In the latter year they had left Barnum, married two sisters, and gone to live in Mt. Airy, North Carolina. Some fourteen years later, finding themselves in need of funds, they came out of retirement and in 1869-70 once again appeared under Barnum's management in New York and London.

Whether or not he ever actually saw Chang and Eng, Mark Twain was obviously fascinated with the idea of Siamese Twins. In 1869, probably inspired by news of their coming out of retirement, he wrote "The Personal Habits of the Siamese Twins," which appeared in *Packard's Monthly* for August of that year. Twenty-two years later he would feature a similar Italian pair in a story that he ultimately split into *Puddn'head Wilson* and *Those Extraordinary Twins*.[17] But in the case of "Some Learned Fables," the inspiration was again immediately contemporary, namely the publicity that followed the death of Chang and Eng on January 17, 1874. An account in the New York *Times* of February 2, for instance, presented not only a lengthy biographical sketch, but a detailed medical report based on the autopsy, complete with diagrams showing exactly how the pair was connected, what organs they shared, and the like. There is little doubt, then, that Twain saw this or a similar article and thus was moved to include the fabulous twins among the "scientific wonders" in "Some Learned Fables."

The other major item with immediately contemporary overtones involves the "Mayoritish Stone," the marker commemorating the great flood. Since I have been unable to locate references to a particular flood of 1847, I suggest that Mark Twain merely reversed the figures for the year in which he wrote the story. There were two serious floods

145

in New England in the winter and spring of 1874. In January, the worst one in twenty years struck Connecticut's Naugatuck and Housatonic River Valleys, washing out many bridges and putting most of four towns under water. Then in mid-May, probably before Twain had finished "Some Learned Fables," rising waters burst the dam at Mill River Reservoir, some ninety-five miles northwest of Boston, causing widespread damage and the loss of at least 140 lives.[18]

As for the marker that allowed Professor Woodlouse to translate the strange language of the creature called Man, one might immediately think of the Rosetta Stone. But the parallel here is to a much more recent event, the discovery and translation of the so-called Moabite Stone.[19] This was a black basalt stele, some 3 and 1/2 feet high and 1 and 3/4 feet wide bearing thirty-four lines of Hebrew-Phoenician characters. Then the earliest text in the characters that formed the basis for the Greek and Roman alphabets, the Moabite Stone, which dates from about 900 B.C., was first discovered at ancient Dibon of Moab in 1868. In 1870, Charles Clermont-Ganneau, a French orientalist, made an impression of the text. While negotiations for purchase were going on, the Arabs broke the stone into pieces, but Clermont-Ganneau was finally able to retrieve them. His translation, made with the aid of his earlier impression and an eight-line segment copied before the stone was broken, showed the passage to be part of an account by the Moabite King Mesha of his battle with the Israelites.

Clermont-Ganneau's discovery and his procurement of the stone for France had received a great deal of publicity, especially in 1871 when biblical scholar Christian D. Ginsburg's book, *The Moabite Stone*, provided a facsimile and translation of the inscription, along with a historical and critical commentary stressing the tremendous importance of this document.[20] If Mark Twain did not know Ginsburg's book at first hand, he may well have seen the review in *Littell's Living Age* for February, 1871. And nearer the time of his story, he perhaps read the reports in 1873 that Clermont-Ganneau had assembled the fragments of the stele for display in the Louvre. In February, 1874, too, U.S. newspapers carried the story of the latter's revelation (in December, 1873) that the alleged Moabite inscriptions in the Shapira collection in Berlin were forgeries.[21]

Because of the condition of the Moabite Stone the message was partially obliterated, a situation that Mark Twain turned to humorous purposes in Professor Woodlouse's "translation." Moreover, if the humorist saw the review of Ginsburg's book in *Littell's Living Age*, one of its quotations may have suggested the idea of having his own "inscription bear a plea for divine assistance. Toward the end of the article, the reviewer quotes Ginsburg's comment that in setting up the stele, Mesha "seems to have Samuel's words in view when he put up his pillar between Mispeh and Shem, in memorial of the Divine help afforded him in defeating the Philistines."[22] And when Mark Twain remarks that Professor Woodlouse's accomplishment in making the translation caused "every seat of learning in his native land" to confer upon him "a degree of the most illustrious grade," he perhaps had in mind the not inconsiderable honors bestowed on Clermont-Ganneau.[23]

In the juxtaposition of a flood and "ancient inscriptions" it is also tempting to find reflections of still another archaeological discovery in 1872 and 1873. On December 3, 1872, at a meeting of the British Society of Biblical Archaeology, George Smith, an Assyriologist at the British Museum, had quietly announced a sensational find. From his translation of cuneiform tablets containing the ancient Epic of Gilgamesh, he read a portion which paralleled in almost every respect the Biblical story of Noah. This "Chaldean Account of the Deluge" caused such widespread reaction that the London *Daily Telegraph* offered a prize of 1000 guineas to the man who could find the missing portion of one of the tablets on which the Flood story appeared. Smith himself undertook the quest, and in May, 1873, was able to report his almost miraculous good luck in finding the very fragment he sought in the ruins of ancient Nineveh. That September the *Daily Telegraph* announced the safe arrival of Smith's large collection of tablets and artifacts at the British Museum, and in October published the translation of the missing portion of the "Deluge" story.[24] Because of the relative furor that Smith's translation caused, especially among Biblical literalists, it is difficult to believe that Mark Twain, who was in London during the autumn of 1873, would not have known about the matter. Thus, George Smith, too, becomes a possible prototype for Professor Woodlouse.

In addition to these major allusions, several miscellaneous references to other activities in science and pseudo-science are worthy of mention. When "the naturalist of the expedition" builds his skeleton of the "colossal spider" from "a fragment of its vertebrae," the reference is clearly to the palaeontological practices resulting from the work of Georges Cuvier (1769-1832), who has been credited with having essentially created and established the department of palaeontology dealing with Mammalia. Mark Twain's comment that the naturalist, from the fragment, "knew exactly what the creature looked like and what its habits and its preferences were, by this simple evidence alone" seems almost an exaggerated paraphrase of Cuvier's own statement that from a single bone he was able "with diligence and intelligent resort to analogy and effective comparison, to determine all of these things [the other parts of the animal] as surely as if we possessed the entire animal."[25]

When examining the various strata of Old Red Sandstone (bricks) the explorers find evidence of "fossil ants and tumblebugs (the latter accompanied by their peculiar goods)" in the very bottom layer, they declare this discovery to be proof that "these vulgar laborers belonged to the first and lowest order of created beings." But they also find "something repulsive in the reflection that the perfect and exquisite creatures of the modern uppermost order owed their origin to such ignominious beings through the mysterious law of Development of Species."

The "law of Development of Species" alludes of course to the evolutionary theories propounded by Darwin and his followers. Mark Twain's library contained a copy of Darwin's *Descent of Man*, which the humorist probably obtained and read in 1871, the year of its first publication. I have not, however, encountered the exact phrase "law of Development of Species" among the works of the early evolutionists. Most of them speak of *theories* rather than *laws*. Still, several of the titles in Alfred Russel Wallace's collected essays, *Contributions to the Theory of Natural Selection* (New York, 1871), might have been significant. Among these appear such chapters as "On the Law which Has Regulated the Introduction of New Species," and "On Creation by Law," which speaks of "the Law of Population of Species." Another piece speaks of "the Law of Natural Selection."

Another possible reference to Darwin occurs when Professor Woodlouse glances into the "ancient record" and translates the sentence: "In truth it is believed by many that the lower animals reason and talk together." It is at this point that the astonished scientists conclude that, strange as it might seem, there must be animals even lower than Man. On page 45 of *The Descent of Man* (Vol. I), Darwin says that "Few persons any longer dispute that animals possess some powers of reasoning. Animals may constantly be seen to pause, deliberate, and resolve." Three pages later, where the author further discusses the acquisition of learning by animals, Mark Twain wrote in the margin of his own copy of the book: "War-horses learn the bugle-notes—Firehorses rush at the fire alarm. That is educated excitement and interest, and inspiration, and memory."[26]

In the realm of pseudo-science, the "inscriptions" near the "caverns" reflect something of the popular culture of Mark Twain's time in the advertisements for various patent medicines. "Try Brandreth's Pills" refers to a well-known cathartic. "Keno" was probably a trade name for a product containing *kino*, an astringent used in controlling dysentery, diarrhea, and other diseases of the bowels. "S.T.—1860—X" is the allegedly ubiquitous trademark for "Plantation Bitters," one of the popular "booze nostrums," so-called because they contained a negligible proportion of medicinal agents in a large proportion of alcohol.[27]

The attribution of the cow manure "Monument" to the Mound Builders reflects the current popular interest in the earthwork mounds left by the Indians in the Mississippi Valley, the Gulf States, and the Great Lakes region. Some of these were burial mounds, altar mounds, or totemic representations (e.g. the famous Serpent Mound in Ohio). Others were fortresses or foundations for buildings. The oldest go back some two thousand years, while some are post-Columbian. At the time of Mark Twain's story they were still generally thought to be the work of a race that had preceded the Indians.

As with so many of these items, still another contemporary occurrence probably inspired the humorist to include this detail. In August of 1873 the Sixth Annual Report of the Peabody Museum at Yale University featured the researches of Henry Gilman in the Mounds near the Detroit River, Lake St. Clair, and southern Lake Huron. Given widespread publicity—2 and 1/3 columns in the New York *Times* of August 29, for example—the report described in great detail the characteristics of the mounds, skeletons, and other artifacts in much the same sort of language that Twain burlesques in "Some Learned Fables."

Though Twain may not have seen the *Times* story, since he was in England at the time, the details he uses suggest that he may well have had some knowledge of the Peabody report. The attention given to the skeletons in the mounds and to the various tools and simple implements buried with them seems mirrored in Lord Longlegs' conclusion that the absence of "skeletons . . . and the rude implements which the creatures used in life" proved that "the mysterious and forgotten race of Mound Builders did not always erect these edifices as mausoleums." And the care with which the Peabody report catalogued the contents of the various mounds seems to find a counterpart when the draughtsmen of the expedition make "views of the monument from different standpoints," while Professor Woodlouse, in a "frenzy of scientific zeal" travels all over it, hoping to find an inscription. At which point the author says "But if there had ever been one it had decayed or been removed by some vandal as a relic."

Finally, the plea of Mark Twain's "savants" that the king "immediately appoint a commission and command it to rest not nor spare expense until the search for this hitherto unsuspected race of the creatures of God [i.e. the creatures that were even lower than Man] be crowned with success," as well as the reactions of the "vulgar and ignorant carpers" like the Tumble-Bug, is very much like the similar plea for a new Arctic expedition in the British *Contemporary Review* (mentioned earlier). The writer of that article began by commending the government's support of the "Challenger" voyage and noted England's keen interest in the African explorations of Baker and Livingstone. Stressing the importance of such ventures for general knowledge rather than for trade, he deplored the efforts of the "croakers" to "raise the cry of danger" by citing the fate of Sir John Franklin, and concluded by appealing to England in the name of all the gallant explorers of history, again sneering at the "timid and ignorant alarmists."

Whether or not Mark Twain had actually seen that particular article, it was out of the amalgam of all these matters that "Some Learned Fables" emerged to ridicule some of the more extravagant claims of the scientists and those enthusiasts who urged more and more explorations. Still, it was not science and scientists *per se* that aroused the humorist's skepticism. Certainly in many instances he was simply having fun with the details he introduced. Neither should we take at face value the Tumble-Bug's pious injunction that investigators not "go prying into the august secrets of the Deity." As in so many of his works, Twain was primarily attacking human presumption and gullibility, as reflected both in the scientists' building their "mountain of demonstrated fact" from "a spoonful of supposition" and in the public's ready acceptance of these "marvels." There is a strong suggestion that genuine scientific achievements were often insufficiently rewarded. But what is most interesting of all, in my opinion, is the realization of how many of Mark Twain's jibes owed their inspiration to immediately contemporary events and discoveries.

[1] See Edgar M. Branch, *The Literary Apprenticeship of Mark Twain* (Urbana, Ill., 1950), pp. 63, 105-109; Gladys Bellamy, "Mark Twain's Indebtedness to John Phoenix," *American Literature*, 13 (March 1941), 29-43; and Hamlin Hill, "Mark Twain's 'Brace of Brief Lectures on Science,'" *New England Quarterly*, 34 (1961), 228-239. John Phoenix was the pseudonym of George Horatio Derby, and Dan DeQuille was William Wright, Twain's friend and fellow-newspaperman in Virginia City, Nevada.

[2] See Twain's own commentary on this story, "The Petrified Man," *Galaxy*, 9 (May 1870), 47. "A Washoe Joke" first appeared in the Virginia City *Territorial Enterprise*, Oct. 5, 1862

[3] *Alta California*, Nov. 11, 1864, p. 1. Silliman, Jr. (1816-85) was the son of Benjamin Silliman (1779-1864), famous Yale professor of chemistry and natural history and founder in 1818 of the *American Journal of Science and the Arts*. For Silliman, Jr's. presence in Nevada and California, see San Francisco *Call*, Apr. 10, Sept. 1, 1864; For other mentions of "meteoric showers" see *Alta California*, Nov. 12, 15. I am most grateful to Edgar M. Branch, who provided me with this latter information and references.

[4] All quotations from "Some Learned Fables" here and hereafter are from *Mark Twain's Sketches, New and Old* (Hartford, 1875), pp. 126-148.

[5] SLC to WDH, Sept. 8, 1874, *Mark Twain-Howells Letters*, ed. H. N. Smith and W. M. Gibson (Cambridge, Mass., 1960), Vol. 1, 24.

[6] Among other items that could have contributed their bit to Twain's general "scientific" construct, one might note that in March, 1874, the American Association for the Advancement of Science (a continuation of the American Assn. of Geologists and Naturalists, founded 1840) was chartered in Massachusetts.

[7] *Britannica*, Eleventh Edition, 5 (1910), 808. To conserve space I shall not hereafter document information gathered from such standard references as *Encyclopaedia*

Howard Baetzhold

Britannica, *Dictionary of American Biography*, and *Dictionary of National Biography*.

[8] Reginald Waterfield, *One Hundred Years of Astronomy* (New York, 1938), p. 47; "The Approaching Transit of Venus," *Littell's Living Age*, 116 (March 15, 1873), 702-704 (reprinted from the *Spectator*).

[9] Mark Twain's fascination with the search for Franklin was later to find indirect voice in chapter 10 of *A Connecticut Yankee* (1889), when the Yankee refers to the Holy Grail as "just the Northwest Passage of that day," and remarks that "every year expeditions went out Holy Grailing, and next year relief expeditions went out to hunt for *them*."

[10] London *Times* item reprinted in New York *Times*, Nov. 5, 1873; *Contemporary Review* article reprinted in *Littell's Living Age*, 119 (November 8, 1873), 341-346.

[11] It seems that by calling his Arctic explorer *Dr.* Bull Frog and his "rill" explorer *Sir* Grass Hopper, Twain was trying to make the identification of Sir John Franklin and Dr. Livingstone a little less obvious, perhaps to avoid any legal repercussions from the families of those explorers.

[12] Mark Twain had met Stanley in 1867, when the latter had reported one of the humorist's lectures in St. Louis (A. B. Paine, *Mark Twain's Biography*, I, 460n; see also III, 1214). Hartford *Courant* article, July 20, 1872, p. 2, col. 2; "On Stanley and Livingstone," *Mark Twain's Speeches* (New York, 1910), pp. 154-156. In 1873 Twain added to his library Josiah Taylor's *Livingstone Lost and Found; or, Africa and Its Explorers* (Hartford, 1873), which contains the above-mentioned speech on pp. 641-642 (*Catalogue of Mark Twain's Books Sold at Auction, 1911*, Anderson Auction Co., New York, p. 65).

[13] SLC to OLC, October 25 [1872], in Mark Twain Papers. See also Paine, *Biography*, I, 464, 466.

[14] *Autobiography of Mark Twain*, ed. Charles Neider (New York, 1959), p. 83; Paine, *Biography*, I, 436. The Old Red Sandstone period was the name originally given to the geological era that followed the Silurian and preceded the Carboniferous (in N. America, the Mississippian). The name derives from red sandstone deposits in Britain and parts of northwest Europe. At the same time the marine strata were named the Devonian. Soon all of the strata of that era came to be called Devonian.

[15] Irving Wallace, *The Fabulous Showman* (New York, 1959), *passim*, supplemented and corrected from New York *Times*, July 14, Sept. 6, 1865; Mar. 15, 1868; Feb. 11, 12, Apr. 25, 28, 1874).

[16] *Mark Twain's Travels with Mr. Brown*, ed. F. Walker and G. E. Dane (New York, 1940), pp. 84, 116-117. Barnum's presence in "a center seat in the front rows" at Twain's London lecture is mentioned in a clipping from the Darlington (England) *Northern Echo*, Oct. 14, 1873, in a scrapbook in the Mark Twain Papers.

[17] Twain wrote "The Personal Habits of the Siamese Twins" on May 13, 1869 (*Love Letters of Mark Twain*, p. 358) and later collected the piece in *Sketches New and Old* (1875). I have been unable to find evidence that Twain ever saw the twins, but his interest was obvious. The immediate inspiration for "Those Extraordinary Twins," as Robert Wiggins has pointed out, was probably a picture of Giovanni and Giacomo Tocci in the *Scientific American*, December, 1891 ("The Original of Mark Twain's 'Those Extraordinary Twins,'" *American Literature*,

23, November, 1951, 355-357). But in the story itself Twain combined traits suggested in the article on the Italian twins with those he had already described in his 1869 article about Chang and Eng.

[18] New York *Times*, Jan. 9, 1874 (story of the Connecticut flood, with a *Hartford* dateline). For Mill River dam stories, see New York *Times*, May 17-27.

[19] This identification is certain, for the manuscript of the story in Berg Collection, New York Public Library, shows that following the word "Mayor," Twain originally wrote, and later deleted, the name "John Moab."

[20] In 1872 Ginsburg himself, at the invitation of the British Archaeological Society, made an expedition to Trans-Jordan to follow up the discovery of the Moabite Stone, but his efforts proved largely unsuccessful.

[21] See New York *Times*, Feb. 9, 1874, p. 2, col. 3.

[22] *Littell's Living Age*, 108 (February 1871), 334.

[23] The additional remark at this point that "it was believed that if he had been a soldier and had turned his splendid talents to the extermination of a remote tribe of reptiles, the king would have ennobled him or made him rich," sneers generally at the seemingly greater respect accorded to military conquest than to intellectual achievement. Frequent in the news at the time Twain was writing his story were accounts of Sir Garnet Wolseley's much-lauded war against the Ashanti tribe in Africa (Oct. 1873-Feb. 1874). Sir Garnet was not, however, ennobled at the time, though later, after other military exploits, he was made Baron, and then Viscount. More generally, Twain could also have had in mind Napoleon's practice of raising his generals to the nobility, or even to the kingship of conquered nations.

[24] See reports from *Daily Telegraph* in New York *Times*, Jan. 2, May 11, 21, Sept. 7, Oct. 6, 1873.

[25] Quoted by William Coleman, *Georges Cuvier, Geologist* (Cambridge, Mass., 1964), p. 121.

[26] Copyright © 1971 by the Mark Twain Company. My thanks to Frederick Anderson and the trustees of the Mark Twain Estate for permission to quote this passage.

[27] See Samuel O. Potter, *Handbook of Materia Medica, Etc.*, 8th ed. (Philadelphia, 1901), p. 899; *Nostrums and Quackery*, ed. Arthur J. Cramp, M. D., 2nd ed., I, 587. For the identification of the "S.T.—1860—X" trademark, I am grateful to Leon Dickinson, who pointed out Howells' use of the symbol in chapter 1 of *The Rise of Silas Lapham* (1885), when Bartley Hubbard queries Lapham about the "NL f. 1835, SL t. 1855" on his Nehemiah Lapham Mineral Paint labels, and says " 'S.T.—1860—X' business." To which Lapham replies, "Yes, but I hadn't heard of Plantation Bitters then, and I hadn't seen any of the fellow's labels."

IX

THE NARRATOR IN HENRY JAMES'S
THE SACRED FOUNT

W. R. MACNAUGHTON

J AMES'S ONLY FIRST-PERSON NOVEL HAS
vexed and perplexed critics and readers since it was published in 1901. The reaction of W. C. Brownell, who read
the manuscript for Scribner's and reported on it, probably
typified that of the majority of the few readers who subsequently puzzled their way through the book: "It is like trying
to make out page after page of illegible writing. The sense
of effort becomes acutely exasperating."[1] William Dean Howells responded to the intellectual challenge of the book and
eventually said that he had come to understand it;[2] he died,
however, without revealing his discovery to the world—an
unkind decease reminiscent of George Corvick's in "The Figure in the Carpet." Rebecca West's epitome is classic and,
though familiar, deserves to be quoted again: "A week-end
guest spends more intellectual force than Kant can have
used on *The Critique of Pure Reason* in an unsuccessful
attempt to discover whether there exists between certain of
his fellow-guests a relationship not more interesting among
these vacuous people than it is among sparrows."[3]

Since her remarks, numerous critical articles have been
written about *The Sacred Fount*, one of the first really acute
ones being by Edmund Wilson, who compared the novel

to "The Turn of the Screw," indicating how the ambiguities in both works derive from the various discrepancies which exist between the interpretations offered by the respective narrators and the facts suggested to the careful reader.[4] Unlike Leon Edel, however, whose 1953 introduction to his edition of *The Sacred Fount* is the next significant discussion about it, Wilson argued that James probably did not realize the problems created for the reader by his treatment of the narrator. Edel argued otherwise as a result of his close analysis of the narrator's characterization of himself, concluding that James had intentionally created an unreliable observer.[5] Edel's essay had the virtue of compelling later critics to take the narrator seriously as a character. The results of criticism based upon this approach, however, have been ambiguous and a few areas of controversy still exist. Critics debate, for example, the reliability of the narrator; is he a Paul Pry or a sensitive man engaged in a humane endeavor?[6] They also debate the extent to which the novel can be construed as a parable about art.[7] As well, there is a question about the essential tone of the story: is it, as James said, a *jeu d'esprit*, and is the tone basically humorous; or is it fundamentally an extremely pessimistic book, depicting, as Walter Isle argues, failure "of perception, of communication, of belief . . . madness, alienation, the inability to feel, and the loneliness of freedom"?[8]

A few critics have helped us to understand the book by demonstrating that it is part of a Jamesian fictional tradition. Jean Blackall, for example, argues that James's essentially comic treatment of a limited observer in *The Sacred Fount* is a culmination of his experiments in the 1890s, e.g., *What Maisie Knew*, and "In the Cage."[9] Walter Isle relates the dramatic qualities of the novel to James's experiments with the scenic method, e.g., *The Awkward Age*; and its complicated analysis to the author's treatment of the "centres of consciousness" in his late fiction.[10] Leon Edel points to the resemblance between this novel and James's tales of obsession, e.g., "The Figure in the Carpet," "The Aspern Papers," "The Turn of the Screw."[11] All of these analogues are useful in helping the reader understand and appreciate the thematic and technical peculiarities of *The Sacred Fount.*

There are also other analogues, however, of which the reader should be aware. My own point of view regarding *The Sacred Fount* is to see in it techniques and attitudes that are manifest in a great deal of James's first-person fiction,[12] not simply the obvious stories about obsession. This narrator, for example, like almost all of James's observers in his fifty first-person stories, is "clever and critical,"[13] yet imaginative and occasionally kind and sympathetic. Moreover, the path which he follows into extreme involvement is similar to that traced by almost all of the first-person narrators: originally he is sceptical about the theorizing of Ford Obert and Mrs. Brissenden; then, he becomes enamoured of the problem and makes it his own. One of his motives in examining the "sacred fount" theory is also similar to other of James's narrators, notably those in "The Private Life"[14] and "The Figure in the Carpet": he responds to the intellectual challenge of the game. Yet, there is also the complicating emotional involvement—here, the narrator's sympathy for May Server (the narrator in "The Private Life" had also voiced his sympathy for Lord and Lady Mellifont). His attitude toward those characters whom he often treats as *ficelles,* e.g., Ford Obert, Mrs. Brissenden, Lady John, is reminiscent of the narrator's attitude toward his *ficelle* in "Europe" (published two years before *The Sacred Fount*): he takes what they give him as long as it fits his perspective; if not, he ignores their remarks.[15] Often through the narrator's conversations with other characters, however, the reader recognizes his limitations, a "corrective" technique that James almost always employs. Another corrective technique common to *The Sacred Fount* and the other first-person fiction is the narrator's occasional recognition of his own errors. Finally, the narrator in this novel is similar to many of

James's other first-person narrators in his ability to impress us with the force, beauty, and truth of many of his observations, even while we recognize that such observations emanate from a limited individual. (The "publishing scoundrel" of "The Aspern Papers" is a good example of this type of narrator.) We note, for example, his awareness of the potential tragedy in May Server's life, or his poetic appreciations of Newmarch. But there is one major difference between James's treatment of his narrator in this novel and in the majority of his non-controversial first-person fiction, a difference which in part explains why it is that this narrator has been the subject of so much commentary, and why the majority of his narrators have been regarded as merely compositional devices.[16] The difference is that in *The Sacred Fount* earlier techniques and attitudes are exaggerated and intensified: what *seems* peripheral elsewhere is patently central here and thus serves to emphasize that this narrator is *not* a camera, but the photographer himself, carefully manipulating the resources of his medium in order to create a highly subjective (and therefore suspect) "truth."

At the beginning of *The Sacred Fount* the reader becomes aware that a quest of discovery—or more mundanely, an attempt at detection[17]—is to be the plot interest, and that he is to be privy to all of the information available to the central searcher. We also realize that the theory of the detective is to be pitted against that of another one, Mrs. Brissenden, whose acuity we have already been asked to respect. Almost immediately, therefore, we are not only encouraged to look very carefully for evidence, but to judge our representative's interpretation of it. Most important, before actually beginning the search, we are given obvious evidence that, although our delegate thinks highly of his own intelligence and analytic prowess, we should be wary of trusting him too completely; we observe, for example, that although the narrator thinks that Mrs. Brissenden's husband ("poor Briss," as he is condescendingly referred to throughout) has aged considerably, Gilbert Long notices no difference in him—in fact, he angrily retorts "No, confound you!" (22) when the narrator tries to prod him into acknowledging a change. That Long later agrees with the narrator is not important, for the effect has already been achieved: we are sceptical about the narrator, a tendency which is accentuated when Mrs. Brissenden says in response to his derogatory remarks about Lady John: "It proves nothing, you know, that you don't like her" (29). The opening sections of all of James's first-person stories achieve one of the purposes achieved by the first few chapters here: the reader's interest is aroused in what the narrator will observe. And the stress put here upon the intellectual quest and the competitive nature of it resembles a few of the other stories, e.g., "The Private Life" and "The Aspern Papers." But, in the rest of the first-person fiction, only in "The Figure in the Carpet" are these other ingredients combined with the strong early hints for us not to be too impressed by the narrator's perspicuity. In *The Sacred Fount* we are therefore pulled in two directions almost from the beginning of the story—toward identifying with the narrator (this is the effect intrinsic to the first-person form) and toward remaining aloof from him. For the rest of the novel, James intensifies this ambivalent pull.

I have mentioned before how in this novel James tends to exaggerate certain aspects of his characteristic treatment of other narrators: the narrator's movement from disinterested observer to embroiled participant, the necessity for him to observe more than one character well, his ostensibly legitimate motives, his proclivity to criticize himself, the use of *ficelles* as correctives, etc. Some of this exaggeration can be attributed to the extreme compression of time in *The Sacred Fount* (the important action occurs in thirty-six hours), a compression which is almost unique in James's fiction.[18] One of the effects achieved and desired is to intensify the dramatic quality of the novel, particularly in its last section.[19]

Another effect (also desired, I believe) is to make the narrator's change from sceptical observer to committed participant seem extremely, unnaturally, even ludicrously rapid to the reader. The limited time also compels the narrator to observe almost frenetically in order to see what he hopes to see. We watch him straining to observe meaningful collocations of individuals at supper, at lunch, and in the music room; peering out of windows; strolling in the woods and trying to appear casual as he meets those whom he has planned to meet; asking Ford Obert near the end of the novel: " 'Did you happen to count them?' 'Count whom?' 'Why, the ladies as they filed up.' " (161) The image of the narrator created through such actions is a ludicrous one. What contributes to the image is the fact that he seldom actually talks to the individuals who interest him most deeply. This is not only because he is reticent but because the pact between him and Ford Obert demands that their search depend "on psychologic signs alone" (52): they are to observe appearances and not to stoop to crass open investigation to validate their theories. The conditions imposed by and upon the narrator, therefore, tend to encourage him to become an absurd Paul Pry. Such conditions, moreover, make his sporadic extreme confidence regarding the validity of his own theories and his contempt for the ignorance of others seem even more ridiculous[20]: "I made up my mind on the spot. . . . I saw it all" (25); "The cleverest man of the party? . . . Hardly that, perhaps—for don't you see the proofs I'm myself giving you?" (31); "I had achieved my flight into luminous ether and, alighting gracefully on my feet, reported myself at my post.(199) Krishna Vaid has commented upon James's tendency to grant his narrators extraordinarily acute intuitive ability in order to overcome some of the limitations of the first-person form.[21] The problem with this narrator is that the conditions of his search combined with his egoistic confidence cause him to intuit continually: he reads meaning into people's eyes (e.g., 42, 73, 122), into the fact that certain people are together, that they seek the company of others, that they desire solitude—he even finds meanings implicit in Mrs. Brissenden's turned back:

> I seem in other words to recall that I received in that brush the very liveliest impression and that is my reason for speaking of myself as having at the juncture in question "studied" Mrs. Brissenden's back. Study of a profound sort would appear needed in truth to account for it. . . . Didn't what I saw strike me as saying straight *at* me, as far as possible, "I *am* young —I am and I *will* be; see, *see* if I'm not; there, there, there!" with "there's" as insistent and rhythmical as the undulations of her fleeting presence, as the bejewelled nod of her averted bow? (151-152).

One possible effect of such intuitive flights is to make the reader laugh at this romantic observer.

And there are still other factors which encourage us to respond this way. Many of James's narrators in the stories whose actions stretch over long periods of time make retrospective discoveries about episodes and characters; thus their momentary ignorance is overcome by future knowledge. In *The Sacred Fount*, however, there is almost no sense of retrospection; the narrator discovers *nothing*, between the time when the action took place and the time when he tells the story, about the real truth regarding the characters whom he observes. Certainly one of the reasons why James has his story told this way is to increase the immediacy and thus the dramatic quality of the novel. Another effect, however, is to leave the reader ingloriously in the dark even while the narrator brags about the efflorescence of his light. We vacillate between finding this disparity irritating and amusing. Perhaps the most important difference between this novel and the rest of James's first-person fiction is the extent to which the author uses other characters to indicate the narrator's weaknesses. Early in the story, for example, when the narrator at Newmarch eagerly encourages both Gilbert Long and Mrs. Brissenden to continue the discussions which took place coming down on the train, neither individual remembers the subjects of these conversations: "He had quite forgotten" (22); "Then, as my listener seemed not quite to remember where we had been, I came to her help" (27). These subtle indications invite the reader to question the narrator's avidity. Later in the novel, numerous other characters openly criticize his theorizing and ultimately his sanity. Lady John says, for example, "It might be . . . if I had, as you appear to, the imagination of atrocity" (136). And: "Well, all the same, give up, for a quiet life, the attempt to be a providence. You can't be a providence and not be a bore. A real providence *knows*; whereas you . . . have to find out—and to find out even by asking 'the likes of' *me*" (138-139). May Server challenges his presumptuous theory about her friendship with "poor Briss" by bridling at his suggestion. "Poor Briss" does not even understand what the narrator is talking about. Climactically, Mrs. Brissenden[22] enunciates ideas that many readers will have been thinking for a number of pages: "You talk too much!" (203); "I mean you're carried away—you're abused by a fine fancy: so that, with your art of putting things, one doesn't know where one is—nor, if you'll allow me to say so, do I quite think *you* always do. . . . You build up houses of cards" (204); "I think you're crazy" (217); "My poor dear, you *are* crazy, and I bid you good night!" (248). Finally, there is one other important technique by which James makes his readers recognize the narrator's weaknesses. In his stories, James often allows his characters to cast doubt upon their own reliability. Here, the narrator does this constantly—continually vacillates between a wild overconfidence and an almost abject awareness of failure. Compare, for example, "I struck myself as knowing again the joy of the intellectual mastery of things unnameable, that joy of determining, almost creating results" (168), with "Things in the real had a way of not balancing; it was all an affair, this fine symmetry, of artificial proportion" (143); or with "*I* stood for the hollow chatter of the vulgar world" (177). As the last example suggests, moreover, the narrator's self-doubts are not limited to the *validity* of his theories, but also to other aspects of them, i.e., those relating to manners, psychology, and morals: "Singular perhaps that only then—yet quite certainly then— the curiosity to which I had so freely surrendered myself began to strike me as wanting in taste" (37); "Had I myself suddenly fallen so much in love with Mrs. Server that the care for her reputation had become with me an obsession?" (49); "I remember indeed that on separating from Mrs. Brissenden I took a lively resolve to get rid of my ridiculous obsession. It was absurd to have consented to such an immersion, intellectually speaking, in the affairs of other people" (71); "It was none of my business; how little was anything, when it came to that, my business!" (87); "I said to myself during dinner that these were scenes in which a transcendent intelligence had after all no application, and that, in short, any preposterous acuteness might easily suffer among them such a loss of dignity as overtakes the newspaperman kicked out" (123-124). What magnifies the tendency of the reader to respond negatively to the narrator—sometimes we laugh, sometimes we are antagonized by him—is that after such statements he will almost immediately swing back to the acme of overconfidence. In some instances, in fact, the awareness of limitation and the ridiculous pride will exist almost simultaneously. Compare "transcendent intelligence" with "preposterous acuteness," for example. Never, in any of James's stories does he make his narrator so self-incriminating; never does he surround his narrator with so many unsympathetic *ficelles*. Often, we must read very closely to discern the irony in James's treatment of his narrators, because he is subtle in dropping his clues. In *The Sacred Fount*, however, the possibility that the narrator is a dupe,[23] an immoral man, a madman is not suggested; it is trumpeted.

Given this kind of treatment of the narrator, the reader may ask why anyone should have taken him to be an admirable individual sympathetically regarded by his creator. Why indeed? One reason is because of the seductiveness of the first-person voice; no matter how much evidence a writer may provide, no matter how many techniques he may employ to undermine his narrator, the character may circumvent the author's purposes,[24] particularly if he possesses good qualities. In *The Sacred Fount* the narrator undoubtedly does have admirable qualities. His propensity to acknowledge his own mistakes, for example, may cause the reader to admire his honesty rather than to find him ridiculous when he again considers himself omniscient. His sympathy for May Server, and his sense of responsibility are also commendable (even if perhaps not totally justifiable): "I hadn't in the least had it in mind to 'compromise' an individual; but an individual would be compromised if I didn't now take care" (38). Such an attitude contrasts with that of Ford Obert, and contrasts to the narrator's benefit, I believe. Obert says, "I assure you I decline all responsibility. I see the responsibility as quite beautifully yours" (166), although throughout he too has been engaged in the inquiry. The narrator's sensitivity is from one point of view ridiculous, culpable, even obscene because it leads him to imagine multifarious relationships which probably do not exist. From another point of view, however, it is admirable because it causes him to sympathize with individuals who may deserve sympathy.[25] Moreover, it is this sensitive perceptiveness which enables him to bring us pleasure when he describes Newmarch, descriptions which succeed almost in poetizing reality: "There was a general shade in all the lower reaches—a fine clear dusk in garden and grove, a thin suffusion of twilight out of which the greater things, the high treetops and pinnacles, the long crests of motionless wood and chimneyed roof, rose into golden air. The last call of birds sounded extraordinarily loud; they were like the timed, serious splashes, in wide, still water of divers not expecting to rise again" (101). Read carefully, of course, this description provides additional evidence of the narrator's "imagination of atrocity" (note the final simile); but the description nevertheless is somberly beautiful. The narrator's imagination and intellect are overwrought, but at times they help create the atmosphere of a melancholy fairyland.[26] Given this effect, it is perhaps not surprising that critics have failed to recognize the comedy in the novel and have seen it as a profoundly serious work; nor is it surprising that readers have reacted so variously to the narrator.

I think that James consciously created the heterogeneous tone of this novel, that he consciously attempted to produce this ambivalent response in his reader.[27] We are asked to laugh at this man often or to despise his foolish pride, but James always wants us to listen to him. He wants us to be partly infected by his enthusiasm for his search because the "vampire" theme, or more generally the whole question of the effects of interpersonal relationships, is one that had always fascinated the author. What James hopes to achieve therefore is for the enthusiasm of the first-person voice to pull the reader toward the theme of the novel, and for the numerous indications that the voice is deluded to pull the reader away in order to judge. Moreover, there are certain pictures in the novel that James wants us to be moved by, most notably the dilemma of May Server.[28] During the scene in the woods, for example, we cannot fail to be influenced by the narrator's descriptions of the lady, particularly since we have just learned that all three of her children are dead:[29] "Beautiful, abysmal, involuntary, her exquisite weakness simply opened up the depths it would have closed. . . . I saw as I had never seen before what consuming passion can make of the marked mortal on whom, with fixed beak and claws, it has settled as on a prey. She reminded me of a sponge wrung dry and with fine pores agape. Voided and scraped of everything, her shell was merely crushable. So it was brought home to me that the victim could be abased, and so it disengaged itself from these things that the abasement could be conscious. That was Mrs. Server's tragedy, that her consciousness survived—survived with a force that made it struggle and dissemble" (106-107). We may believe that at this point the narrator exaggerates, but the light of truth glimmers through the hyperbole. The effect of his following observation is quite similar:

> What . . . I most made out was the beauty and the terror of conditions so highly organized that under their rule her small lonely fight with disintegration could go on without a gasp or a shriek, and with no worse tell-tale contortion of lip or brow than the vibration, on its golden stem, of that constantly renewed flower of amenity which my observation had so often and so mercilessly detached only to find again in its place. (131-132)

In this instance, his desire to make Mrs. Server an Aristotelian tragic heroine is almost comic, yet our sense of the ridiculous aspect of his attempt does not destroy our appreciation of the basic facts that James wants us to recognize: this lady is in a difficult situation and should be treated kindly. We are meant to remember such descriptions later in the novel, I believe, when Ford Obert says that Mrs. Server is again all right, and when Mrs. Brissenden says that she is "horrid" (247). How can she be "all right," how can she be "horrid," we ask, considering her situation, the pathetic-tragic aspects of which the narrator has already made us feel? Another effect of our ability to compare the remarks made by Ford Obert and Mrs. Brissenden with our sense of the reality of May Server's plight should be to recognize the artist's superficiality and the woman's occasional cruelty, a cruelty of which the narrator has previously made us aware: "My interlocutress stared, and I had at this moment, I remember, an almost intolerable sense of her fatuity and cruelty. . . . She seemed to recall to me nobly the fact that *she* hadn't a lover. No, she was only eating poor Briss up inch by inch, but she hadn't a lover" (56-57).

But Mrs. Brissenden is not only cruel, she is also magnificent; and it is because of the narrator's ability to appreciate both of these aspects (particularly in the climactic long scene between the two characters) that she appears to us in all her complexity as a worthy progenitor of the James villainess:[30] "She might have been a large, fair, rich, prosperous person of twenty-five; she was at any rate near enough to it to put me for ever in my place. It was a success, on her part, that, though I couldn't as yet fully measure it, there could be no doubt of whatever, any more than of my somehow paying for it" (187). Our response to this final scene will be even more complicated if we have read the novel closely and recognize the possibility that Mrs. Brissenden is really fighting for her social survival: she and Long have been carrying on a liaison, she fears the narrator suspects this, and she must deceive him.[31] The general effect of the reader's ambivalent reactions towards the narrator, in sum, is similar to that of James's story called "Glasses." There, the narrator's point of view helped the reader sympathize with characters—helped dignify them as well—who from another point of view could easily have been made to appear *only* sordid or trivial. In *The Sacred Fount*, the situation of May Server and Mrs. Brissenden could easily have been depicted as inconsequential or meretricious. Viewed from the perspective of the narrator, however, they are much more than this; and the reader responds emotionally to the "more" even while recognizing intellectually the "less." Although the narrator is essentially unreliable and the tone of the story is most often comic, therefore, more positive responses toward the man are legitimate and the tone of the novel is at times exceedingly complex.

There remains to be discussed the relationship between the themes of this novel and other of James's recurring ones, particularly the aesthetic theme. It would seem that, through his treatment of the narrator and through his inclusion of the scene centering on the painting of The Man with the

Mask, James wanted to make it obvious that his work was crucially concerned with the theme of appearance and reality. It also seems evident that what the author wishes to suggest about this theme is not that the individual is doomed to remain in a solipsistic dungeon because ultimate reality cannot be understood, but that certain "lesser" realities—social, personal, etc.—are far more complex than most people are prepared to recognize. Each person who looks at The Man with the Mask interprets it differently, and, judging from the objective facts[32] which we learn about the picture this is inevitable; the picture seems to invite idiosyncratic responses. In such a context, the viewer is justified in saying, "my interpretation is valid, but so is yours." Throughout the novel there are numerous liaisons that are hinted at, but about which there is no conclusive evidence; in such situations,[33] the patently unwise thing to do is to leap to conclusions, a mental act which the narrator often performs. We *know* that Lord Luttley and Lady Froome are carrying on an affair because they flaunt its existence. Such an attitude and such a situation act as foils for the other possible affairs in the novel, foils which invite the reader to be dubious about anyone who judges quickly about this deceptive society. It is implied that a similar attitude is the proper one to assume in judging change in character and the reasons for it. May Server is described in the course of the novel as "charming" (17), "unhappy" (17), "stupid" (77), "all right" (166), "horrid" (247), and "clever" (248); Long is obtuse (4), perceptive (14, 44), and a "prize fool" (227). Given the existence of these extreme responses, the reader is warned to doubt their validity because such opinions can depend upon factors that change from moment to moment. This implied attitude toward the various realities in the novel relates as well to the central reality in whose exploration the narrator is engaged—his theory of the "sacred fount"—the idea that in interpersonal relationships some people benefit while others are "simply sacrificed." Again the reader is warned of the dangers of oversimplifying, something which the narrator does constantly, and of erecting intricate structures upon the flimsiest of foundations. The reader and the narrator know objectively that Mrs. Brissenden seems younger whereas "poor Briss" seems to have aged considerably. We also suspect that Gilbert Long and May Server are somehow changed. What we should also recognize, therefore, is the foolishness in building up houses of cards and calling them skyscrapers. Perhaps Mr. and Mrs. Brissenden change simply as a natural effect of their marriage, perhaps Mrs. Brissenden seems younger and Guy seems older because she is having an affair and he discovers it, perhaps. . . . We cannot say definitely, but what is suggested is that all of these factors may affect the respective "sacred founts" of these individuals.

What the novel also succeeds in dramatizing is the effect of the *moment* on one's "sacred fount" (or, as I interpret the term, one's appreciation of life).[34] Certainly even the memory of the narrator's own searches has the effect of constantly vitalizing his fount, and the fluctuation of minor victories and defeats replenishes and depletes it, e.g., "I didn't after all—it appeared part of my smash—know the weight of her husband's years, but I knew the weight of my own. They might have been a thousand, and nothing but the sense of them would in a moment, I saw, be left me" (248). In his scene in the forest with May Server, the narrator, in order to gloss over some indiscreet remarks, asks, "But isn't there such a state also as being in love by the day?" (116). By this question, he points unwittingly to what the novel seems to be saying about the nature of the "sacred fount": that its vitality can be nourished or diminished by ephemera which cannot be calculated—cannot be set down in a rigid formula as the narrator tries to do.

In the narrator's final meeting with Ford Obert, the artist describes their mutual quest in the following terms: "I've blown on my torch, in other words, till, flaring and smoking, it guided me, through a magnificent chiaroscuro of colour and shadow, out into the light of day" (173-174). And the narrator responds, "Your image is splendid . . . you're being out of the cave" (174). The metaphor here is surely meant to remind the reader ironically of Plato's parable of the cave in *The Republic*.[35] In *The Republic*, the observer is chained within the cave by his ignorance. The philosopher-king can leave the cave and achieve a vision of the world of forms, but only after he has studied long and arduously and after he has come to understand a series of lesser realities. The problem with the characters (particularly the narrator) in this novel is that they try to pierce through to something which is ultimate on the most specious of evidence and in the minimum of time. The importance of dialogue in this novel is obvious, and there are, in it, examples of teacher-student imagery, e.g., "I felt a little like a teacher encouraging an apt pupil; but I could only go on with the lesson" (29); " 'Tell me,' I pleaded, 'and teach me.' Equally with her voice her face echoed me again. 'Teach you?' " Such evidence, combined with the metaphor of the cave and the importance of the appearance–reality theme, suggests the possibility that in *The Sacred Fount*, James has created a kind of ironic Platonic dialogue,[36] at the end of which Socrates (the narrator) is confounded by his erstwhile pupil because he lacks her "tone" although he possesses "three times her method" (249). "Tone" or attitude as a convincing force, however, is all-important in a world so far removed from the ideal: point of view or perspective is crucial in a society where no one formula can encompass a series of minor, but nonetheless complex, realities, and where logic cannot be used to guarantee truth.

The final problem to discuss is that of the relationship between this novel and James's aesthetics. From what I have argued thus far it is evident that I do not think that the narrator is really James himself or an ideal novelist, as a few critics have contended.[37] What I think James meant to create in his narrator was a person who resembled a creative individual—not just an artist, but a scientist and logician[38] as well—yet one who misuses his gifts by applying them to a real life situation to which they were either not meant to apply or for which there is insufficient evidence to make their application meaningful. In some respects, the narrator resembles a kind of Jamesian type gone mad: he has the imagination of the novelist but he cannot control it—"my imagination rides me" (216)—he has superior analytic powers but misuses them by trying to turn life into art. Seen from this perspective, the narrator becomes almost a parody of the Jamesian novelist[39]—discovering his *donnée* and working it out, fitting his characters into the pattern demanded by the *donnée*, fitting his milieu as well into this pattern. The *donnée* is the idea of the "sacred fount"; in the "novel" which the ersatz novelist tries to create in order to exemplify this *donnée*, May Server becomes the tragic heroine—the Mme. de Vionnet type who is used by others but who fights to prevent her consciousness from being obliterated.[40] Gilbert Long becomes a Chad Newsome figure who has benefited from his Mme. de Vionnet, but about whom the narrator–novelist is perplexed because of Long's deleterious effect on the lady. The would-be novelist has no difficulty in deciding the role of Lady John: she is the fool because of whose presence the brilliance of the other characters is illuminated more brightly; the narrator says, "Lady John had a vision as closed as Obert's was open. It didn't suit *my book* [my italics] for both these observers to have been affected in the same way" (179). Ford Obert is the "touchstone" (23), the intelligent *ficelle*. The narrator is at once novelist and observer-hero in the novel he creates—a Strether type who hovers over these characters and whose "sense of reality" (27) gives their experience meaning. The narrator finally cannot decide about the worth of Mrs. Brissenden: he is impressed by her "generosity" (11); admires the "miracle" of her youth, her "wonderful sense of success and well-being" (25); but also is repelled by her "fatuity and cruelty" (56), "her simplified egotism" (57). Is she to be a kindly listener—a sympathetic *ficelle*—or an ambiguous Kate Croy?

The problem with the situation and these characters is that they continually explode. One critic argues that the narrator in *The Sacred Fount* contends with a reality which refuses to be idealized.[41] I would like to express his insight in terms of my context: the narrator is confronting lives which refuse to be fictionalized. Lady John, "poor Briss"— the fools of the novel (although the narrator can never quite decide how to categorize Guy Brissenden)—refuse to remain pinned on his manuscript page; they somehow wriggle free and occasionally astound the narrator with insights that he believes to be out of character; he thinks, for example, after one of Guy's remarks: "There was a certain surprise for me in so much acuteness" (92). Long refuses to fit his pattern because the reactions of others toward him make the narrator wonder briefly if a pattern ever really existed; if Long is "always amusing" (47) as Obert says, then the narrator's theory that he has immensely improved by drinking from an unidentified woman's "sacred fount" is chimerical. The condition of May Server at the end of the novel, if we are to believe Obert or Mrs. Brissenden, is definitely not tragic. Mrs. Briss, who comes to the narrator in the novel's final scene ready to be his *ficelle*, is driven by him to accept the heroine's part. And Ford Obert, the supposedly sensitive artist-observer, refuses to admit any responsibility for his actions, alternately gives up and resumes the chase, and, in general, shows himself to be anything but perceptive. This fact should not seem unusual to readers familiar with James's treatment of the society-artist narrators in "The Special Type," "The Tone of Time," and "The Beldonald Holbein," all written within a year of *The Sacred Fount*; such individuals are too superficial, too self-centered, too comfortable in society to be trusted to discover truth in a complex inquiry. Moreover, the society in which these people move is not as remarkable as the narrator would like to think, a fact which he admits to himself on a few occasions, e.g., "it was something to talk as hard as possible with other persons and on other subjects, to mingle in groups much more superficial than they supposed themselves" (72). He continually glamorizes this society, however, in order to make it worthy of his *donnée*. The resources are here, it is true; there is the magnificent country house setting replete with the best of literature, music, and art. But the people who move within the setting cannot wear with ease the garb in which he dresses them. They are dressed in borrowed robes and are perhaps more appropriate subjects for satire than for tragedy, a fact which the reader gradually discerns as he comes to see how these people frivolously use one another. It is this negative undercurrent in the novel which has provoked some critics to argue that, in its fashion, *The Sacred Fount* presents an extremely critical picture of English society.[42] I believe, however, that read properly, James's handling of his first-person narrator creates the paradoxical effect that I have discussed earlier: even while we see beyond the narrator and recognize the faults that he does not usually wish to observe, we are still sufficiently affected by his vision to respond to the potential for tragedy, for nobility, that even this society of masks cannot conceal.

In a sense, therefore, James satirizes someone with gifts and interests similar to his own through his treatment of his narrator. What James seems to have done is to ask himself, "What if a person somewhat like myself tried to make a real English country house group fit a novelistic conception?" and then work out the fictional answer to the question. As I have mentioned before, however, the narrator is not only a "novelist"; he also has definite affinities with the philosopher and the scientist. Scientific and philosophical terminology pervade the novel; the narrator explains the purpose of his quest as follows, for example: "I was just conscious, vaguely, of being on the track of a law, a law that would fit, that

173

would strike me as governing the delicate phenomena—delicate though so marked—that my imagination found itself playing with" (19). He constantly looks for "evidence" (32), praises his "analogy" (53), objects to the "extravagant inferences" of others (60), recognizes his "frenzied fallacy" (130), searches throughout for the "law" (149), notes Ford Obert's "erroneous assumption" and "misconception" (183), admits temporarily that he and Mrs. Brissenden lack "collateral support" (193), characterizes his enjoyment as "purely intellectual" (224), and checks the validity of his intuitions by "the scientific method" (231). His "sacred fount" theory of the relations between the sexes, moreover, is Darwinian in its implications as is evinced by the narrator's following description of May Server, a potential loser in the English country house jungle: "I saw as I had never seen before what consuming passion can make of the marked mortal on whom, with fixed beak and claws, it has settled as on a prey. . . . This was Mrs. Server's tragedy, that her consciousness survived—survived with a force that made it struggle and dissemble" (107).

There are also other characteristics of the narrator which suggest more the satirized scientist than the satirized analytic novelist. There is the tendency suggested by his language on the first page of the book, for example, a tendency which is exemplified throughout [my italics]: "It was an occasion, I felt . . . to look out at the station for others, *possible friends and even possible enemies*, who might be going. Such premonitions, it was true, *bred fears when they failed to breed hopes.* . . . "

"I had met him Gilbert Long at Newmarch only—a place of a charm so special as to create rather a bond among its guests; but he had always, in the interval, so failed to know me *that I could only hold him as stupid unless I held him as impertinent*" (3). This sensitive narrator has an "either-or" mentality. Therefore, whichever extreme he happens to choose tends toward the simplistic, the stereotyped

—stereotypes, moreover, which are formed largely for subjective reasons. Gilbert Long, for example, is a "piece of human furniture" (4), primarily, it is suggested only because he once snubbed the narrator.[43] When Long begins to pay attention to him, he goes to the other extreme, exaggerating good qualities which Long always possessed in order to create a new stereotype. As the narrator becomes more and more fascinated with his theory, he willfully ignores or distorts evidence so that his structure will not be decimated. Almost all the while, however, he defends his objectivity, and the purely intellectual pleasure that he derives from his search. What the novel succeeds wonderfully in dramatizing is the emotional appeal of the supposedly intellectual pursuit. What it also depicts is the problem inherent in applying the "scientific" method to this social environment. We notice the insistent use of the words, "natural" (e.g., 41, 44, 46, 47, 50, 52, 59, 226, 230, 240) and "simplify" or "simple" (e.g., 132, 155, 180, 218, 221, 222, 240), and come to realize that to base a theory upon what is "natural" in this society of "screens" (30), to attempt to discover a principle which will "simplify" its heterogeneity is to accomplish one definite result —to make oneself grotesque. Moreover, to identify a defense of one's theory with a defense of one's honor as the narrator finally does (236), and to sacrifice one's sympathy for other human beings to the exigencies of the theory is ultimately immoral: "There was no point at which my assurance could, by the scientific method, judge itself complete enough not to regard feeling as an interference and, in consequence, as a possible check. If I had to go I knew well who went with it, but I wasn't there to save *them.* I was there to save my priceless pearl of an inquiry and to harden, to that end, my heart" (231). What the novel has to say, therefore, is related not only to the novelist, but to the creative man in general—to any man, in fact, who wishes to force the world into his conception of it. *The Sacred Fount* is about "Only an intelligent man gone wrong" (228).[44] The tone of

the book is essentially comic because, although the narrator
is occasionally aware and occasionally dangerous, in general
he is an invulnerably egoistic ineffectual fool; that he retains
these qualities even to the end of his experience is exemplified
by his wonderful last statement: "I *should* certainly never
again, on the spot, quite hang together, even though it wasn't
really that I hadn't three times her method. What I too
fatally lacked was her tone" (240). The ironic novelist-scientist-
philosopher-intelligent man stumbles from his sophisticated
jungle, bloody but unbowed.

[1] Quoted in Oscar Cargill, *The Novels of Henry James* (New York, 1961), p.
282. Cargill's excellent review of criticism in his chapter on *The Sacred Fount*
contains a number of amusing quotations culled from the comments of exasperated
early readers of the novel.

[2] Howells said in 1903, "I have mastered the secret, though for the present I
am not going to divulge it." Quoted in Sidney Finklestein, "The 'Mystery' of Henry
James's *The Sacred Fount*," *The Massachusetts Review*, 3 (summer 1962), 753.

[3] Rebecca West, *Henry James* (New York, 1916), pp. 107-108.

[4] Edmund Wilson, "The Ambiguity of Henry James," *Hound and Horn*, (April-
May 1943), 385-406. The commentary of Wilson Follett and R. P. Blackmur is
also provocative. Follett argues that in *The Sacred Fount* James was probably
parodying himself, though Follett cannot seem to make up his mind whether James
wanted to laugh at his own practices (by pointing out the folly of trying to make
life mirror art) or show them to advantage (by contrasting the symmetry of art
with the chaos of life). See Follett, "The Simplicity of Henry James," *American
Review*, 1 (May-June 1923), 315-325; and "Henry James's Portrait of Henry James,"
N.Y. Times Book Review (Aug. 23, 1936), 2, 16. R. P. Blackmur first argues,
in "*The Sacred Fount*," *Kenyon Review*, 4 (autumn 1942), 328-352, that the narrator
is the hidden conscience of the other characters, and as such acts as the author's
delegate. In a later article, however, his brief comments suggest that he did not
think that James was really sure what he was trying to do in this novel. See
Blackmur, "In the Country of the Blue," *Kenyon Review*, 5 (autumn 1943), 597.

[5] Leon Edel, "An Introductory Essay," *The Sacred Fount* by Henry James (New
York, 1953), pp. v-xxxii.

[6] The majority of recent critics condemn the narrator to a greater or lesser degree,
e.g., Jean Frantz Blackall, *Jamesian Ambiguity and The Sacred Fount* (Ithaca,
N. Y., 1965); Landon C. Burns Jr., "Henry James's Mysterious Fount," *Texas
Studies in Literature and Language*, 2 (winter 1961), 520-528; Oscar Cargill; James
K. Folsom, "Archimago's Well: An Interpretation of *The Sacred Fount*," *Modern
Fiction Studies*, 7 (Summer 1961), 136-144; Arnold P. Hinchliffe, "Henry James's

The Sacred Fount," *Texas Studies in Literature and Language*, 2 (spring 1960), 88-94; S. Gorley Putt, *Henry James: A Reader's Guide* (Ithaca, N. Y., 1966); Norma Phillips, "*The Sacred Fount*: The Narrator and the Vampires," *PMLA*, 76 (Sept. 1961), 1407-1412; Ralph A. Ranald, "*The Sacred Fount*: James's Portrait of the Artist *Manqué*," *Nineteenth-Century Fiction*, 15 (Dec. 1960), 239-248. The following three critics, however, defend the aims and methods of the narrator: Finklestein; Naomi Lebowitz, *The Imagination of Loving: Henry James's Legacy to the Novel* (Detroit, 1965); and James Reaney, "The Condition of Light: Henry James's *The Sacred Fount*," *Univ. of Toronto Quarterly*, 31 (Jan. 1962), 136-151.

[7] The majority of critics see it as a parable about life and art. A few critics, however, believe the thematic focus is elsewhere. Elizabeth Stevenson in *The Crooked Corridor* (New York, 1949), p. 47, for example, suggests that it may be a parable about how people use one another; Osborne Andreas in *Henry James and the Expanding Horizon* (Seattle, 1948), p. 76, stresses the significance of the theme of love; and Robert J. Andreach in "Henry James's *The Sacred Fount*: The Existential Predicament," *Nineteenth-Century Fiction*, 17 (Dec. 1962), 216, says that the adventures of its hero prefigure the contemporary interest in modern man's existential predicament.

[8] Walter Isle, *Experiments in Form: Henry James's Novels, 1896-1901* (Cambridge, Mass., 1968), p. 232. The majority of recent critics ignore the comic aspects of the novel. Jean Blackall is the only critic who sees it as essentially comic in its treatment of the narrator though Walter Wright in his *The Madness of Art: A Study of Henry James* (Lincoln, Neb., 1962), p. 186, refers briefly to the "comic bafflement" of the narrator. Norma Phillips (op. cit., note 6) refers to the "bizarre comedy" in the delineation of the "egocentric excesses of its central figure" (412), but her article does not focus on the comedy. Sidney Finklestein notices the early light comedy but argues that the tone becomes progressively more serious as the story unfolds (768). Maxwell Geismar in *Henry James and the Jacobites* (Boston, 1963), p. 199 also refers to the comedy in the novel, but does not give evidence of it. Naomi Lebowitz is, other than Mrs. Blackall, really the only critic who emphasizes the humor in *The Sacred Fount*, but she argues that the narrator is not a comic butt. He is, instead, James himself good naturedly permitting his characters to develop their possibilities and, in so doing, to have, occasionally, a joke at his expense (Lebowitz, pp. 121-122).

[9] See Chapter 6, "*The Sacred Fount* in James's Fiction," of Mrs. Blackall's book.

[10] Isle, pp. 207-209.

[11] Edel, pp. xxii-xxiii.

[12] Oscar Cargill suggests a relationship between *The Sacred Fount* and the short fiction, but does not develop it, i.e., "In *The Spoils of Poynton*, in *What Maisie Knew*, and in *The Awkward Age* (to say nothing about shorter things) James tried out various points of view; why not suppose that he continued his trials with *The Sacred Fount* and regard it as an experiment with telling a story through a narrator who has an obsession?" (p. 283).

[13] Henry James, *The Sacred Fount* (London, 1923), p. 8. *The Sacred Fount* was first published in 1901.

[14] A few critics have observed the resemblance between "The Private Life" and

this novel, e.g., Q. D. Leavis says in "Henry James: The Stories," *Scrutiny*, 14 (spring 1947), 223, " 'The Private Life' is an earlier exercise, I should say, for *The Sacred Fount*, and is silly in the same way."

[15] The narrator in "Europe" ignores statements from the *ficelle* which tend either to lessen the guilt of Mrs. Rimmle or to make Jane Rimmle's "rebirth" in Europe look ridiculous.

[16] Jean Blackall, for example, who condemns the narrator as being unreliable, refers to the other narrators as follows: 'The functional narrator is a stock character of the short stories of the nineties. Those in "Collaboration" (1892), "The Next Time" (1895), "Glasses" (1896), "Europe" (1899), "The Special Type" (1900), and "The Beldonald Holbein" (1901) are all anonymous, and all exist on the periphery of the episodes they record, having no personal stake in the plot beyond that of a storyteller's interest or sympathy' (p. 155).

[17] Numerous critics have pointed to the "psychological detective story" aspect of the narrative, e.g., H. S. Canby, *Turn West, Turn East: Mark Twain and Henry James* (Boston, 1951), pp. 219; Robert A. Perlongo, " *The Sacred Fount*: Labyrinth or Parable," *Kenyon Review*, 22 (autumn 1960), 636; Edward Sackville-West, *Inclinations* (London, 1949), p. 66.

[18] Only in "The Private Life," of the first-person stories, are the events confined to such a brief period of time.

[19] Walter Isle (op. cit., note 8) comments perceptively about the dramatic qualities of the novel. It is true, of course, that one must read this novel very closely in order to become involved enough to be able to appreciate its drama; but one of the important positive effects of the recent critical attention given to *The Sacred Fount* is to encourage readers to give the book just this kind of attention.

[20] Jean Blackall says, "James's joke was meant to depend on the reader's gradually being able to see through the narrator, whose wilful self-deception would therefore become amusing, and whose downfall would be a satisfying denouement because it is the legitimate reward of a fool" (p. 12).

[21] Krishna Baldev Vaid, *Technique in the Tales of Henry James* (Cambridge, Mass., 1964), p. 18.

[22] James Reaney (op. cit., note 6) who thinks that the narrator is not insane, but whose theorizing is "in actuality very much connected with life, its preservation and betterment" (139), argues that Mrs. Brissenden is obviously lying at the end of the novel and that the truth of the narrator's structure is not destroyed (147-148). Perhaps, but the reader cannot be certain of this fact; moreover, since the narrator does not effectively counter her arguments, the reader must be impressed by their potential validity. Most important, her charges culminate a series of accusations made by various characters, and therefore possess the force which naturally attaches to arguments appearing at a climactic position.

[23] Jean Blackall argues that the narrator's tendency to use undignified metaphors, e.g., games imagery, to describe what he is doing also contributes to James's satiric treatment of him. See, in particular, Chapters 3 and 4 in her book.

[24] Mrs. Blackall also refers to the effect of the first-person voice (pp. 12-13), deriving most of her arguments from Wayne Booth.

[25] Sidney Finklestein (op. cit., note 2) praises the narrator's ethical responsibility and contrasts his attitude with Obert's (763), then goes on to argue that, "the

narrator's morality, with its sensitivity to human suffering and resentment of human cruelty, is James's morality" (769).

[26] Walter Isle admires the narrator's "painting of reality with sticks of beauty, strangeness, enchantment, wizardry" (p. 215).

[27] A few critics, while not definitely agreeing with my argument that James consciously tried to create this tone or that he consciously attempted to make the reader react ambivalently, are sensitive to the positive effects of the narrator's sensibility, even while recognizing that he is ultimately unreliable, e.g., Walter Isle; Laurence Bedwell Holland, *The Expense of Vision: Essays in the Craft of Henry James* (Princeton, 1964), pp. 183-226; and D. W. Jefferson, *Henry James* (Edinburgh and London, 1960), pp. 56-57. Jefferson says, for example, that sometimes the effect of the narrator's obsessed vision is to suggest "uncanny possibilities lurking beneath the appearances fostered by a society so schooled" (p. 56). Jean Blackall, on the other hand, considers this ambivalence to be a weakness in the novel, arguing that it derives primarily from James's unsuccessful attempt to fuse a "humorous frame story" with a *donnée* (the idea of the sacred fount) that is essentially serious (pp. 17-18). Miriam Allott also argues that James's attempts to fuse the tragic and the ironic are unsuccessful. See Allott, "Symbol and Image in the Later Work of Henry James," *Essays in Criticism*, 3 (July 1953), 328.

[28] Oscar Cargill disagrees with my point of view: "We do not even feel for May Server as we should, for the simple reason that the obsessed mind . . . sees the whole company at Newmarch in the terms of psychologic algebra. Vaguely affected by May Server, he has no real love, sympathy, or understanding for her" (p. 295). By the end of the story, it is true, the narrator is more enamoured of his theory than of May Server; before this time, however, particularly in the scene in the woods, his sensitive comments do make us feel sympathy for her.

[29] She also has no man to look after her. Perhaps she is a widow, perhaps divorced from her husband. In any event, she is *alone*.

[30] Observe also the narrator's contrasting pictures of May Server and Mrs. Brissenden: "What was actually before me was the positive pride of life and expansion, the amplitude of conscious action and design; not the arid channel foresaken by the stream, but the full-current, the flooded banks into which the source had swelled" (191). Yet even here, the narrator is somewhat comic in the way in which he allows himself to be carried away by the flood of his own rhetoric.

[31] This theory that Mrs. Brissenden and Gilbert Long are actually having an affair was first briefly advanced by Oscar Cargill (pp. 293-294) and developed by Jean Blackall (pp. 61-68). Ironically, the narrator believes that Mrs. Brissenden and Long are united, but not in order to prevent him from discovering their sexual liaison. The result of his belief, however, is to make him extremely appreciative of Mrs. Brissenden's style in defending her secret. A concomitant effect is that, because of the narrator, we too are able to respond to Mrs. Brissenden—to admire her—even though we may recognize that she is culpable, and even though we may sense that the narrator's interpretations of her motives are wrong.

[32] James Folsom (op. cit., note 6) argues that the observer is not even justified in concluding that there is definitely a relation between the Man and the Mask in the painting, as all of the observers in the novel conclude (differing in their interpretations of this relation). The relation is only "apparent," Folsom argues,

and the observers are therefore wrong to conclude that there *must* be a relation (140), just as the narrator is foolish in assuming that there *must* be cause and effect relationships between the various changed characters in the novel (143).

[33] One cannot completely exclude the possibility that James *was* trying to make a metaphysical point about the individual's inability to understand reality. There are a number of factors in the novel, however, which suggest that an individual who tries to discover anything *ultimate* in such a context is foolish. These factors suggest to me that James's focus is not on ambiguity deriving from metaphysical causes, but from social ones. Dorothea Krook writes, "In *The Sacred Fount* what each principal—including, of course, the narrator—sees and does not see is determined partly indeed by his or her character but chiefly by the relation in which he or she stands, or appears to stand, to the other principals; and since these relations, whether real or delusory, are very much more intricate than those in *The Turn of the Screw*, the motives of the principals are correspondingly more intricate, the incentives to deception and self-deception correspondingly stronger, and the ambiguities springing from these deeper and subtler." See Krook, *The Ordeal of Consciousness in Henry James* (New York, 1962), p. 175. That the ambiguities deriving from this context are "deep" and "subtle" is perhaps true, but I do not think that James's attitude toward this situation is pessimistic as some critics (e.g., Isle) have argued. The narrator's attempts to simplify—to pierce through the ambiguity—are defeated, it is true; but his defeat is comic, not tragic.

[34] See Blackall, pp. 126-127, note 5 for an extensive list of different critical interpretations of the meaning of the phrase, "the sacred fount."

[35] James Reaney (op. cit., note 6) also notices the echo of *The Republic* here, but he interprets it as being still another indication of the dignity of the narrator's purposes (141).

[36] We note the progressive inversion of the true Socratic purposes, as well. At the beginning of the novel, the narrator disinterestedly wishes to discover truth; at its end, he simply wants to protect his theory for egoistic reasons.

[37] To Naomi Lebowitz, for example (op. cit., note 6) the narrator is James himself and the novel "is a critical preface in action." James projects himself "into a fantasy of relationship with his characters, only to find that they, in their independent spontaneity, worry his original concepts of them by flexing the muscles of their possibilities." James accepts a "mock defeat" at the end but is really superior to Mrs. Brissenden "in his refusal, and her acceptance, of a limitation of consciousness in relationship only to the shallows" (pp. 120-121).

[38] Brother Joseph Wiesenfarth says: "The novel is not a problem in metaphysics; it is, rather, a study in logic and semiosis"; it is not about a truth "but the correct reasoning about signs." See Wiesenfarth, *Henry James and the Dramatic Analogy: A Study of the Major Novels of the Middle Period* (New York, 1963), p. 97. He really gives no textual evidence for this theory, however. As far as I know, no critic has seen that the narrator also has affinities with the scientist.

[39] My general point of view is very similar to that of Laurence Holland, who also uses the term "parody" to refer to James's strategy here. Through writing this novel, Holland argues, James came to grips with the "unintended parody" that his art threatened to become and was able to measure the forces (primarily the desire to escape the chaos of life through the order of art) that were compelling

his art toward this unintentional parody (p. 183). A few other critics see the narrator as a type of "artist *manqué*" but do not see any element of self-parody in James's treatment of him, e.g., Landon C. Burns (op. cit., note 6), Jean Blackall, Ralph A. Ranald (op. cit., note 6). It seems to me that there is an element of self-satire in James's treatment of *many* of his narrators.

[40] A few other critics, most notably Julian B. Kayne in "*The Awkward Age, The Sacred Fount* and *The Ambassadors*: Another Figure in the Carpet," *Nineteenth-Century Fiction*, 17 (March 1963), 339-351, have noticed resemblances between this novel and *The Ambassadors*, but no one has viewed these resemblances from the analogical perspective that I assume in my discussion.

[41] John Roland Dove in "The Tragic Sense in Henry James," *Texas Studies in Literature and Language*, 2 (autumn 1960), 309, says, "The tragedy at the core of James's novels is the tragedy of a reality that refuses to be idealized." In *The Sacred Fount*, this situation is not tragic, it is essentially comic.

[42] e.g., Walter Isle, Sidney Finklestein, James Reaney, and J. A. Ward, "The Ineffectual Heroes of James's Middle Period," *Texas Studies in Literature and Language*, 2 (autumn 1960), 315-327.

[43] Ford Obert says that Long is "always amusing" (47).

[44] In his early critical grapplings with the novel, R. P. Blackmur said, "For the narrator could be any novelist, and the novelist could in the long run and the same predicament be any man." See "*The Sacred Fount*," 346 (op. cit., note 4). I would argue that the narrator is any *intelligent* man *gone wrong*.

X

FRANK NORRIS' *THE OCTOPUS*:
SOME OBSERVATIONS ON VANAMEE,
SHELGRIM AND ST. PAUL

RICHARD ALLAN DAVISON

WHILE PREPARING TO PUT TOGETHER A COL-
lection[1] of key essays and statements on *The Octopus*,
I surveyed virtually all the extant criticism on Frank Norris
to better my understanding of this, his most celebrated novel.
I discovered how most of the critics have affected each other
as well as how they were all affected by *The Octopus*.[2] Unfortunately, much of the vigorous disagreement that a complex
and stimulating work of art inspires often throws more light
on the critics than on Norris. Least offensive are the critical
weaknesses that come from strong personal viewpoints; worse
by far are those resulting from murky-minded reasoning and
careless reading of the novel. So-called pivotal passages are
read with the blurred subjectivism of an Ishmael seduced
by the artificial light of the try-works. Frequently, like the
proverbial blind men in their encounter with the elephant,
the critics have been seized by a single tentacle of *The Octopus*
and have strangely managed to elude its other wriggling
appendages, not to mention that massive head! that Cyclo-
pean eye! Many of the diverse and contradictory opinions
warrant a brief sampling.[3]

Richard A. Davison

I

The earliest known reviewer of *The Octopus*, Wallace Rice, called the novel "a work of realism" whose "philosophy [was] hideous" and whose "purpose [was] self-defeated." He felt that "the episode of Vanamee and Angèle . . . [had] no possible relevance" to the work and saw Shelgrim's speech as "wholly converting [Presley] the most intelligent character" in the book. Over the next fifteen months or so contemporary reviewers further complicated the issues. F. T. Cooper saw Norris as "farther away from real life in *The Octopus* than he was in *A Man's Woman*, just as in that novel he was farther away than in *McTeague*." William Dean Howells felt each of the characters "most intimately and personally real, physically real, but also psychically real." B. O. Flower saw Norris' novel "exhibiting the strength, power, vividnesses, fidelity to truth, photographic accuracy in description, and marvelous insight in depicting human nature, together with that broad and philosophic grasp of the larger problems of life, that noble passion for justice, that characterizes the greatest work of Emile Zola, without that sexualism or repulsive naturalism which the French writer so frequently forces upon his readers. . . . " Another reviewer felt *The Octopus* "too visibly determined by Zola and often too diligently brutal in style . . . [but] tremendous in strength and scope." The early disagreement over Norris' inclusion of Vanamee and Angèle was even more violent. While the *Overland Monthly* praised "the delicate love Idyll of Vanamee and Angèle Varian, touching upon phases of the most modern psychological thought, the shadowy world of the mind," the *Independent* attacked the subplot for dwindling "away into the regions of the most artificial and unconvincing supernaturalism." Just as William Payne of the *Dial* praised Norris for "the vein of mysticism that. . . . is not only distinctly Zolaesque, but also provides a welcome relief from the oppressive atmosphere of the narra-

tive . . .", so H. H. Boynton of the *Atlantic Monthly* attacked
Norris' handling of Vanamee and Angèle as "the sort of
romantic vulgarity of which only the realist of the French
School is capable." The mass of later criticism has followed
most of these early reviewers' guidelines, if not always their
piety and concern for poetic justice. Until the 1940s *The
Octopus* was generally attacked, particularly for alleged philosophical inconsistencies.

Writing in 1915 Frederick Lewis Pattee claimed *The
Octopus* was "not literature" and came to "no terminus
or conclusion." Eighteen years later Norris' biographer Franklin Walker, while seeing a good deal more merit in the novel
than did Pattee, referred to it as "an imperfect synthesis . . .
a ragout . . . parts of which are nutritious, others indigest-
ible." Granville Hicks wrote, the next year, that "*The Octopus* can scarcely be called a great book; it is too confused, and in the end too false." By the early 1940s H.
Willard Reninger and George Wilbur Meyer had somewhat
cautiously argued for different kinds of philosophical consistency in *The Octopus* but Ernest Marchand in the
second booklength study of Norris (1942) saw the author
bewildered and confused regarding the philosophy of his
novel. To this day critics disagree as to the novel's aesthetic
and philosophic values. Warren French sees philosophical
consistency but flawed structure. Richard Chase has called
The Octopus "a sub-novel" and Kenneth Lynn has
claimed that "measured by any architectonic standard" it
is "a literary chaos." Donald Pizer and William B. Dillingham seem most in agreement about the merits of the novel
but each has certain reservations.[4] Pizer sees philosophical
unity in what he views as a Le Contean reconciliation of
"evolutionary science and religious faith"—a kind of "evolutionary theism" stressing divine immanence in the wheat,
transcendentalism and utilitarianism.[5] His most serious reservations concern Norris' embodiment and reinforcement of
his ideas.

II

Although so many critics have disagreed over *The Oc-topus'* rank in American literature, no one to my knowledge has denied its vast energy, scope and power. Norris may not be a great novelist but he could be a very good one.[6] *The Octopus* almost embraces the greatness it reaches out for. Norris tells an exciting, profoundly compelling story and he tells it well. Furthermore, Norris was more consciously in control of the philosophy and structure of *The Octo-pus* than even the most recent favorable critics seem to believe. Almost all critics agree that the weakest aspects of the novel are in the Vanamee-Angèle episode and the conclu-sion. They are also not sure how to interpret Presley's inter-view with Shelgrim.[7] As interrelated as these issues are they are worth examining, to an extent at least, one at a time. But to provide a broader context for the discussion, a review of Norris' meticulous concern for the unity of his novel may prove enlightening. What Norris thought he was doing in *The Octopus* may help us to evaluate his actual achieve-ment.

Particularly during the last years of his short life Norris evidenced rather acute awareness of the strengths and short-comings of his novels.[8] In his critical essays on the novel in general he demanded a structural concentration that was Aristotelian in its unity. "The Mechanics of Fiction"[9] offers a handbook description of some of the unity Norris believed he had achieved in *The Octopus*.

He calls for "a beginning, and end, which implies a middle, continuity . . . " and then elaborates in some detail:

> . . . it is hard to get away from that thing in every novel which let us call the *pivotal event*. All good novels have one. It is *the peg upon which the fabric of the thing hangs*, the nucleus around which the shifting drifts and currents must—suddenly—coagulate, the sudden releasing of the brake to permit for one instant the entire machinery to labour, full steam,

ahead. *Up to that point the action must lead; from it, it must decline.*

But—and here one holds at least one mechanical problem— *the approach,* the leading up to this pivotal event *must be infinitely slower than the decline.* For the reader's interest in the story centers round it. . . .

The unskilled, impatient of the tedium of meticulous elaboration, will rush at it in a furious gallop of short chapters and hurried episodes, so that he may come the sooner to the purple prose declamation and drama that he is sure he can handle with such tremendous effect.

Not so the masters. Watch them during the first third— say—of their novels. Nothing happens—or at least so you fancy. *People come and go, plans are described, localities, neighborhoods; an incident crops up just for a second for which you can see not reason,* a note sounds that is puzzlingly inappropriate. The novel continues. There seems to be no progress: again that perplexing note, but a little less perplexing. By now we are well into the story. There are no more new people, but the old ones come back again and again, and yet again; you remember them now after they are off stage. You are more intimate with the two main characters. Then comes a series of incidents in which these two are prominent. The action still lags, but little by little you are getting more and more acquainted with these principal actors. Then perhaps comes the first acceleration of movement. The approach begins—ever so little—to rise, *and that same note which seemed at first so out of tune sounds again and this time drops into place in the progression, beautifully harmonious, correlating the whole gamut.* By now all the people are 'on;' by now all the groundwork is prepared. You *know the localities* so well that you could find your way about among them in the dark; *hero and heroine are intimate acquaintances.*

Now the action begins to increase in speed. The *complication* suddenly tightens; all along the line there runs a sudden alert. An episode far back there in the first chapter, an episode with its appropriate group of characters, is brought forward and, coming suddenly to the front, collides with the main line of development and sends it off upon an entirely unlooked for tangent. Another episode of the second chapter—let us suppose—all at once makes common cause with a more recent incident, and the two produce a wholly unlooked for counter influence which swerves the main theme in still another direction, and all this time the action is speeding faster and faster, the complication tightening, and straining to the breaking point, and then *at least a 'motif' that has been in preparation ever since the first paragraph of the first chapter of the novel suddenly comes to a head, and in a twinkling the complication is solved with all the violence of an explosion,* and the *catastrophe, the climax, the pivotal event fairly leaps from the pages* with a rush of action that leaves you stunned, breathless, and overwhelmed with the sheer power of its presentation. And there is a master work of fiction.

The master work of fiction Norris so vigorously described follows the structural patterns of a Greek tragedy with its exposition, inciting action, rising action, climax, catastrophe, and falling action. The novel he actually wrote also follows this basic pattern. The scope of his theme, however, prompted him to add more characters and more fully develop the falling action. In *The Octopus* Norris achieved a "progression" that is "beautifully harmonious" largely through an intricate analogical structure reinforced by what E. M. Forster has called inner stitching or rhythmic repetition with variation.[10] Just as Melville employed countless rhythmic patterns embodying the numerous themes in *Moby Dick* and Twain used incremental repetition to impose form on otherwise picaresque incidents in *Huckleberry Finn*,[11] so Norris coordinated his epic, elemental struggle between the ranchers and Pacific and Southwestern Railroad. He begins the preparation of various of his motifs "in the first paragraph of the first chapter." Norris realizes in *The Octopus* a full artistic development of man's struggles with himself and his society. He portrays a complex world whose inhabitants are clearly responsible for their actions. *The Octopus* (along with *The Pit*) is the culmination of Norris's growing belief in a morally ordered universe. By refining devices already present in earlier works,[12] he reveals the far-reaching implications of St. Paul's optimistic philosophy. As the novel progresses the motifs become increasingly meaningful through his manipulation of repeated comparison, contrasts, ironic juxtapositions, and a masterful handling of detail.[13]

III

The first chapter is largely unified by Presley's bicycle trip over the terrain that is to become so familiar to the reader. Norris included a "Map Of The Country Described In *The Octopus*" that at once enhances the visual conception of his novel and reinforces many of its major images.[14] In the opening sentence of *The Octopus* Presley passes Caraher's saloon (where the anarchist is to press both Dyke and Presley into violence). Derrick's ranch, Los Muertos, is mentioned as the "prolonged blowing" of a railroad whistle reaches Presley's ears. Within the first ten pages Norris established the post harvest time (the "last half of September") and the sparsity of the recent wheat crop. Presley passes the life-giving watering tank on which a fresh sign, "S. Behrman, Real Estate, Mortgages, Main Street, Bonneville, Opposite the Post Office," is "all but finished." Hooven is introduced along with his fear that Magnus Derrick will remove him as tenant; Presley rides past the greyhounds that will participate in the rabbit hunt and massacre following Dyke's capture and preceding the climactic ditch fight. He passes the giant live-oak which remains in towering majesty impervious to changing human circumstances.[15] He passes the Derricks' broken-down, rusting seeders and the Railroad's box cars that are to take the Derricks' new plows on a costly, circuitous route. Presley rides past the unfinished irrigation ditch, potential bringer of water and life, that is to be the site of bloodshed and death. The moral flaws in Minna Hooven are hinted at. Dyke is introduced with news of his recent firing by the Railroad. Presley meets Annixter, who complains of Derrick's exploitive ranching methods. He also announces his own upcoming barn dance. Presley meets Vanamee and Father Sarria and recalls the shepherd's tragic loss of Angèle.

Chapter one ends with the slaughter of Vanamee's neglected sheep by a speeding locomotive.

Throughout chapter two the exposition continues at its slow and steady pace. The inciting action does not occur until chapter three when, at a ranchers' meeting at Derrick's house, Osterman suggests their counter use of bribery to combat the Railroad. With the rising action Norris' novel gains momentum as pivotal incidents pile one upon another: Vanamee's meeting with Father Sarria and rejection of St. Paul's hopeful words; his first attempt to call Angèle from the grave; Annixter's thwarted attempt to kiss Hilma; the celebratory barn dance (where all the characters literally or figuratively join hands and circle round, a device much like the scaffold scenes in *The Scarlet Letter* or the Corey dinner party in *Silas Lapham*);[16] the art show at Lyman Derrick's San Francisco club where the joyful cries of the raffle winner merge with the news of the ranchers' major setback in the higher courts;[17] Annixter's thwarted overtures to Hilma; Dyke's ruin; Annixter's realization of a love beyond the purely physical the same day Presley writes "The Toilers" and Vanamee sees Angèle's daughter for the first time and the young green sprouts of wheat break through the brown earth; Annixter's marriage and Dyke's train robbery; Lyman Derrick's betrayal of the ranchers; Genslinger's blackmail of Derrick; Dyke's capture and the rabbit hunt followed by the climactic irrigation ditch battle. The falling action involves the sorting out of thoughts and the inexorable working out of what human beings have set in motion: the catastrophic scene of Magnus Derrick disgraced and driven from the stage of the opera house to a claustrophobic actress' dressing room that reeks of sachet;[18] Presley's astounding interview with Shelgrim; Minna Hooven's downfall and her mother's starvation; the Gerard dinner party; Vanamee's enlightened restatement of St. Paul to Presley; Behrman's death; Presley's departure on the wheat-filled ship destined to relieve starving people in India and his concluding statements of hope. Norris has carefully developed the implications of Presley's concluding optimistic speech. The omniscient author and the reader can better appreciate the appropriateness of this ending than can the convalescing protagonist and speaker.

IV

Claiming that the "Conclusion" of *The Octopus* is neither prepared for nor convincing, Norris' detractors have inevitably used it to cap their arguments for his muddled philosophy and loose artistic control. Yet Presley's semi-enlightened echo of Vanamee's enlightened restatement of St. Paul represents the culmination of a motif that Norris established in the fourth chapter of the first book of a sixteen-chapter novel. And the seeds of this optimistic philosophy begin their growth in the very first chapter. When Vanamee continues to despair of the loss of Angèle, Father Sarria tries in vain to comfort him by quoting from St. Paul's letter to the Corinthians:[19]

"Thou fool! That which thou sowest is not quickened except it die, and that which thou sowest, thou sowest not that body that shall be, but bare grain. It may chance of wheat, or of some other grain. But God giveth it a body as it hath pleased him, and to every seed his own body. . . . It is sown a natural body; it is raised a spiritual body. It is because you are a natural body that you cannot understand her, nor wish for her as a spiritual body, but when you are both spiritual, then you shall know each other as you are—know as you never knew before. Your grain of wheat is your symbol of immortality. You bury it in the earth. It dies, and rises again a thousand times more beautiful. Vanamee, your dear girl was only a grain of humanity that we have buried here, and the end is not yet. But all this is so old, so old. The world learned it a thousand years ago, and yet each man that has ever stood by the open grave of anyone he loved must learn it all over again from the beginning."

The truth of these words has not yet reached the bereaved lover (I, 139).

Before the end of Book I Vanamee himself draws the parallel between his mystical awareness of what seems to be Angèle's growing presence and " 'the very first little quiver of life that the grain of wheat must feel after it is sown, when it answers to the call of the sun, down there in the dark of the earth. . . . ' " Now it is Vanamee who quotes St. Paul to a noncommittal Presley: " 'That which thou sowest is not quickened except it die . . . ' " (I, 209). But he rather fuzzily associates this phenomenon with a kind of sixth sense until the night Angèle's daughter appears to him in the Mission garden. Then even Sarria's assurance that the beautiful girl is not Angèle but her daughter does not dampen Vanamee's new spiritual affirmation:

> Life out of death, eternity rising from out of dissolution. There was the lesson. Angèle was not the symbol but the proof of immortality. The seed dying, rotting and corrupting in the earth; rising again in life unconquerable, and in immaculate purity. . . . Why had he not had the knowledge of God? Thou fool, that which thou sowest is not quickened except it die. . . . The wheat called forth from out of darkness . . . from out of the grave, from out of corruption, rose triumphant into light and life. So Angèle, so life, so also the resurrection of the dead. . . . (II, 106-107)

By the end of the novel Vanamee has generalized his new awareness into a transcendental philosophy. He reads Presley a lesson that is gradually to dissipate the young poet's confusion and bitterness: " 'the good never dies; evil dies, cruelty, oppression, selfishness, greed—these die; but nobility, but love, but sacrifice, but generosity, but truth . . . —these live forever. . . . Never judge of the whole round of life by the mere segment you see. The whole is, in the end, perfect.' "[20] The words have taken root in Presley's mind by the time he is bound for the open sea and India: "The larger view always and through all shams, all wickednesses, discovers the Truth that will, in the end, prevail, and all things, surely, inevitably, resistlessly work together for good" (II, 361). Throughout Norris' book the moral implications of St. Paul's message grow into a kind of incremental refrain which vibrates through the very backbone of the novel. What is more, St. Paul's statements provide a central frame of reference for almost all of the characters, particularly the major ones.[21]

Early in the novel when Annixter attempts to convince a vacillating Magnus Derrick that bribery is the best way to combat the Railroad, his argument is a kind of mock version of Presley's concluding restatement of St. Paul. Annixter's remarks smack of Shelgrim's sophistry. It is a viewpoint he is to transcend: " 'But, Governor, standards have changed since your time; everybody plays the game now as we are playing it—the most honorable men. You can't play it any other way, and, pshaw! if the right wins out in the end, that's the main thing' " (I, 177). Nowhere in the novel does Norris condone dishonest means as justified by their ends. Annixter, himself, is to repudiate this position.[22] Magnus Derrick's own confusion reveals an inherent misunderstanding of St. Paul's message: "He was hopelessly caught in the mesh. Wrong seemed indissolubly knitted into the texture of Right. He was blinded, dizzied, overwhelmed, caught in the current of events and hurried along, he knew not where. He resigned himself" (II, 8). This is also redolent of Shelgrim's rationalizations concerning the absence of human responsibility amidst the inevitability of Force. Shelgrim's speech to Presley toward the end of the novel contains only the sense of inevitability in St. Paul and none of the hope (II, 283-86). The railroad president's apotheosis of Force is a kind of irony of self-deception, a weak conterpoint to Vanamee's eventual realization and the central truth Presley speaks in the last paragraph of *The Octopus*. Annixter, Magnus Derrick, Vanamee and Presley all repudiate this tissue of expediency and half-truths. And through them so does Norris.

V

Both the Vanamee-Angèle episode and Shelgrim's function are crucial to an understanding of Norris' use of St. Paul and hence the consistency of the novel's conclusion. Vanamee is a much more reliable philosophical frame of reference for the author than is usually granted.[23] His reactions are a barometer for the moral implications of *The Octopus*. Just as Annixter, for a time, may be an externalization of Norris' Victorian struggle with sexuality,[24] Vanamee seems to epitomize the novel's central spiritual struggle. In a letter written just three months before he completed *The Octopus*, Norris expressed strong feelings as to the importance of the Vanamee-Angèle inclusion: "You'll find some things in it that for me—are new departures. It is the most romantic thing I've yet done. One of the secondary subplots is pure romance—oh, even mysticism, if you like, a sort of allegory— I call it the Allegory of the Wheat."[25] Norris places Vanamee in important locations throughout most of the novel. He keeps the "subplot" before the reader as Vanamee gradually changes along with Annixter[26] and, to a lesser extent, Presley. Although there are certain weaknesses in Norris' execution of Vanamee's story, the transformation is rendered convincingly. On close observation even the most questionable facts surrounding Vanamee's career are scarcely unacceptable.[27] It *is* somewhat odd that Vanamee seems unaware of Angèle's growing daughter until the night he first sees her as a full grown replica of her mother. He left for distant wanderings, however, even before Angèle's grave was filled, perhaps without having seen the newborn baby. For sixteen years he stayed away long periods at a time, returning only intermittently. When he meets Presley at the beginning of the novel he has been away for perhaps six years.[28] Since there is no evidence that he ever met Angèle at her home but always rendezvoused in the Mission garden, it is not strange that he does not seek the daughter at her home.[29] Furthermore, he is a loner, a mystic with whom odd habits and strange lapses are as common as his spiritual insight.

Norris continually underlines Vanamee's physical and spiritual resemblance to the Hebraic prophets.[30] He is at the outset an appropriate vehicle for Norris' philosophy in *The*

Octopus, for life in accordance with natural goodness, Christian morality, and St. Paul's statements on immortality. From the beginning he is an editorial spokesman. He registers un-condescendingly positive reactions to the Homeric scene of the ranch workers' feasting and drinking after a hard day's involvement in the planting stage of nature's cycle of growth, its continuum. To Vanamee, but not Presley, the feasting is as natural as the songs and sleep that follow (I, 127).[31] Not so the overindulgence and drunkenness at Annixter's barn dance. The atmosphere and unnatural circumstances cause Vanamee to become "more and more disgusted" (I, 261).[32] Presley merely remains aloof.

Vanamee's importance is evident in many other ways. He is philosophically linked directly or indirectly with almost every major character and many minor ones. It is Vanamee who sparks Presley's thoughts about the great poem of the West (I, 37-39) and to whom Presley takes "The Toilers" for an honest judgment. Norris gives to Vanamee the last prophetic words in Book I,[33] just as his "words" end the novel. It is Vanamee who brings the news of the Railroad's march on the ranchers but remains a neutral pacifistic figure.[34] Even Angèle and Hilma are associated through image motifs and parallelism. Hilma, a continual reinforcement of the goodness that Vanamee attributes to unspoiled nature, is seen in almost constant sunlight.[35] Until the moment Angèle's daughter meets Vanamee she and her mother are continually associated with moonlight. When Vanamee meets the daughter, Norris externalizes the simple profundity of the shepherd's new spiritual insight: "It was no longer an ephemeral illusion of night, evanescent, mystic, but a simple country girl coming to meet her lover. . . . She stood forth in the sunlight a fact, and no longer a fancy."[36] By this point Norris has traced Vanamee's essentially Christian spiritual progression from that of knowledge of evil (Angèle's rape by the Other), to despair (his aimless wanderings and denial of God's goodness), to penance (his ascetic life and the long nights of contemplation in the Mission garden), to rebirth and deepened spiritual insight first realized in the love of Angèle's grown daughter. Vanamee struggles many years before his epiphany. The results of his transformation allow him to throw off self-pity and despair and rejoin the human race with new spiritual breadth. A kind of microcosm of the novel, the Vanamee–Angèle episode in its ultimate "Reality"[37] is an allegorical comment on each of the other plots as well as "the Allegory of the Wheat."

VI

In fact the five most central plots in *The Octopus* are structurally and thematically interwoven. The plots involving Vanamee, Annixter, Hooven, Dyke, and Derrick are all, in varying degrees, microcosms of the novel's major plot, side mirrors for the various attitudes toward the wheat in the struggle between the ranchers and the Railroad.[38] All the characters are thematically linked.[39] Annixter repents of his desire for purely physical gratification and is on his way to spiritual fulfillment in Hilma's love at his death. Vanamee achieves an earthly fulfillment through his love of Angèle and her daughter. Presley is groping toward the truth that he speaks by the novel's end. Magnus Derrick asks God's forgiveness for his dishonesty to others and to himself. The misguided Hooven dies nobly for "the Vaterland," the dwelling place of his wife and children. Dyke alone seems merely pathetic in his attempt to save his family by striking back at the Railroad. But in the context of "the larger view" is the assurance that he, along with Hooven, will rise up out of the earth as did the corrupted wheat.[40] Norris likens the fallen ranchers to the seeds in Paul's letter to the Corinthians; they too await the fulfillment of promised resurrection. The astute reader is not to be taken in by Shelgrim's explanation of the Universe as a combination of mere conditions and forces to which man must acquiesce. Man is responsible for combatting evil and moving toward the good. The Railroad and the wheat are neither responsible nor irresistible as mere forces. It is man's use of these forces that results in evil or good. Men bribe railroad commissioners and exploit the land. Neither tenant farmers nor railroad presidents are immune to responsibility.

Although Shelgrim is physically present in only one scene, it is a vital one. Whenever he is mentioned before this scene there is a suggestion of something worse than S. Behrman, something worse than the Other. He is the Octopus, the embodiment of the Railroad, the title of Norris' novel incarnate. During the first meeting of the ranchers Shelgrim's name falls "squarely in the midst of the conversation" (I, 99). He is described as "a giant figure . . . hated . . . dreaded . . . " with a "colossal intellect operating the width of an entire continent. . . . " After Lyman Derrick has been so speedily elected as the ranchers' railroad commissioner, Annixter is distrustful of such an apparent victory: "It's too easy. . . . No I'm not satisfied. Where's Shelgrim in all this. . . . There's a big fish in these waters somewhere" (II, 8). And just before Presley's interview with Shelgrim Norris again places a nonhuman image before the reader: "How far were the consequences of that dreadful day's work at the irrigating ditch to reach. To what length was the tentacle of the monster to extend" (II, 278).[41] Norris has consciously played up the monstrous aspects of Shelgrim before he is seen. During the interview Presley is mesmerized by the man and his forceful pronouncements. Norris is not; nor, hopefully, is the reader. Consciously satiric description reinforces the suggestion that Norris is undercutting Shelgrim's half-truths.[42] For the gigantic president of the P. and S. W. Railroad is given the physiognomy and attributes of the very creature that gives the novel its title:[43]

> He was large, almost to massiveness. An iron-grey beard and moustache that completely hid the mouth covered the lower part of his face. His eyes were a pale blue, and a little watery; here and there upon his face were moth spots. But

the enormous breadth of the shoulders was what, at first, most vividly forced itself upon Presley's notice. Never had he seen a broader man; *the neck, however, seemed in a manner to have settled into the shoulders,* and furthermore *they were humped* and *rounded,* as if to bear great responsibilities and great abuse.

At the moment he was wearing a silk skull cap. . . . (II, 281)

Presley, his senses never more alive, observed that, *curiously enough, Shelgrim did not move his body. His arms moved, and his head but the great bulk of the man remained immobile in its place,* and as the interview proceeded and this peculiarity emphasized itself, *Presley began to conceive the odd idea that Shelgrim had, as it were, placed his body in the chair to rest, while his head and brain and hands went on working independently.* A saucer of shelled filberts stood near his elbow, and *from time to time he picked up one of these in a great thumb and forefinger and put it between his teeth.* (II, 283)[44]

Norris was undoubtedly aware of precedents for such a portrayal in the numerous political cartoons depicting the actual prototype for Shelgrim (Collis P. Huntington) with the body and tentacles of an octopus. One such cartoon shows his tentacle grasping figures and papers labeled: "Honest Vote, Manufacturer, Farmer, Merchant, Orange Raiser, Subsidized press and the cities of Oakland and San Francisco."[45] Certainly Norris' juxtaposition of Presley's meeting with the fallen Minna Hooven after his meeting with the railroad president gives the lie to Shelgrim's claims that Force and not men are to blame. Even Shelgrim's possibly sentimental gesture to save Tentell's job suggests man's ability to act justly, if he so chooses. That one villain is society's potent Indifference becomes clear as one by one the ambassadors of society—the landlady, the sexton, the flophouse attendant, potential employers, policemen, and people on the street —all turn their backs to the Hoovens' plight. Here indifferent men, not Forces, are to blame.[46] Significantly, it is outside the mansion of Shelgrim's Vice President, Gerard, that Mrs. Hooven starves and her daughters are orphaned.[47]

Norris proposes no easy solution to the agony of living in an imperfect society. But a transcendental view of the world is necessary before his characters can come to terms with themselves. Possibly the social evils can be partially conquered by the Unity of the People aroused from lethargic Indifference. Perhaps this can only be realized through the kind of human sacrifice the ranchers suffer. In Norris' framework, when man acts for the good, even when he dies tragically, he is in harmony with a Christian universe transcending the Railroad and ranches. Regardless of all the vacillating, capricious, or indifferent men, there will always be an Annixter, a Hilma, a Vanamee, an Angèle, a repentant Magnus Derrick. The cause of truth and justice will eventually triumph over evil as certainly as the buried wheat rises to life and Angèle's daughter appears to fulfill Vanamee's love. For, in *The Octopus*, when man lives for goodness or dies tragically aware, he does so in the matrix of a well-ordered universe. But the order is not immediately apparent to all men. In this real world Norris creates, it is possible for a mystic to vibrate with the fecund rhythms of nature—Emersons' or Whitman's vast continuum. It is possible for a man of the dignity and worth of Magnus Derrick to fall tragically and for a lustful, self-centered Annixter to rise through humility. It is also possible for one to be taken in by the high-sounding malarky of a Shelgrim. Norris was saddled with his own frailties. He struggled with personal prejudices that prompted him to see individuals as better or worse than they really were. He, like Presley, was very much at home dining with the Gerards; he was also imaginatively capable of seeing the "frail, delicate . . . fine ladies with their small fingers and slender necks, suddenly transfigured into harpies tearing human flesh" (II, 317). The "clink of wine glasses" could, in his mind, be "drowned in the explosion of revolvers" (II, 317). Norris' personal attitude toward both the ranchers and the railroad owners contained an ambivalence that, transmuted into art, enriched the texture of his epic novel. The complexity of his view of man and the fine artistic embodiment of it are what brings him in *The Octopus* far closer to Hawthorne and Melville than to his contemporary muckrakers.

[1] *The Merrill Studies in The Octopus.* Columbus, Ohio: Charles E. Merrill, 1969.

[2] Among the most perceptive critics of *The Octopus* are Franklin Walker, Ernest Marchand, H. Willard Reninger, George W. Meyer, Warren French, Donald Pizer and William B. Dillingham.

[3] Commentary on *The Octopus* will be surveyed in the following order: *Chicago American Literary and Art Review* (April 16, 1901), 5-6. *Bookman*, 13 (May 1901), 246. *Harper's Monthly*, 103 (October 1901), 824. *Arena*, 27 (May 1902), 542. *Land of Sunshine*, 15 (July 1901) 58. *Overland Monthly*, 37 (May 1901) 1050. *Independent*, 53 (May 16, 1901), 1140. *Dial*, 31 (September 1, 1901), 136. *Atlantic Monthly*, 89 (May 1902), 708. *A History of American Literature Since 1870.* (New York, 1915), 400. *Frank Norris: A Biography* (Garden City: Doubleday, Doran, 1932), 259. *The Great Tradition* (New York: Macmillan, 1933), 172. "Norris Explains *The Octopus*: a Correlation of His Theory and Practice," *American Literature*, 11 (May 1940), 218-27, "A New Interpretation of *The Octopus*," *College English*, 4 (March 1943), 351-59. *Frank Norris: A Study* (Stanford University Press, 1942). *Frank Norris* (New York: Twayne, 1962). *The American Novel and Its Tradition* (Garden City, New York: Doubleday), p. 203. Introduction to *The Octopus* (Boston: Houghton Mifflin, 1958), p. v. *The Novels of Frank Norris* (Bloomington: Indiana University Press, 1966). *Frank Norris: Instinct and Art* (Lincoln: University of Nebraska Press, 1969).

[4] *The Novels of Frank Norris*, p. 160; *Frank Norris: Instinct and Art*, pp. 119-21

[5] "The Concept of Nature in *The Octopus*," *American Quarterly*, 14 (spring 1962), pp. 73-80.

[6] Mr. Pizer is one of many who have made this judgment. See *The Novels of Frank Norris*, p. 179.

[7] Other weaknesses in *The Octopus* frequently attacked, and with some justice, are the treatment of the "little tad," Sidney Dyke, who in her hissings at passing trains is rather frighteningly reminiscent of Elsie Venner; Mrs. Hooven's starvation scene and S. Behrman's death. In the last two instances, particularly Behrman's death, Norris may be descending to melodrama; but his writing is so effective (as it is in "the death in the desert business" in *McTeague*) that the reader is too caught up in it to be adversely critical. If Behrman's suffocation by the wheat seems too contrived, it is an appropriate death. For the greediness that prompts him to lean close to the hold and finger the wheat, as a miser would his gold, has been thoroughly established.

[8] Norris wrote to his friend Isaac Marcosson of the *Louisville Times* insightful statements about two of his novels. Regarding *Moran of the Lady Letty*, he said:

"When I wrote Moran I was, one might say, flying kites, trying to see how high I could go without breaking the string. However I have taken myself more seriously since then and in my next novel [*McTeague*] I have tried to do something really worthwhile." Norris called *A Man's Woman* "a kind of theatrical sort with a lot of niggling analysis to try to justify the violent action of the first few chapters. It is very slovenly put together and there are only two people in all its 100,000 words." See items 9 and 28 in Franklin Walker's edition of *The Letters of Frank Norris* (San Francisco: The Book Club of California, 1956).

[9] *The Responsibilities of the Novelist*, Volume VII, *The Complete Edition of Frank Norris* (Garden City: Doubleday, Doran, 1929) pp. 113-117. Hereafter page references to *The Complete Edition* will be incorporated into the text. *The Octopus* comprised Volumes I and II of this ten-volume edition. The italics are mine.

Norris later admitted that an overly strict adherence to this formula is not always advisable (I, 117).

[10] E. M. Forster, *Aspects of the Novel* (New York: Harcourt, Brace, 1927), Chapter VIII.

[11] See Frank Baldanza's "The Structure of *Huck Finn*," *American Literature*, 27 (November 1955), pp. 347-355.

[12] Norris manages to sustain his control more effectively than in his best earlier novels, *McTeague* and *Vandover and the Brute*, where the control is often sporadic and the technical effects generally more heavy-handed.

[13] Notice how Norris controls the function of such minor details as Annixter's bronco, which is a linking device. Delaney's "breaking" of it in front of Hilma triggers off Annixter's jealousy. Delaney steals the horse and rides it during his humiliating defeat in the gunfight at Annixter's barn dance. Annixter gives the horse to Dyke as he tries unsuccessfully to outride the posse. It carries Annixter to the irrigating ditch and his death. All who ride it suffer some calamity.

[14] Neatly drawn and labeled are, among many other items Norris chose to stress, the watering tank, the live-oak tree, the irrigating ditch and the Long Trestle. It is by the Long Trestle that the sheep are mutilated as Presley dreams. It is underneath the Long Trestle, "an oasis of green shade," that Hilma goes to gather water cresses and receives Annixter's ugly proposition. At the Long Trestle the hot steam of the railroad meets with the cooling waters of the Earth. The climactic gunfight takes place by the irrigating ditch that flows under the railroad tracks in full view of the live-oak tree.

[15] This healthy oak tree is recalled when Mrs. Hooven dies near "a few stunted live-oaks" (II, 319) outside the railroad Vice President's mansion.

[16] In Norris, as well as Hawthorne and Howells, the major characters are changed as a result of these gatherings.

[17] The winner is, significantly, Mrs. Cedarquist: industrialist's wife, philanthropist and do-gooder.

[18] Another indication of Norris' concern for detail in *The Octopus* is in his use of smells. He associates sachet, for example, with downfall or defeat. After the calamity of the barn dance the smell of buckskin (also associated with disaster) is blended with the "stale perfume" of sachet. Magnus Derrick's dishonesty is ex-

posed in a room smelling of "stale grease paint" and sachet. Minna Hooven surrenders her virtue to an enameled madame who exudes an atmosphere that is "impregnated with sachet."

[19] Wallace Rice has pointed out that Norris has a Catholic priest quote from the Protestant King James Version of *The Bible*. This is but one of many relatively unimportant inconsistencies in *The Octopus*. Along with the slips in chronology that Pizer has alluded to (*The Novels of Frank Norris*, p. 196) there is, for example, Norris' comment about Annixter only months before his death: "For years he could with little effort reconstruct the scene [of his fight with Delaney]." (I, 252-53)

[20] For an indication of the transcendental elements in *The Octopus* compare Vanamee's last words with the conclusion of Emerson's "Each and All:" "Beauty through my senses stole;/ I yielded myself to the perfect whole."

[21] Norris underlines the important figures by including, along with his map, a list of "Principal Characters in the Novel."

[22] This is particularly evident when the once volatile Annixter tries to settle matters peacefully just before the bloodshed at the irrigating ditch. (II, 222).

[23] Vanamee proves a far mellower spokesman for Norris than the vacillating, unstable Presley. Except on some literary matters Presley's judgment is almost consistently unreliable. See, for instance, I, p. 10 and II, pp. 275-76.

[24] See, for instance, Kenneth Lynn's "Introduction" to *The Octopus* for mention of repressed sexuality in Norris' characters.

[25] Franklin Walker, *Letters*, pp. 67-68. Norris was writing to Isaac Marcosson on September 13, 1901.

[26] Although there is some preparation for Annixter's transformation it is more sudden than Vanamee's.

[27] For the more popular opinion see Donald Pizer's *Novels of Frank Norris*, p. 160. It may be strange that Vanamee has never noticed Angèle's daughter; but then only at the end does he seek her in the light of day.

[28] See, for example, I, pp. 31, 36-37, 139-140, and 146.

[29] There is also some confusion concerning Angèle's home life. Presley remembers her "as a girl of sixteen . . . , who lived with an aged aunt in the Seed ranch back of the Mission." (I, 33) But the "little babe was taken by Angèle's parents. . . . " I, 36) Neither the aunt nor the parents are again mentioned.

[30] Father Sarria, Presley and the narrator all point this out at various times.

[31] As Presley grows toward Vanamee's insights he becomes more tolerant of such natural activities. (II, 216)

[32] See also I, 240-241.

[33] "I think . . . , I think that there was rain in Brussels the night before Waterloo." Rain falls on the ranchers as they leave Annixter's barn.

[34] Vanamee is conspicuous by his absence from the rabbit slaughter.

[35] Sunlight represents the truth and reality Vanamee and Annixter came to realize in the light of day.

[36] Not only does Angèle move towards Hilma's sun (as Hilma gains some of the complexity of darkness) in a symbolic sense; she, as well as Hilma, is described

as a sensuously attractive woman of flesh and blood. (I, 79-80, 150-51, 144, 233-34; II, 347). The parallel between Hilma's strong simple love and Angèle's becomes vividly apparent.

[37] Norris emphasizes the importance of seeing Vanamee and Angèle's daughter as real flesh and blood human beings rather than ethereal creatures subsumed in the realm of the fantastic. They are spiritually *and* physically united. See II, pp. 346-47.

[38] Presley, like Magnus Derrick, Dyke and S. Behrman, has understood the wheat purely in physical terms. Only later does he begin to realize the spiritual significance that is at the core of St. Paul's letter.

[39] Dyke's train robbery parallels Derrick's moral compromise. Hooven's shot which precipitates the ditch battle underlines Annixter's early impulsiveness.

[40] Dyke is essentially a good man who is misguided and directed toward evil deeds. His "Eden" (security and happiness for Sidney and his mother) has been violated along with Magnus' (personal integrity and his love for his son), Annixter's (Quien Sabe and his love for Hilma), Hooven's ("The Vaterland"—wherever "der wife and der kinder" are) and Vanamee's (his idyllic relationship with Angèle). According to St. Paul, in the end the good that is a part of all of these men will triumph.

[41] The phrase "nucleus of the web" (II, 279), describing Shelgrim's office, gives him a spidery dimension but this is not the dominant image. Shelgrim is also described in passing as an ogre and a tiger, with both animals seemingly transformed into an octopus: " 'It is an ogre's vitality' he [Presley] said to himself. 'Just so is the man-eating tiger strong. The man should have energy who has sucked the life-blood from an entire People.' " (II, 280). Norris' later description of a broken Magnus Derrick is a kind of pathetic analogue to the vital picture of Shelgrim. (II, 331)

[42] Shelgrim's speech has been prepared for by similarly deceptive words and actions by many other men, including Osterman, and all the Derricks, excepting Annie. I cannot agree with Mr. French's claim (*Frank Norris*, p. 94.) that the Shelgrim interview distorts "the structure of the novel and begins to make us suspect the artistic integrity of a writer who peremptorily introduces a new viewpoint into a nearly completed work."

The core of Shelgrim's claims is as follows:

"You are dealing with forces, young man, when you speak of Wheat and the Railroads, not with men. There is the Wheat, the supply. It must be carried to feed the People. There is the demand. The Wheat is one force, the Railroad, another, and there is the law that governs them—supply and demand. Men have only little to do in the whole business. . . . If you want to fasten the blame of the affair at Los Muertos on any one person, you will make a mistake. Blame conditions, not men" (II, 285)

[43] Another student of Harry Hayden Clark, Marston LaFrance, first brought Norris' device to my attention. It is the same technique that Norris uses to draw parallels between both Angèles and stalks of wheat. See I, pp. 33-34, 136-37; II, pp. 104-05 and 347.

[44] The italics are mine.

Richard A. Davison

[45] For samples of these cartoons see Oscar Lewis' *The Big Four* (New York: Alfred A. Knopf), pp. 136-137. Huntington died in August, 1900, some four months before Norris completed *The Octopus*.

[46] The theme of Indifference is first discussed by Cedarquist. (II, 19-22).

[47] Shelgrim's earlier gesture to Tentell may be as insidious as Indifference in its capricious paternalism.

XI

GERTRUDE STEIN: NON-EXPATRIATE

BENJAMIN T. SPENCER

"All things are breathing.
Can you see me.
Hurrah for America."[1]

I. THE CONTEXT OF NATIONALITY

AMONG GERTRUDE STEIN'S OFT-REITERATED declarations or dicta, such as "When this you see remember me," is the following: "After all anybody is as their land and air is. Anybody is as the sky is low or high, the air heavy or clear and anybody is as there is wind or no wind there. It is that which makes them and the arts they make and and [*sic*] the work they do and the way they eat. . . . " In repeating this statement she made only slight variations. In "What Are Masterpieces" she added that she was "an American" who had lived half her life in Paris, "not the half that made me but the half in which I made what I made." In *Everybody's Autobiography* she shifted the phrasing to note that "everybody is as their food and weather is" and that American college football players and red Indians move alike. In *Wars I Have Seen* she shifts the pronoun from "anybody" and "everybody" to "every one" and more specifically includes the mountains and rivers and oceans, the rain and snow and ice, as formative indigenous influences on "their way to act their way to think and their way to be subtle . . . any American knows that."[2]

The sense of diversity in all such national qualities, Miss Stein remarked in her last years, had been impressed upon her even as a child in Vienna, where she had a Czech tutor and a Hungarian governess; and this sense was subsequently intensified by the various ethnic strains which had converged in the California of her school days. Here she learned that "Germans are as they are and French and Greeks and Chinamen and Japs," and that though people may develop, they do not change. Every nation, she concluded, "has a way of being of being [*sic*] that nation that makes it that nation," and any important person "in the development of that nation has to be some way somehow like that." Throughout her life she was intent on discovering the indices that showed the way a nation had of "being that nation," whether it was the dogs, which "resemble the nation that creates them," or distinctive foods and colors and houses.[3]

In her preoccupation with "The Psychology of Nations or What Are You Looking At"—to use the title of one of her "plays"—she often found her most revealing clues in the servant class. Though in *The Making of Americans* she had consistently attached the epithet "german" [*sic*] to the central family of Herslands in the manuscript version, it is through the female servants, whether Irish or Mexican or German, that national diversity is most explicitly projected; and in the servant girls of *Three Lives*, as Michael Hoffman has observed, German frugality is contrasted with Irish free-hearted impulsiveness. Though such contrasts are Miss Stein's normal mode of disclosing dominant national traits, she occasionally noted salient correspondences. Both Spain and America, she observed, are "abstract and cruel," and they are the "only two western nations that can realise abstraction," which Spain expresses by ritual and America by "disembodiedness, in literature and machinery." Similarly, in contrast to England where "the dead are not dead because they remain connected with others living," both Spain and America "make them alive and they make them dead"; and, indeed, Mark Twain's ability to "make a dead man dead" seemed to her "a great American thing to do."[4]

In her more frequent employment of cultural contrasts, however, France and England served as the dominant foils in Miss Stein's attempts to define American nationality. French life, she discovered, could afford a proper stimulus to the American imagination because "the french [*sic*] and the Americans do not have the sense of going on together," whereas "living in England does not free the American the way living in France frees him. . . . England to an American [*sic*] English writing to an American is not in this sense a foreign thing." Unlike the Americans, she said, the French do not glamorize or worry about the twentieth century, for they are wholly concerned with their "daily life." Always aware of the "earth," they paint it but do not "poetize" it. Rather they are committed to "logic and fashion," and with the English they will civilize the twentieth century and "make it a time when anybody can be free, free to be civilized and to be."[5]

Though Gertrude Stein felt that England was too much like America to provide stimulus and perspective for cisatlantic writers, she repeatedly pondered the contrasting effects of the geography of the two countries on their cultures. As an island culture England may well need to absorb the similar culture of the Greeks, she remarked to Bertrand Russell, but "America needed essentially the culture of a continent which was of necessity latin [*sic*]." Indeed, America's continental expanse seemed to her to have determined much of the national psychology and behavior. In answer to her own question of why "Americans [are] different from others," she emphasized their mobile homelessness and their pioneer experience and heritage. Because "waiting is a part of earning a living and there is no waiting in an American," she somewhat abstrusely argued in writing of Grant, Americans can succeed (i.e. earn a living) only because they "are part European." And if she could find a distinctive restlessness nurtured by the empty American continent, she could also understand American religion as lacking a sky such as European religion had. In asserting that Americans had only air and not a sky above them, she apparently intended a metaphor to suggest a confident or even defiant egalitarianism in which "heaven" has disappeared and there is "no over all" and "Each one is all." In her attempts to define the national character, however, Miss Stein did not ignore the more generally acknowledged traits such as pragmatism: Americans "know what they are . . . by looking at what they do." Thus George Washington, observing America's geographical uniqueness, "began a novel . . . the great American novel"; he did "do what a novel is."[6]

Yet it was attachment to freedom, the corollary of uncircumscribed physical space, that Miss Stein finally stressed as primarily and emphatically American and accordingly judged both Presidents Roosevelt atypical because "They do not feel America to be a very large country around which anybody can wander." In general she accepted this influence of American space as a positive one. The pioneer experience had necessitated and bred optimism, she argued; but after the economic depression of the 1930s she began to fear that her country would "never be so young again" since, lacking the old pioneer venturesomeness, Americans would increasingly be content to "feel themselves employed and not potential employers." Viewing the mid-twentieth century as the crucial period for America since the Civil War, she warned that Americans "have to fight a spiritual pioneer fight or we will go poor as England and other industrial countries. . . ."[7]

The ultimate interpretation of American nationality which emerged from Miss Stein's lifelong concern with her country was thus not merely a conceptual one but an affective one as well—an affirmative acceptance of her cisatlantic heritage.

More ingenuously and explicitly than her venerated Henry James, she not only recognized the "complex fate" of her nativity but also confidently assimilated and examined it. "It made me wonder a lot about what it is to be an American," she said after speaking at New England colleges and observing that those that had been "made to make missionaries were more interesting than those that had been made to make culture. . . . " Repeatedly she attached the epithet "American" to herself to explain her behavior or tastes, such as her indifference to African sculpture because its primitiveness seemed not "savage" enough; or, in expressing her love for France and the French people, she felt impelled to add: "but after all I am an American, and it always comes back to that . . . one's native land is one's native land. . . . "[8]

In her early novel *Things as They Are* (1903) Adele, the narrator who generally reflects Miss Stein herself, observes that she and her two friends are "distinctively American"; Helen is the "American version of the English handsome girl," and Sophie's "long angular body . . . betrayed her New England origin." Though Adele alludes to James's Kate Croy in *The Wings of the Dove*, in her staunchly American loyalties and attitudes she herself rather resembles his Isabel Archer or Henrietta Stackpole in *The Portrait of a Lady*, convinced as she is that "no passion [is] more dominant and instinctive in the human spirit than the need of the country to which one belongs"—a passion that Gertrude Stein admitted as her own. In the fog and soggy streets of London Adele, like James's Henrietta, felt nostalgic for the "clean blue distance" and the "clean-cut cold" of her native land. In New York, on the other hand, she rejoiced in the functional simplicity of the "undecorated houses" and the elevated railway. With a more personal involvement in Boston she "steeped herself in the very essence of clear eyed Americanism" and with native pride observed both the "passionless intelligence of the faces" about her and also the "ready intercourse, free comments and airy persiflage all without double meaning" in the street-cars. Such, indeed, was the national consciousness of the James-Stein heroine of the early 1900s.[9]

In *The Making of Americans* (1906-1908) Miss Stein's concern with the national character found its most sustained and extended utterance. From the experience of her California girlhood she attempted to depict "the new people made out of the old" and the creation of a national "tradition" in "scarcely sixty years." The epic quality of her fictive record emerges not only from its extensive interweaving of the lives of the Dehning and Hersland families through three generations in the late nineteenth century but also from her expressed conviction—and one alien to the expatriate temper—that it is "a rare privilege" to be "a real American" involved in the creation of a new culture such as the book cumulatively portrays. Though her ultimate focus of reference may be that of universal psychological types (such as dependent-independent), these very types are integrally related to their Western milieu. Thus Julia Dehning at eighteen "showed in all its vigor, the self-satisfied crude domineering American girlhood that was strong inside her" yet did not "attain quite altogether that crude virginity that makes the American girl safe in all her liberty." And on Julia, as on many a Jamesian heroine, her culture had impressed a "moral idealism, the only form of culture the spare American imagination takes refuge in." Even the dull, hopeless red and green shades of Julia's living rooms Miss Stein correlates with the "ethically aesthetic aspiration of the spare American emotion."[10]

The psychological concern of *The Making of Americans* thus constantly veers toward social psychology—toward hypotheses concerning American mores and ethical and religious attitudes underlying American behavior: "In American teaching marrying is just loving . . . "; religion in the West can be like "eating and sleeping," or like "washing" or "believing," "like breathing," or "like loving"; education can be redirected, as by the Herslands and Wymans, so that California children will have "american training" for outdoor living and thus be "brought up american." Such hypotheses, however, persistently suggest an imaginative flight beyond clinical observation, as does the memorable conclusion to her description of western college life: the "american mind accustomed to waste happiness and be reckless of joy finds morality more important than ecstacy [*sic*]. . . . To our new world feeling the sadness of pain has more dignity than the beauty of joy." Thus there remained for Gertrude Stein during her first decade in France a sense of a distinctively "western morality" and a "new world humanity." And there was also, more concretely and affectively, a recollection of the "real country living" experienced by the Hersland children in contrast to their father, the urban-oriented fortune seeker who felt himself "as big as all the world" around him—a "real feeling of wind blowing in the country" and of fruit trees and vegetable gardening, of ploughing and haymaking.[11]

Thus in Gertrude Stein's work over almost half a century both her persistent resort to the concept of nationality and her especial concern with the formation and values of the national character are evident. Convinced of the ineluctable impress of one's native land, she happily affirmed her own American heritage. "Our roots can be anywhere and . . . we take our roots with us," she said after her American visit. "The essential thing is to have the feeling that they exist. . . . " Though America was her "well-nourished home," it was "not a place to work," she had written earlier in *transition*—a judgment which she further explained by asserting that though America is the oldest country and the mother of modern civilization, one wishes to be born in the country that has "attained" and to live in the countries that are "attaining." In conjunction with her more famous pronouncement that "America is my country and Paris is my home town," she affirmed the need of "every one who makes anything inside themselves" to have both their native civilization and also one "that has nothing to do with them." Or, in a later version in *Paris FRANCE*: ". . . writers have to have two countries, the one where they belong, and the one in which they live really. The second one is romantic, it is separate from themselves, it is not real but it is really there." Hence, residing in Paris she became a European, as she said, only "for the purposes of daily living." On the more profound level of cultural alienation from her native land, she was surely justified in disclaiming expatriation: "For one thing, for all the time I've been in France, I have never been called an expatriate and that is the thing I am proud of. I proved you could be a good American anywhere in the world." And so she did.[12]

II. THE CORRELATIVE OF STYLE

Beyond the evidence of Miss Stein's non-expatriated mind in her own substantive remarks, however, lies the subtler confirmation of the impress of her native land and air on her aesthetic theory and the modes of her writing. It was on the level of style in the most comprehensive sense—a projection of felt experience through linguistic forms and structure—that she saw her own work as indubitably American. Thus *The Making of Americans* seemed to her "an essentially American book" not primarily because of its California setting and its developing New World characters but rather because of its attempt to express "something strictly American . . . a space of time that is filled always filled [*sic*] with moving." Proceeding beyond the use of idea and image and even myth, therefore, she sought through such stylistic devices as the enlargement of paragraphs to recreate the innermost sense that an American has of "what is inside this space of time."[13]

To correlate Miss Stein's style with defensible conclusions about the American psyche, however, becomes a difficult endeavor for several reasons: the difficulty of validly establishing any nation's distinctive character, the appreciable changes in her own style during nearly half a century, and the intuitive and often whimsical or simplistic nature of her dicta on America. Moreover, she implies for herself a partial release from the nationalistic determinism which she so generally perceived in other artists such as Picasso; for in reviewing her life in the United States and abroad she makes a distinction between "the half [of her life in America] that made me" and "the half in which I made what I made." Thus she posits a "freedom inside yourself" which life in an alien culture permits, while "in your own civilization you are apt to mix yourself up too much with your civilization." In reiterating her contention that writers "interested in living inside themselves" need a country "to be free in," Miss Stein is surely implying that there are aspects and qualities of her work that do not bear the stamp of their author's American nurture. It is therefore not judicious to assume that her resistance to expatriation permitted her to achieve some impersonally pure national style. Indeed, it may be said of her style, as she said of the bias of one of her character types in *The Making of Americans*: "In a way it is a personal thing for them, in a way it is a family affair in them, in a way it is a way of living in a national way for them, in a way . . . of the local way in them, in a way . . . their kind in men and women have in being in living."[14]

Although Gertrude Stein declared that "any nation's literature is a homogeneous thing" throughout its history, she made virtually no observations on the presence or nature of this homogeneity in such major ante-bellum authors as Emerson, Thoreau, Melville, and Whitman. Indeed, so far as explicit comments are concerned, the authentic national mode in her view was rather embodied in the varied realism of Twain, Howells, and Henry James; and of these it was James who took up where English literature left off because "it had no further to go." His "disembodied way of disconnecting something from anything . . . was the American one," she said, and this way "had a future feeling." In fact, she came to recognize him as the only nineteenth-century American writer who "felt the method of the twentieth century"; and, despite her insistence in the Toklas autobiography that in her formative years she had neither read nor cared for his work, the point of view, structure, and characterizations of her early *Things As They Are*, as Michael Hoffman has convincingly argued, attest James's strong influence. Later her recognition of his brilliant fictional strategies—his ability to write simultaneously both "what you are writing" and "what you are going to be writing"—prompted her fantasy of him as a "general," though as a general, she concedes, "he was a European." Yet far more cogent than this capricious portrait is her tribute to his creation of a "whole paragraph" structure which "was detached [*sic*] what it said from what it did, what it was from what it held, and over it all something floated. . . ."[15]

Miss Stein's relationship to other American forebears and contemporaries in the "homogeneous" national literature generally eludes firm or substantial definition. Undoubtedly the psychological and philosophical views of her preceptor William James left their deep imprint upon her—both his earlier concept of consciousness as an entity which determines character types (implicit in *The Making of Americans*) and his later idea of the unpredictable "stream" of consciousness (implicit in *Tender Buttons* and the portraits). Although her psychological emphasis and stylistic patterns thus owe much to the brothers James, her early settings and characters also reflect current trends among the naturalists. "I have to content myself with niggers and servant girls and the foreign population generally," she wrote after completing *Three Lives*; yet in treating such characters she was generally indifferent to the humanitarian concern that motivated much of the naturalists' fiction, and she dispensed with their heavy reliance on quotidian data and colloquial idiom in favor of an exploration of states of mind or psychological types. Apparently, therefore, she was indifferent to "Melanctha" in *Three Lives* as an innovative projection of the Negro into American fiction, for she rather valued the book as a "noble combination of Swift and Matisse." Moreover, she declared that since her "very simple and very vulgar" materials would not "interest the great American public," she could "never write the great American novel." (She was later willing to pronounce Wilder's *Heaven's My Destination* to be "*the* American novel.") Thus, though in the early 1900's she had affiliations with the naturalists and felt that American "life needed a clean and resistant realism," she also realized that both her literary purposes and the American temper required larger dimensions than realism encouraged. There was also the need to "move around," she observed, and this moving involved "feeling romantic." Hence she spent the early part of her life, as she said, escaping the nineteenth century with its reliance on science and technology, its belief in progress, and its ultimate literary creed nurtured by a positivistic philosophy. It may be that, as Miss Allegra Stewart contends, Gertrude Stein's "romanticism" finally brought her in "Doctor Faustus Lights the Lights" close to "an authentic American tradition as expressed by Emerson, Thoreau, and Whitman"—a tradition which fused "Oriental and Occidental spirituality"; but if so, her affinity with the three nineteenth-century figures must be non-derivative and hence illustrative of her view of the inherent homogeneity of national literatures. Her admission of any significant indebtedness to their works is not a matter of record.[16]

If Miss Stein found little of a "usable past" in American letters before 1900, she nevertheless deduced from her own comprehensive observation of American behavior and attitudes the qualities that characterized the national imagination and issued in a distinctive national style. Primary among these traits was the American proclivity toward abstraction. To Bertrand Russell she eloquently asserted the "disembodied abstract quality of the american [*sic*] character" and cited automobiles and Emerson as typical American "products." Later, in her *Lectures in America*, she correlated this abstractionism with the absence in her native land of that "daily island life" which had held English literature close to the earth and the emotions. Accordingly, in "all persistent American writing" she found "a separation from what is chosen to what is that from which it has been chosen," and she asserted that Irving, Whitman, and James (among others) showed that what "makes what American literature" is this lack of "connection with that from which it is choosing."[17]

The validity of Miss Stein's generalized insistence on the American penchant for such "disembodiedness" is indeed dubious. One may suspect that she has prejudicially posited the Hawthorne–James tradition as the authentically American one and has casually dismissed the strong empirical strain of Irving's genre pieces, of Whitman's extensional richness and devotion to identity, of Twain's principle and practice of "founding on fact," of Dreiser's massive naturalism. Her own graduate training and experiments in psychology had of course instilled in her an ultimate concern for the generalized "what" rather than the concrete "it." Later in Europe her predilection for the abstract was attested by her especial affinity for Spanish landscapes and art and culture—an affinity which arose, as she said, "because I was expressing the same thing in literature" and because Spaniards and Americans, unlike other Europeans and Orientals, "do not need religion or mysticism not to believe in reality as all the world knows it . . . . and that is why there are skyscrapers and American literature and Spanish painting and literature." Hence, too, her admiration for Picasso's cubism, for if it properly concerned itself with "visible things," it nevertheless projected a "visible world" not as everybody sees it but as an intuited essence or rhythm, or as what Mabel Dodge praised as "the 'noumenon' captured" in *The Making of Americans*. Similarly in her portraits, as Miss Stein explained, she had "tried to tell what each one is without telling stories," and in the early plays she had likewise dispensed with narration in order to evoke the "essence of what happened." Accordingly in

Geography and Plays the "essence" of France is presumably suggested by a collage of aphorisms such as "To be afraid is not near sighted," or "One special absence does not make any place empty"; and America is even more tenuously adumbrated by "Pow word, a pow word is organic and sectional and an old man's company," or by "America key, america key."[18]

The complex relationship of Miss Stein's style to Continental aesthetics during the two decades following 1910 has already received thoughtful treatment by several critics, including Edmund Wilson, Donald Sutherland, and J. M. Brinnin. Only one aspect of that relationship is relevant here: the extent to which Miss Stein's residence abroad diverted her from the native influences which she so assiduously delineated and explicitly embraced. At least one tendency would seem persistently clear: whatever she did in her cumulative experimentation she always related to the American mind. Thus if she was drawn toward abstraction (as she was from the beginning), she assured herself and others that Americans are generally so inclined. Hence cubism was for her confirmative, not formative. Viewing America as the creative founder of twentieth-century culture, she accordingly construed her innovations in style to be the prophetic vehicles and agents of the inclusive mutation initiated by her country. Thus the patterns in the lines and quarter sections of the landscape observed during her plane flights across the States, she said, "made it right that I had always been with cubism and everything that followed after."[19]

Although her notorious *Tender Buttons* (1914) scarcely impresses most readers as a distinctively American product, Miss Stein has essentially provided from time to time the critical assumptions for arguing that the work is actually a complex of stylistic tendencies markedly cisatlantic. At its center lies its use of the word as, in her view, it was transformed by New World experience. After *The Making of Americans*, as Michael Hoffman has discovered from an autobiographical statement in one of her unpublished essays, she felt a new sense of the creative possibilities inherent in her native language. Indeed, as she said, she found herself "plunged into a vortex of words, burning words, cleansing words, liberating words, feeling words, and the words were all ours and it was enough that we held them in our hands to play with them; . . . and this was the beginning of knowing; of all Americans [*sic*] knowing, that it [*sic*] could play and play with words and the words were all ours all ours." In her later lectures in America she further observed that though England and America had the same words and grammatical construction, they had "come to be telling things that have nothing whatever in common." The English language, made as it was "to tell the story of the soothing of living every minute," had proved uncongenial to the restive temper of the New World; hence "in American writing" the old English words began to reflect a new "consciousness of completely moving, they began to detach themselves from the solidity of anything" and to have a different pressure put upon them." Sensing this verbal liberation, Emerson, Whitman, Hawthorne, and Twain, she asserted, had all shown that the old words could be pressed and shaped into doing what was needed. In *Tender Buttons*, therefore, Miss Stein was at least indulging a native propensity to play with words, to make them move in any and every direction, and to enjoy "the feeling of words doing as they want to do and as they have to do when they live where they have to live. . . . " Americans could adapt their linguistic heritage to their needs, she later observed in *Wars I Have Seen*, only by choosing words they liked best, "by putting words next to each other in a different way . . . , by shoving language around." Sherwood Anderson therefore seems justified in the early 1920s in viewing Miss Stein as "an American woman of the old sort" creatively living "among the little housekeeping words" in "her word kitchen in Paris."[20]

How far the verbal play of *Tender Buttons* can be translated

into paraphrasable or discursive or subliminal meanings re-
flecting an American genesis or influence is not easily established. During this cubistic phase of her writing her reiterated intention was to strip words of their overtones and
associations and to treat them as plastic entities, as colors
on her palette, and therein she dissents from the linguistic
assumptions of contemporary symbolists and of Joyce and
Eliot. As early as 1920 Richard Aldington had traced this
autotelic word play to its cisatlantic source. Asserting that
Tender Buttons constituted with "The Raven" and *Leaves
of Grass* one of the "three impingements of American genius
upon the mind of Europe," he characterized Miss Stein's
style as that of the new "American calculated facetiousness"—
a conclusion in which most readers are inclined probably
to concur. Yet assuming psychic processes involving a complexity and depth far beyond "calculated facetiousness," Miss
Allegra Stewart has recently argued that the diction and
verbal patterns of *Tender Buttons* were media to the unconscious through which she attained profound insights into
the nature of reality and the self. Through an awareness
of the root meanings of key words (such as the seven in
"A Caraffe") and through meditations generated by these
words, Miss Stewart learnedly argues, Miss Stein was enabled
to touch the mythic and ritual depths of human experience
and to achieve flashes of "subliminal intuition." The "tender
buttons," in effect, are the "living words [which] seem to
put forth like green buds in the spring," and, like all vegeta-
tion, contain "the secret force of life." In this essentially
mythic reading of *Tender Buttons* the American quality of
the work is found to lie in its reassertion of the Emersonian
quest for the authentic self and in the process of "denudation"
whereby Miss Stein achieves the transcendence of an "Emersonian transparent eyeball."[21]

Between these alleged American matrices of "calculated
obsequiousness" and "subliminal intuition" one may also
perceive in *Tender Buttons* that "naivety of vision," with

its collages of objects and its consequent paratactic style, which Tony Tanner has convincingly shown to be a persistent characteristic of American writing. According to this version of a cisatlantic mode Miss Stein sustains the "innocent eye" of Emerson, Thoreau, and Whitman, with its simple delight in discrete objects which achieve coherence chiefly through the naïve "wonder" in the mind of the observer. Though this "wonder" did not necessarily involve Jungian insights or archetypes such as Miss Stewart finds inherent in *Tender Buttons*, it did involve the responses of what Miss Stein called "human nature," with its impure concern for the self and identity as revealed in the context of memory and time. This context Miss Stein renounced more decisively than did the Transcendental exponents of the "innocent eye." Great literature, she insisted, is the product rather of the "human mind" liberated from the contingencies of "human nature" and from the sense of identity and localization imposed by valleys and hills. On such assumptions she could prophesy that America, with its vast flatlands, would produce a civilization capable of releasing the "human mind" from "local assertion" and of nurturing thereby a literature that would express "the way the earth is and looks." In the impersonality and objectivity of *Tender Buttons*, therefore, she may well have felt her writing to be distinctively American in its projection of the literary mode of that future civilization where pure reality is revealed by the "human mind" unalloyed by facts or meaning or a sense of time.[22]

In addition to the abstract perspective and the liberated diction (but related to these two aspects), Miss Stein remarked a third distinguishing element: a new feeling for space-time induced by American experience. "It is singularly a sense for combination within a conception of the existence of a given space of time," she wrote in explaining the genesis and style of *The Making of Americans*, "that makes the American thing the American thing . . . "; it is "something strictly American to conceive a space that is . . . always filled with moving . . . ," and as "an American," she testifies, she "felt this thing, and . . . made a continuous effort to create this thing in every paragraph. . . . " Since Americans unlike the English have "no daily life at all," she further explained in *Narration*, they want everything to be "exciting, and to move as everything moves." This "vitality of movement" she supposed she had projected in her portraits and in *Four in America* by a kind of cinematic process—by a "continuous succession of the statement of what that person was until I had not many things but one thing." Thus through the slight phrasal variations in a series of sentences, comparable to the changing images in successive frames of a cinematic film, and by ignoring what a character does or says in favor of disclosing "the intensity of movement" inside him, she sought to create a "continuous present" untainted by distracting associations and memory. Through this "more and more listening to repeating," she asserted, she allowed each of her characters to become a "whole one" for whom she had achieved a "loving feeling" and a "completed understanding."[23]

In place of the old Aristotelian reliance on a causally sequential plot, Miss Stein therefore proposed the assumption of a "continuous present" as the corollary of a twentieth-century culture nurtured primarily by her native land. As "an American," she said, she had gradually discovered "that anything that everything has a beginning and a middle and an ending," and that "American writing has been . . . an existing without the necessary feeling of one thing succeeding another thing. . . . " In the 1920s she had asserted that "composition" is based on the "thing seen," which changes from generation to generation, and she later added that "the business of Art . . . is to live in . . . and to completely express that complete actual present." Her emphasis on the reality of the continuous present was therefore neither pragmatic nor humanitarian but rather epistemological in origin. Knowledge to her was "what you know at the time . . . you really know anything," and hence "knowing has not succession" since it is always contingent on the "time you are knowing it." Her addiction to the present participle in *The Making of Americans*, she explained, was an aspect of her effort to escape the assumption that meaning resides in beginning and middle and ending and to posit it in the only valid matrix of knowledge—that of the continuous present. And this sense of the present seemed to her, as did the penchant for abstraction and the transformation of English diction, essentially an "American thing."[24]

III. THE FINAL PHASE

Though during the first third of the century Miss Stein made a continuous attempt to comprehend the American mind and to disclose its distinctive voice both by critical analysis and literary experiment, the final dozen or so years of her life were marked by a more inclusive involvement and synthesis. Even in the late 1920s before she made her single return to the States, her concern for dispassionate abstraction had begun to yield, as Virgil Thomson has observed, to the more "visceral" and emotional vein of "Patriarchal Poetry" (1927) and *Lucy Church Amiably* (1927), a "Novel of Romantic beauty" (as she calls it) which occasionally resorts to such whimsical American-oriented word play as "Atchison Topeka and Santa Fé when this is not the month of May." Moreover, in *Stanzas in Meditation* (1932) she moved from the still lifes and household objects of *Tender Buttons* to pastoral imagery and landscapes— to manifold and specific animals, flowers, birds, and trees, and to human relationships often described in ethical terms. With the Toklas autobiography (1932) she had for the first time, she said, "felt something outside me while I was writing"; and soon thereafter in *Four in America* (1933) she had again turned to the history and characters of her native land as the matrix of an entire book.[25]

Coming as it did following her shift toward romanticism

and extroversion, Miss Stein's visit to America induced an almost rhapsodic involvement with a culture and people and landscape upon which she had reflected for over thirty years from abroad. Her "Meditations on Being About to Visit My Native Land" (1934) reveals a mingling of childlike eagerness with small anxieties and concerns that her country will not be "really different," that she will prove to be "a good American," and that she can "see and talk to and listen to Americans as they come and go." With her triumphal lecture tour her hopes and expectations were so superlatively realized that she could pronounce "everything" to be "wonderful" and could express the desire "to stay in U.S.A. for ever [*sic*]." Entranced by the cultural differences among the various states, by the landscapes as viewed from the air, and especially by the wooden houses and their windows ("the most interesting thing in America"), she confessed on her return to Paris that she was already "homesick for America," and that, indeed, she was "married; I mean I am married to America, it is so beautiful." So contagious was her enthusiasm in these years that Thornton Wilder, after reading *The Geographical History of America* (1935) felt impelled to write her from Vienna: "Yes, I'm crazy about America. And you did that to me, too. . . . " In view of such warm and ingenuous reponses on Miss Stein's part, it is difficult to concur in John Peale Bishop's indictment of her as an "emotional invalid."[26]

Delighted during her visit that America was not merely the same country she had left a generation earlier but that, in fact, "now it's more so," Miss Stein inevitably tended to reconsider many of the national traits that she had with more detachment discovered in her youth and had later assessed from her Parisian perspective. Yet the late 1930s and the 1940s bred fears that her compatriots were losing something of their former individualism and initiative, as evidenced by the fiscal policies of the New Deal and the rise of an "employee mentality," which her fictional G.I.s Brewsie and

Henry find displacing the distinctive American propensity "to pioneer." But as Whitman had found a reassuring integrity and humanity in the soldiers of the Civil War, so did Miss Stein in the G.I.s of the 1940s; and if in her later romantic vein she relegated the grosser aspects of American army life to generalized illusion, she perhaps did so, like Whitman, in order to disclose and reaffirm what she deemed to be the more durable and positive traits of the national character. Prominent among these were an independence of mind, a tolerant and skeptical common sense, and an interest in disputation which impels the G.I.s to "just keep on thinking and talking" and to admit that "we dont [*sic*] think we know that all America is just so. . . . " Miss Stein's occupation forces probe the American character—its hubris, its evolution, and its current liabilities; and their discussions, she confessed in a postscript entitled "To Americans," "made me come all over patriotic. . . . I was always in my way a Civil War veteran, but in between, there were other things, but now there are no other things."[27]

Yet, on a level of perception and understanding below that of the G.I.s' discussion of the American character and destiny, lay Miss Stein's own rich fund of responses and reflections accrued through two generations of experience with American persons and things. Hence the reiterated fascination that American voices held for her in the last years of the war: the radio Voice of America, with its broadcasts beginning with "poetry and fire" and modulating to "modesty and good neighborliness," thereby revealing the conduct of the war itself; or, in the soldiers' responses to her persistent inquiry about their native state and occupation, the tonal diversity of regional and urban voices whereby the sound not only of Colorado but also of Chicago, Baltimore, and Detroit could become "music to the ear." The "thing I like most," she declared, "are [*sic*] the names of all the states. . . . They make music and they are poetry. . . . " Indeed, after the first world war she had projected a long book or poem about how each state differed from the others—how each had "its own character, its own accent" like the ancient French provinces, and yet was American. The delight afforded by the talk of the "G.I. Joes," however, involved beyond its "music" a linguistic pride. They had completed the necessary transformation of the English tongue, she said; they had not merely possessed their language but had also dominated it, and in making it "all theirs" they had both "become men" and also "become more American." Surely implicit in these responses to the music and poetry and vitality of the G.I. vernacular is an almost complete reversal of Miss Stein's linguistic views during the cubistic period. Words are no longer merely plastic entities to be liberated from time and memory in behalf of a pure expression of the "human mind"; "human nature," with its involvement with identity and the local has finally reasserted itself, and Miss Stein's writing, despite earlier dicta, is no longer indifferent to "meaning" and "remembering," to "beginning" and "ending."[28]

Even at the end of her life, therefore, Gertrude Stein not only retained her belief in the ineluctable imprint of nationality but also affirmed the native roots of her own writing. Since "a nation is even stronger than the personality of any one," she concluded, "it certainly is so nations must go on, they certainly must." Such a concession to nationality seems to some of her critics to have led her to an "uncritical patriotism"; but Mary Ellen Chase, visiting with her in England in 1936, perhaps more validly construed her attitude as a belief in "some stout American dream, massive, like herself, rather than sentimental, but to her, clearly real and even possible of fulfillment." No doubt much of her final view of the essential national character is contained in her admonitions at the end of *Brewsie and Willie*: avoid being "yes or no men," "learn to express complication," and "go as easy as you can." It was, indeed, her adherence to such maxims that enabled her to resist a modish immersion in the expatriate temper during her decades abroad. Incisively and persistently probing the phenomena of American history and experience, she fashioned an organically national literary style and aesthetics the pervasive influence of which on her country's literature is a matter of record.[29]

[1] G. Stein, *Geography and Plays* (New York, 1968), p. 392

[2] G. Stein, *Geography and Plays*, p. 419; *What Are Masterpieces* (Los Angeles, 1940), pp. 61-62; *Everybody's Autobiography* (New York, 1937), p. 198; *Wars I Have Seen* (New York, 1945), p. 250.

[3] G. Stein, *Wars I Have Seen*, pp. 5, 8; *Painted Lace* . . . (New Haven, 1955), p. 72; *Paris FRANCE* (London, 1940), pp. 33-36.

[4] G. Stein, *Geography and Plays*, p. 416; M. J. Hoffman, *The Development of Abstractionism in the Writings of Gertrude Stein* (Philadelphia, 1965), pp. 69, 100-102; G. Stein, *The Autobiography of Alice B. Toklas,* in *Selected Writings,* ed. Carl Van Vechten (New York, 1946), p. 76; *Picasso* (Boston, 1959), pp. 12, 16, 18; *Everybody's Autobiography*, pp. 110, 270; *Painted Lace* . . . , p. 316.

[5] G. Stein, *What Are Masterpieces*, pp. 64, 68; *Paris FRANCE*, pp. 2, 22, 24, 43.

[6] G. Stein, *Selected Writings*, p. 126; *Four in America* (New Haven, 1947), pp. 10, 16, 30, 32, 167, 169, 195.

[7] G. Stein, *Painted Lace* . . . , p. 74; *Everybody's Autobiography*, pp. 105, 233; *Brewsie and Willie* (New York, 1946), p. 113.

[8] G. Stein, *Everybody's Autobiography,* p. 239; *Selected Writings*, pp. 53-54; *Wars I Have Seen*, p. 132.

[9] G. Stein, *Things As They Are* (Pawlet, Vt., 1950), pp. 4, 53-55, 75

[10] G. Stein, *The Making of Americans* (New York, 1966), pp. 3, 14-15, 22, 31.

[11] *Ibid.*, pp. 68, 110-112, 118, 132-133, 240, 280, 438

[12] See J. M. Brinnin, *The Third Rose: Gertrude Stein and Her World* (Boston, 1959), pp. 276, 339; *transition* #28 (fall, 1928), quoted in G. A. Harrison, *Gertrude Stein's America* (Washington, 1965), p. 68; W. G. Rogers, *When this you see* [*sic*] . . . (New York, 1948), pp. 45, 46; G. Stein, *Paris FRANCE*, p. 2; *What Are Masterpieces*, pp. 61-62, 64, 68; *Wars I Have Seen*, p. 56.

[13] G. Stein, *Selected Writings*, pp. 225-226.

[14] G. Stein, *What Are Masterpieces*, pp. 61-63; *Paris FRANCE*, pp. 2-3; *The Making of Americans*, p. 718.

[15] G. Stein, *Narration* (Chicago, 1935, 1969), p. 3; *Lectures in America* (New York, 1935), pp. 52-54; *Selected Writings*, p. 65; M. J. Hoffman, *op. cit.*, pp. 32-36; R. Bridgman, *The Colloquial Style in America* (New York, 1966), pp. 165ff.; G. Stein, *Four in America*, pp. 127, 137-139.

[16] See M. J. Hoffman, *Personalist*, 67 (Spring 1966), 227-232; E. Sprigge, *Gertrude Stein/ Her Life and Work* (New York, 1957), pp. 57-58; J. M. Brinnin, *The Third Rose*, p. 338; M. J. Hoffman, *The Development of Abstractionism in* . . . *Stein,*

pp. 80-86; G. Stein, *Wars I Have Seen*, pp. 44, 48, 80; Allegra Stewart, *Gertrude Stein and the Present* (Cambridge, Mass., 1967), pp. 143-144.

[17] G. Stein, *Selected Writings*, p. 126; *Lectures in America*, pp. 46-47, 50, 51, 53.

[18] G. Stein, *Picasso*, pp. 15-18, 38; *Selected Writings*, p. 99; D. Gallup, ed., *The Flowers of Friendship/ Letters . . . to . . . Stein* (New York, 1953), p. 52; P. Meyerowitz, ed., *Gertrude Stein/ Writings and Lectures* (London, 1967), p. 75; G. Stein, *Geography and Plays*, pp. 28, 41, 44.

[19] D. Sutherland, Preface to Stein's *Stanzas in Meditation* (New Haven, 1956), pp. v ff.; E. Wilson, *Axel's Castle* (New York, 1959), pp. 241 ff.; J. M. Brinnin, *The Third Rose*, pp. 130-165; G. Stein, *Everybody's Autobiography*, pp. 191-192.

[20] M. J. Hoffman, *The Development of Abstractionism in . . . Stein*, p. 154; G. Stein, *Narration*, pp. 13-15; *Wars I Have Seen*, p. 239; S. Anderson, Introduction to Stein's *Geography and Plays*, pp. 7-8; *New Republic*, 32 (Oct. 11, 1922), 171.

[21] F. W. Dupee, "Gertrude Stein," *Commentary*, 33 (June, 1962), 521; R. Aldington, *Poetry*, 17 (Oct., 1920), 35-37; A. Stewart, *Gertrude Stein and the Present*, Chap. 3, especially pp. 91, 107, 112-113, 132. B. F. Skinner (*Atlantic Monthly*, 153 [Jan., 1934], 50-57) and Francis Russell (*Three Studies in Twentieth Century Obscurity* (Aldington, Kent, 1954), pp. 76-77) also link the style with Miss Stein's experiments in automatic writing but ignore the question of its wider American provenance.

[22] T. Tanner, *The Reign of Wonder* (Cambridge, 1965), pp. 190ff.; G. Stein, *What Are Masterpieces*, pp. 83-86; *The Geographical History of America . . .* , Introduction by T. Wilder (New York, 1936), pp. 8, 14, 51, 54, 114. See also J. M. Brinnin, *The Third Rose*, pp. 135, 142, 156ff., and D. Sutherland, Preface to *Stanzas in Meditation*, pp. x-xi, xiv; R. Bridgman, *op cit.*, pp. 11-12.

[23] G. Stein, *Selected Writings*, pp. 225-226; *Lectures in America*, pp. 170-172, 173, 176-178, 183, 184-185, 224; *Narration*, p. 6; T. Tanner, *op. cit.*, pp. 192-193; G. Stein, *The Making of Americans*, pp. 291-292.

[24] G. Stein, *Narration*, pp. 20, 23-25; *Selected Writings*, pp. 453, 455-457; *What Are Masterpieces*, pp. 17, 26, 27; P. Meyerowitz, ed., *Gertrude Stein/ Writings and Lectures*, p. 65. A somewhat similar exhortation to live in a non-sequential present came from Emerson in "Self-Reliance" in his exaltation of the rose, which makes no reference to former roses, while man lives time-bound by past memories and future prospects. Cf. Riverside edition of Emerson: *Selections*, p. 157.

[25] G. Stein, *Bee Time Vine . . .* , ed. V. Thomson (New Haven, 1953), pp. 251-252, 256, 258, 270, 272; *Lucy Church Amiably* (New York, 1969), p. 35; *Stanzas in Meditation*, pp. v-vi, xii, 22-25, 36-37; *Lectures in America*, p. 205.

[26] G. Stein, *Painted Lace . . .* , pp. 255, 256; *Everybody's Autobiography*, pp. 182-185; W. G. Rogers, *op. cit.*, pp. 123, 130-134, 152; D. Gallup, *op. cit.*, pp. 305-306; J. P. Bishop, *Collected Essays* (New York, 1948), p. 387.

[27] W. G. Rogers, *op. cit.*, pp. 130-131; G. Stein, *Painted Lace*, pp. 71-72; *Brewsie and Willie*, pp. 11, 63-65, 82, 96, 97, 113, Chap. VIII passim; *Wars I Have Seen*, pp. 251, 252.

[28] G. Stein, *Wars I Have Seen*, pp. 155-156, 201, 246, 249-250, 259; *What Are Masterpieces*, pp. 83ff.; *The Geographical History of America*, pp. 8, 54, 69, 114, 174.

Benjamin T. Spencer

[29] G. Stein, *Wars I Have Seen*, pp. 132, 156; F. Russell, op. cit., p. 70; M. E. Chase, *Massachusetts Review*, 3 (spring 1962), 513-514; G. Stein, *Brewsie and Willie*, pp. 113-114.

APPENDIX

A LIST OF THE PUBLISHED WRITINGS
OF HARRY HAYDEN CLARK

A LIST OF THE PUBLISHED WRITINGS
OF HARRY HAYDEN CLARK

BOOKS AND EDITIONS

An Outline of English Literature and Its Reflection of Tendencies Political, Religious and Social. Ann Arbor, Mich.: Edwards Brothers, 1926.

Poems of Freneau. Edited, with introduction (51 pp.), by Harry Hayden Clark. New York: Harcourt, Brace, 1929. lxiii, 425 pp. Reprint. New York: Hafner Publishing Co., 1960.

American Writers Series. General Editor, Harry Hayden Clark. New York: American Book Co., 1934-50. 26 vols.

American Literature Series. General Editor, Harry Hayden Clark. New York: American Book Co., 1934-56. 10 vols.

Major American Poets. Edited, with notes (170 pp.), by Harry Hayden Clark. (American Literature Series.) New York: American Book Co., 1936. xiv, 964 pp.

American Fiction Series. General Editor, Harry Hayden Clark. New York: American Book Co., 1937-39. 6 vols.

Six New Letters of Thomas Paine. Edited, with introduction and notes, by Harry Hayden Clark. Madison: University of Wisconsin Press, 1939. xxxii, 63 pp.

Literary Criticism: Pope to Croce. Edited by Gay Wilson Allen and Harry Hayden Clark. New York: American Book Co., 1941. x, 659 pp. Reprint. Detroit: Wayne State University Press, 1962.

Thomas Paine: Representative Selections. Edited, with introduction (141 pp.) and notes (28 pp.), by Harry Hayden Clark. (American Writers Series.) New York: American Book Co., 1944. cli, 436 pp. Revised edition. (American Century Series.) New York: Hill & Wang, 1961. clxiii, 436 pp.

Bibliography

James Russell Lowell: Representative Selections. Edited, with introduction (156 pp.) and notes (32 pp.), by Harry Hayden Clark and Norman Foerster. (American Writers Series.) New York: American Book Co., 1947. clxvi, 498 pp.

Whittier on Writers and Writing: The Uncollected Critical Writings of John Greenleaf Whittier. Edited by Edwin Harrison Cady and Harry Hayden Clark. Syracuse: Syracuse University Press, 1950. 219 pp.

Transitions in American Literary History. Edited, with introduction, by Harry Hayden Clark. Durham, N.C.: Duke University Press, 1953. xi, 479 pp. Reprint. New York: Octagon Books, 1967.

Survey of American Literature I: Instructor's Course Outline MC408.4. Madison, Wis.: United States Armed Forces Institute, 1956. 96 pp.

Instructor's Guide D409.4: Survey of American Literature II. Madison, Wis.: United States Armed Forces Institute, 1960. 95 pp.

American Literature: Poe through Garland. (Goldentree Bibliographies in Language and Literature.) New York: Appleton-Century-Crofts, 1971. xii, 148 pp.

CONTRIBUTIONS TO BOOKS

"American Literary History and American Literature," in *The Reinterpretation of American Literature*, ed. Norman Foerster. New York: Harcourt, Brace, 1928, pp. 181-213. Reprint (with preface by Robert P. Falk). New York: Russell & Russell, 1959.

"Freneau, Philip Morin," in *Encyclopaedia Britannica*, 14th ed. London: Encyclopaedia Britannica, 1929, vol. 9: 832-33. Reprinted in later editions through 1959.

"Pandora's Box in American Fiction," in *Humanism and America: Essays on the Outlook of Modern Civilization*, ed. Norman Foerster. New York: Farrar & Rinehart, 1930, pp. 170-204. Reprint. Port Washington, N.Y.: Kennikat Press, 1967.

"Foreword," in Harry Hartwick, *The Foreground of American Fiction.* New York: American Book Co., 1934, pp. v-vii. Reprint. New York: Gordian Press, 1967.

[Chapter 30], in *Irving Babbitt: Man and Teacher*, ed. Frederick Manchester and Odell Shepard. New York: Putnam, 1941, pp. 264-70. Reprint. New York: Greenwood Press, 1969.

Bibliography

"Introduction" and "Bibliographical Note," in Philip Freneau, *Letters on Various Interesting and Important Subjects*. New York: Scholars' Facsimiles and Reprints, 1943, pp. iii-vi.

"American Criticism, to 1919," in *Dictionary of World Literature*, ed. Joseph T. Shipley. New York: Philosophical Library, 1943, pp. 23-27. Revised edition. New York: Philosophical Library, 1953, pp. 15-19. [HHC also contributed about 70 brief unsigned entries to this work.]

"Paine, Thomas," in *Collier's Encyclopedia*. New York: P. F. Collier, 1950, vol. 15: 319-20. Reprinted in later editions.

"Introduction," in William Dean Howells, *The Rise of Silas Lapham*. New York: Modern Library, 1951, pp. v-xxii.

"Foreword: Why Is Literary Criticism in America Worth Studying?" in *The Achievement of American Criticism*, ed. Clarence Arthur Brown. New York: Ronald Press Co., 1954, pp. xiii-xxii.

"Changing Attitudes in Early American Literary Criticism: 1800-1840," in *The Development of American Literary Criticism*, ed. Floyd Stovall. Chapel Hill: University of North Carolina Press, 1955, pp. 15-73. Reprint. New Haven: College and University Press, 1965.

"Mark Twain," in *Eight American Authors: A Review of Research and Criticism*, ed. Floyd Stovall. New York: Modern Language Association of America, 1956, pp. 319-63. Reprint (with supplement by J. Chesley Mathews). New York: Norton, 1963.

"More, Paul Elmer," in *Dictionary of American Biography, Supplement Two*. New York: Scribner, 1958, pp. 471-73.

"Paine, Thomas," in *Encyclopaedia Britannica*. Chicago: Encyclopaedia Britannica, 1958, vol. 17: 33-34. Reprinted in later editions.

[Articles on American authors], in *The World Book Encyclopedia*. Chicago: Field Enterprises Educational Corp., 1960. Reprinted in certain later editions. [HHC contributed articles on the following writers in 1960 (with dates of last appearance in parentheses for those not in the current edition): Anderson (1970), Bacheller (1970), Bierce, Chambers (1967), Churchill, Crane (1970), Dreiser (1967), Fisher, Gale, Garland (1970), O. Henry, London (1970), Morrow, Nicholson (1964), Page (1968), Poole, Stedman, Sinclair (1970), Tarkington, Van Dyke, Wharton, Wister.]

"Lowell, James Russell," in *Encyclopaedia Britannica*. Chicago: Encyclopaedia Britannica, 1961, vol. 14: 440-41. Reprinted in later editions.

Bibliography

"Conservative and Mediatory Emphases in Emerson's Thought," in *Transcendentalism and Its Legacy*, ed. Myron Simon and Thornton H. Parsons. Ann Arbor: University of Michigan Press, 1966, pp. 25-62.

"Hawthorne: Tradition versus Innovation," in *Patterns of Commitment in American Literature*, ed. Marston La France. Toronto: University of Toronto Press, 1967, pp. 19-37.

"The Growth of Whittier's Mind—Three Phases," in *Memorabilia of John Greenleaf Whittier*, ed. John B. Pickard. Hartford: Emerson Society, 1968, pp. 119-26. Also issued as *Emerson Society Quarterly*, No. 50 (first quarter, 1968).

ARTICLES AND NOTES

"A Study of Melancholy in Edward Young," *Modern Language Notes*, 39 (March, April 1924), 129-36, 193-202.

"The Literary Influences of Philip Freneau," *Studies in Philology*, 22 (Jan. 1925), 1-33.

"Lowell's Criticism of Romantic Literature," *Publications of the Modern Language Association*, 41 (March 1926), 209-28.

"The Romanticism of Edward Young," *Transactions of the Wisconsin Academy*, 24 (1929), 1-45.

"What Made Freneau the Father of American Poetry?" *Studies in Philology*, 26 (Jan. 1929), 1-22.

"Reply to Mr. Kallen [letter]," *Saturday Review of Literature*, 5 (26 Jan. 1929), 628.

"What Made Freneau the Father of American Prose?" *Transactions of the Wisconsin Academy*, 25 (1930), 39-50.

"Lowell—Humanitarian, Nationalist, or Humanist?" *Studies in Philology*, 27 (July 1930), 411-41.

"Emerson and Science," *Philological Quarterly*, 10 (July 1931), 225-60.

"Thomas Paine's Relation to Voltaire and Rousseau," *Revue Anglo-Américaine*, 9 (April, June 1932), 305-18, 393-405.

"Thomas Paine's Theories of Rhetoric," *Transactions of the Wisconsin Academy*, 28 (1933), 307-39.

"An Historical Interpretation of Thomas Paine's Religion," *University of California Chronicle*, 35 (Jan. 1933), 56-87.

"Toward a Reinterpretation of Thomas Paine," *American Literature*, 5 (May 1933), 133-45.

Bibliography

"Nationalism in American Literature," *University of Toronto Quarterly*, 2 (July 1933), 492-519.

"Thomas Paine [letter]," *Saturday Review of Literature*, 10 (31 March 1934), 588.

"Factors to Be Investigated in American Literary History from 1787 to 1800." *English Journal* (*College Edition*), 23 (June 1934), 481-87.

"Dr. Holmes: A Re-interpretation," *New England Quarterly*, 12 (March 1939), 19-34.

"Intellectual History and Its Relation to a Balanced Study of American Literature," *English Institute Annual 1940*, pp. 115-29.

"Literary Criticism in the *North American Review*, 1815-1835," *Transactions of the Wisconsin Academy*, 32 (1940), 299-350.

"Suggestions Concerning a History of American Literature," *American Literature*, 12 (Nov. 1940), 288-96.

"The Vogue of Macaulay in America," *Transactions of the Wisconsin Academy*, 34 (1942), 237-92.

"The Influence of Science on American Ideas, from 1775 to 1809," *Transactions of the Wisconsin Academy*, 35 (1943), 305-49.

"The Role of Science in the Thought of W. D. Howells," *Transactions of the Wisconsin Academy*, 42 (1953), 263-303.

"The Influence of Science on American Literary Criticism, 1860-1910, Including the Vogue of Taine," *Transactions of the Wisconsin Academy*, 44 (1955), 109-64.

"Fenimore Cooper and Science," *Transactions of the Wisconsin Academy*, 48 (1959), 179-204; 49 (1960), 249-82.

"Hawthorne's Literary and Aesthetic Doctrines as Embodied in His Tales," *Transactions of the Wisconsin Academy*, 50 (1961), 251-75.

"Henry James and Science: *The Wings of the Dove*," *Transactions of the Wisconsin Academy*, 52 (1963), 1-15.

"Influential Teachers of Literature at the University of Wisconsin," *Transactions of the Wisconsin Academy*, 55 (1966), 1-9.

"The Growth of Whittier's Mind—Three Phases," *Emerson Society Quarterly*, No. 50 (first quarter 1968), 119-26. [See above, under "Contributions to Books."]

BOOK REVIEWS

[Amy L. Reed, *The Background of Gray's "Elegy"*], *Saturday Review of Literature*, 1 (27 Dec. 1924), 416.

Bibliography

[L. A. Sherman, *How to Describe and Narrate Visually*], *Saturday Review of Literature*, 2 (26 June 1926), 888.

[Brooks Atkinson, *Henry Thoreau*], *Saturday Review of Literature*, 4 (28 Jan. 1928), 555.

[E. Sculley Bradley, *George Henry Boker*], *Saturday Review of Literature*, 4 (16 June 1928), 971.

[Norman Foerster, *American Criticism*], *American Literature*, 1 (May 1929), 206-12.

[G. R. Elliott, *The Cycle of Modern Poetry*], *Saturday Review of Literature*, 6 (17 Aug. 1929), 52.

[Ernest E. Leisy, *American Literature*], *Saturday Review of Literature*, 6 (17 Aug. 1929), 63. [Unsigned.]

[Norman Foerster, *The American Scholar*], *Saturday Review of Literature*, 6 (28 Dec. 1929), 602.

[E. Sculley Bradley (ed.), George Henry Boker's *Sonnets* and *Nydia*], *Saturday Review of Literature*, 6 (8 Feb. 1930), 709.

[F. O. Matthiessen, *Sarah Orne Jewett*; Newton Arvin, *Hawthorne*], *Yale Review*, n.s., 19 (March 1930), 633-35.

[Ludwig Lewisohn, *Stephen Escott*], *Bookman*, 71 (April-May 1930), 209-10.

[F. O. Matthiessen, *Sarah Orne Jewett*], *Saturday Review of Literature*, 6 (3 May 1930), 1011.

[Aldous Huxley, *Brief Candles*], *Bookman*, 71 (July 1930), 438-39.

[Stephen Hudson, *A True Story*], *Bookman*, 71 (Aug. 1930), 541-42.

[Hermann Sudermann, *The Dance of Youth*], *Bookman*, 72 (Oct. 1930), 167-68.

[Stark Young, *The Street of the Islands*], *Bookman*, 72 (Oct. 1930), 165-67.

[Alfred Cobban, *Edmund Burke and the Revolt against the Eighteenth Century*], *Saturday Review of Literature*, 7 (18 Oct. 1930), 246-47.

[Nelson F. Adkins, *Fitz-Greene Halleck*], *Bookman*, 72 (Nov. 1930), 324-25.

[Dorothy Canfield, *The Deepening Stream*], *Bookman*, 72 (Nov. 1930), 300-01.

[Phillips Russell, *Emerson, the Wisest American*; Regis Michaud, *Emerson, the Enraptured Yankee*], *Saturday Review of Literature*, 7 (24 Jan. 1931), 552.

Bibliography

[Vernon L. Parrington, *The Beginnings of Critical Realism in America*], *Bookman,* 72 (Feb. 1931), 652-54.

[Fred L. Pattee, *The New American Literature*], *Bookman,* 72 (Feb. 1931), 650-52.

[Jean-Richard Bloch, *A Night in Kurdistan*], *Bookman,* 73 (March 1931), 74-75.

[Llewelyn Powys, *A Pagan's Pilgrimage*], *Bookman,* 73 (April 1931), 214-16.

[Henry W. Boynton, *James Fenimore Cooper*], *Bookman,* 73 (Aug. 1931), 645-47.

[T. R. Ybarra, *Cervantes*], *Bookman,* 74 (Nov. 1931), 334-35.

[Stanley T. Williams (ed.), *Journal of Washington Irving*], *Bookman,* 74 (Oct. 1931), 210-11.

[Gordon Haight, *Mrs. Sigourney*], *Saturday Review of Literature,* 8 (9 Jan. 1932), 441.

[S. Foster Damon, *Thomas Holley Chivers*], *Saturday Review of Literature,* 8 (5 March 1932), 571.

[Baron de Lahontan, *Dialogue Curieux*], *Saturday Review of Literature,* 8 (14 May 1932), 733.

[Bliss Perry (ed.), *The Heart of Emerson's Essays*], *Saturday Review of Literature,* 10 (7 Oct. 1933), 173. [Signed H. H. C.]

[Gertrude H. Brownell (ed.), *William Crary Brownell*], *American Review,* 2 (Dec. 1933), 237-41.

[N. Bryllion Fagin, *William Bartram*], *New York Herald Tribune Books,* (10 Dec. 1933), p. 10. [Unsigned.]

[Adolf Koch, *Republican Religion*], *American Review,* 2 (Jan. 1934), 371-74.

[A. S. Turberville (ed.), *Johnson's England*], *American Review,* 2 (Feb. 1934), 504-08.

[Adolf Koch, *Republican Religion*], *Journal of Philosophy,* 31 (1 March 1934), 135-38.

[Albert Mordell, *Quaker Militant*], *American Literature,* 6 (May 1934), 206-10.

[A. S. Turberville (ed.), *Johnson's England*], *Saturday Review of Literature,* 10 (23 June 1934), 770.

[Albert Keiser, *The Indian in American Literature*], *New England Quarterly,* 7 (Sept. 1934), 600-02.

[Herbert M. Morais, *Deism in Eighteenth Century America*], *American Literature,* 6 (Jan. 1935), 467-69.

[J. W. H. Atkins, *Literary Criticism in Antiquity*], *American Review,* 4 (March 1935), 633-36.

[Fred L. Pattee, *The First Century of American Literature*], *Saturday Review of Literature*, 12 (20 July 1935), 18.

[Robert Shafer, *Paul Elmer More and American Criticism*], *American Review,* 5 (Sept. 1935), 492-96.

[Robert E. Spiller, *James Fenimore Cooper*], *Eleusis of Chi Omega*, February 1936, pp. 64-67.

[Nathan G. Goodman, *Benjamin Rush*], *American Literature*, 8 (May 1936), 236-37.

[Harry R. Warfel, *Noah Webster*], *Saturday Review of Literature*, 14 (9 May 1936), 11.

[Alexander Cowie, *John Trumbull*], *Saturday Review of Literature*, 14 (1 Aug. 1936), 18.

[Norman Foerster, *The American State University*], *Yale Review*, n.s., 26 (March 1937), 622-24.

[Norman Foerster, *The American State University*], *Daily Cardinal* (Univ. of Wisconsin), 2 March 1937, p. 4.

[*The Huntington Library Bulletin*, No. 10, Oct. 1936], *New England Quarterly*, 10 (June 1937), 411,

[Howard M. Jones, *The Harp That Once*; L. A. G. Strong, *The Minstrel Boy*], *Yale Review*, n.s., 27 (Dec. 1937), 411-13.

[*The Huntington Library Bulletin*, No. 11, April 1937], *New England Quarterly*, 11 (March 1938), 212.

[Townsend Scudder, *The Lonely Wayfaring Man*], *Modern Language Notes*, 53 (April 1938), 312-13.

[Ervin C. Shoemaker, *Noah Webster*], *Modern Language Notes*, 53 (April 1938), 317.

[Hope J. Vernon (ed.), *The Poems of Maria Lowell*], *American Literature*, 10 (May 1938), 237.

[Thomas F. Currier, *A Bibliography of John Greenleaf Whittier*], *American Literature*, 11 (May 1939), 222-24.

[Dumas Malone, *Saints in Action*], *Journal of Bible and Religion*, 8 (May 1940), 98-99.

[Ralph H. Gabriel, *The Course of American Democratic Thought*], *Journal of Bible and Religion*, 8 (Nov. 1940), 220-21.

[Perry Miller, *The New England Mind*], *Journal of Bible and Religion*, 8 (Nov. 1940), 221-22.

[Lewis Leary, *That Rascal Freneau*], *American Literature*, 14 (March 1942), 82-84.

[Russel B. Nye, *George Bancroft*], *Wisconsin Alumnus*, 46 (15 Dec. 1944), 6.

[Howard M. Jones, *Ideas in America*], *American Literature*, 18 (May 1946), 170-73.

Bibliography

[Philip S. Foner (ed.), *The Complete Writings of Thomas Paine*], *American Historical Review*, 51 (July 1946), 724-25.

[Charles R. Anderson (ed.), *The Centennial Edition of the Works of Sidney Lanier*], *U. S. Quarterly Book List*, 2 (Sept. 1946), 172-73. [Unsigned.]

[Philip S. Foner (ed.), *The Complete Writings of Thomas Paine*; W. E. Woodward, *Tom Paine*], *Political Science Quarterly*, 61 (Sept. 1946), 455-56.

[Lewis Leary (ed.), *The Last Poems of Philip Freneau*], *American Literature*, 19 (May 1947), 18-86.

[Maurice le Breton (ed.), *Anthologie de la poésie américaine contemporaine*], *American Literature*, 20 (Nov. 1948), 360.

[Nelson F. Adkins, *Philip Freneau and the Cosmic Enigma*], *U. S. Quarterly Book List*, 5 (Dec. 1949), 458-59. [Unsigned.]

[Ralph L. Rusk, *The Life of Ralph Waldo Emerson*], *American Historical Review*, 55 (Jan. 1950), 381-82.

[Nelson F. Adkins, *Philip Freneau and the Cosmic Enigma*], *William and Mary Quarterly*, 3rd ser., 7 (April 1950), 329-30.

[William S. Clark (ed.), *Lowell: Essays, Poems, and Letters*], *American Literature*, 22 (May 1950), 200-02.

[Frederick W. Conner, *Cosmic Optimism*], *American Literature*, 22 (May 1950), 189-92.

[Harry R. Warfel, *Charles Brockden Brown*], *William and Mary Quarterly*, 3rd ser., 7 (July 1950), 503-04.

[Lionel Trilling, *The Liberal Imagination*], *U. S. Quarterly Book Review*, 6 (Sept. 1950), 279. [Unsigned.]

[John A. Pollard, *John Greenleaf Whittier*], *American Literature*, 22 (Nov. 1950), 360-62.

[Stow Persons (ed.), *Evolutionary Thought in America*], *U. S. Quarterly Book Review*, 7 (March 1951), 37-38. [Unsigned.]

[Agnes M. Sibley, *Alexander Pope's Prestige in America, 1725-1835*], *American Literature*, 23 (March 1951), 141-42.

[Thelma M. Smith (ed.), *Uncollected Poems of James Russell Lowell*], *U. S. Quarterly Book Review*, 7 (March 1951), 26-27. [Unsigned.]

[Harry R. Warfel, *Charles Brockden Brown*], *American Historical Review*, 56 (April 1951), 668.

[Joseph Beaver, *Walt Whitman*], *U. S. Quarterly Book Review*, 7 (June 1951), 139-40. [Unsigned.]

[Florence B. Freedman (ed.), *Walt Whitman Looks at the Schools*], *U. S. Quarterly Book Review*, 7 (June 1951), 158-59. [Unsigned.]

[Arthur H. Quinn (ed.), *The Literature of the American People*], *U. S. Quarterly Book Review*, 7 (Sept. 1951), 239. [Unsigned.]

[Arthur H. Quinn (ed.), *The Literature of the American People*], *American Literature*, 23 (Nov. 1951), 367-71.

[Alfred O. Aldridge, *Shaftesbury and the Deist Manifesto*], *U. S. Quarterly Book Review*, 7 (Dec. 1951), 360-61. [Unsigned.]

[L. H. Butterfield (ed.), *Letters of Benjamin Rush*], *U. S. Quarterly Book Review*, 7 (Dec. 1951), 342. [Unsigned.]

[David Mead, *Yankee Eloquence in the Middle West*], *American Historical Review*, 57 (Jan. 1952), 556-57.

[Lawrance R. Thompson, *Melville's Quarrel with God*], *U. S. Quarterly Book Review*, 8 (June 1952), 135. [Unsigned.]

[William H. Jordy, *Henry Adams*], *U. S. Quarterly Book Review*, 8 (Sept. 1952), 236. [Unsigned.]

[Mary C. S. Oliphant, A. T. Odell, and T. C. D. Eaves (eds.), *The Letters of William Gilmore Simms*], *U. S. Quarterly Book Review*, 8 (Sept. 1952), 240-42. [Unsigned.]

[Stow Persons (ed.), *Evolutionary Thought in America*], *American Literature*, 24 (Nov. 1952), 394-96.

[Leon Howard, *Victorian Knight-Errant*], *U. S. Quarterly Book Review*, 8 (Dec. 1952), 367. [Unsigned.]

[Van Wyck Brooks, *The Confident Years*], *Wisconsin Magazine of History*, 36 (Winter 1952-53), 137.

[David L. Clark, *Charles Brockden Brown*], *U. S. Quarterly Book Review*, 9 (June 1953), 111. [Unsigned.]

[Mary C. S. Oliphant, A. T. Odell, and T. C. D. Eaves (eds.), *The Letters of William Gilmore Simms*, vol. 2], *U. S. Quarterly Book Review*, 9 (Sept. 1953), 265-66. [Unsigned.]

[Roy H. Pearce, *The Savages of America*], *U. S. Quarterly Book Review*, 9 (Sept. 1953), 278-79. [Unsigned.]

[Edward A. White, *Science and Religion in American Thought*], *American Literature*, 25 (Jan. 1954), 528.

[Leon Howard, *Victorian Knight-Errant*], *Modern Language Notes*, 69 (March 1954), 214-15.

[Morris R. Cohen, *American Thought*], *U. S. Quarterly Book Review*, 10 (Dec. 1954), 513-14. [Unsigned.]

[Mary C. S. Oliphant, A. T. Odell, and T. C. D. Eaves (eds.), *The Letters of William Gilmore Simms*, vol. 3], *U. S. Quarterly Book Review*, 10 (Dec. 1954), 470. [Unsigned.]

[Grant C. Knight, *The Strenuous Age in American Literature*], *U. S. Quarterly Book Review*, 11 (March 1955), 60. [Unsigned.]

[Lewis Leary, *Articles on American Literature*], *U. S. Quarterly Book Review*, 11 (March 1955), 153 [Unsigned.]

Bibliography

[Stanley M. Vogel, *German Literary Influences on the American Transcendentalists*], *U. S. Quarterly Book Review*, 11 (June 1955), 212. [Unsigned.]

[Edward Wagenknecht, *Longfellow*], *Chicago Sunday Tribune Magazine of Books*, (23 Oct. 1955), 1-2.

[Mary C. S. Oliphant, A. T. Odell, and T. C. D. Eaves (eds.), *The Letters of William Gilmore Simms*, vol. 4], *U. S. Quarterly Book Review*, 11 (Dec. 1955), 444-45. [Unsigned.]

[Alfred Kazin, *The Inmost Leaf*], *U. S. Quarterly Book Review*, 12 (March 1956), 38-39. [Unsigned.]

[Robert E. Spiller, *The Cycle of American Literature*], *U. S. Quarterly Book Review*, 12 (March 1956), 40-41. [Unsigned.]

[Edward Wagenknecht, *Longfellow*], *U. S. Quarterly Book Review*, 12 (March 1956), 10-11. [Unsigned.]

[Leonard J. Fick, *The Light Beyond*], *U..S. Quarterly Book Review*, 12 (June 1956), 181-82. [Unsigned.]

[John P. Pritchard, *Criticism in America*], *U. S. Quarterly Book Review*, 12 (June 1956), 173-74. [Unsigned.]

[Jean Holloway, *Edward Everett Hale*], *Wisconsin Magazine of History*, 41 (Winter 1957-58), 150.

[E. Hudson Long, *Mark Twain Handbook*], *American Literature*, 30 (Jan. 1959), 543-44.

[Sherman Paul, *The Shores of America*; Walter Harding and Carl Bode (eds.), *The Correspondence of Henry David Thoreau*], *American Quarterly*, 11 (Fall 1959), 429-31.

[Christof Wegelin, *The Image of Europe in Henry James*], *Comparative Literature*, 11 (Fall 1959), 375-76.

[Oscar Cargill, *The Novels of Henry James*], *Wisconsin Studies in Contemporary Literature*, 3 (Winter 1962), 71-73.

[Thomas Philbrick, *James Fenimore Cooper and the Development of American Sea Fiction*], *Journal of English and Germanic Philology*, 62 (Jan. 1963), 236-38.

[Lewis Leary, *John Greenleaf Whittier*], *American Literature*, 35 (March 1963), 93-94.

[Walter F. Wright, *The Madness of Art*], *American Literature*, 35 (Nov. 1963), 379-81.

[Lewis P. Simpson (ed.), *The Federalist Literary Mind*], *Western Humanities Review*, 17 (Winter 1963), 92-93.

[Edd W. Parks, *Ante-Bellum Southern Literary Critics*], *Mississippi Quarterly*, 17 (Winter 1963-64), 50-51.

[Millicent Bell, *Hawthorne's View of the Artist*], *New England Quarterly*, 37 (March 1964), 108-10.

[Alfred R. Ferguson (ed.), *The Journals and Miscellaneous Note-*

books of Ralph Waldo Emerson, vol. 4], *American Literature*, 37 (March 1965), 78-79.

[Ernest Samuels, *Henry Adams: The Major Phase*], *American Literature*, 37 (Nov. 1965), 324-25.

[Maurice Gonnaud, *Individu et Société dans l'Oeuvre de Ralph Waldo Emerson*], *American Literature*, 38 (May 1966), 249-50.

[Sydney J. Krause (ed.), *Essays on Determinism in American Literature*], *Criticism*, 8 (Summer 1966), 300-02.

[Joel Porte, *Emerson and Thoreau*], *American Literature*, 38 (Jan. 1967), 562-64.

[G. Thomas Tanselle, *Royall Tyler*], *American Historical Review*, 73 (Oct. 1967), 221-22.

[Edward Wagenknecht, *John Greenleaf Whittier*], *American Literature*, 40 (May 1968), 240-41.

[James T. Callow, *Kindred Spirits*], *American Historical Review*, 73 (June 1968), 1634-35.

[Richard Cary (ed.), *Edwin Arlington Robinson's Letters to Edith Brower*], *CEA Critic* (Feb. 1969).

[Edward Wagenknecht, *John Greenleaf Whittier*], *South Atlantic Quarterly*, 68 (Spring 1969), 272-73.

[Howard P. Vincent (ed.), *Melville and Hawthorne in the Berkshires*], *American Literature*, 41 (May 1969), 284-85.

[Joel Porte, *The Romance in America*], *American Literature*, 43 (May 1971), 310-11.

[James Woodress, *Willa Cather*], *Contemporary Literature*, 13 (Spring 1972), 258-60.

LIST OF CONTRIBUTORS

Edwin H. Cady is Professor of English and Associate Editor of *American Literature*, Duke University.

Neal Frank Doubleday is Professor Emeritus of English, Millikin University.

Merton M. Sealts, Jr. is Professor of English, University of Wisconsin.

Gay Wilson Allen is Professor Emeritus of English, New York University.

Alexander C. Kern is Professor of English, University of Iowa.

Richard D. Rust is Professor of English, University of North Carolina.

John Stephen Martin is Associate Professor of English, University of Calgary (Canada).

Howard Baetzhold is Professor of English, Butler University.

W. R. Macnaughton is Assistant Professor of English, University of Waterloo (Canada).

Richard A. Davison is Professor of English, University of Delaware.

Benjamin T. Spencer is Professor of English, Ohio Wesleyan University.

G. Thomas Tanselle is Professor of English, University of Wisconsin.